The Strange Story c

Mór Jókai

Alpha Editions

This edition published in 2024

ISBN : 9789362994318

Design and Setting By
Alpha Editions
www.alphaedis.com
Email - info@alphaedis.com

As per information held with us this book is in Public Domain.
This book is a reproduction of an important historical work. Alpha Editions uses the best technology to reproduce historical work in the same manner it was first published to preserve its original nature. Any marks or number seen are left intentionally to preserve its true form.

Contents

PREFACE. ....- 1 -

INTRODUCTION. ....- 4 -

CHAPTER I. ....- 7 -

CHAPTER II. ....- 10 -

CHAPTER III. ....- 13 -

CHAPTER IV. ....- 16 -

CHAPTER V. ....- 22 -

CHAPTER VI. ....- 28 -

CHAPTER VII. ....- 33 -

CHAPTER VIII. ....- 35 -

CHAPTER IX. ....- 40 -

CHAPTER X. ....- 44 -

CHAPTER XI. ....- 48 -

CHAPTER XII. ....- 55 -

CHAPTER XIII. ....- 57 -

CHAPTER XIV. ....- 63 -

CHAPTER XV...- 68 -

CHAPTER XVI. ....- 73 -

CHAPTER XVII. ....- 84 -

CHAPTER XVIII. ....- 90 -

CHAPTER XIX. ....- 96 -

CHAPTER XX. ....- 101 -

CHAPTER XXI. ....- 109 -

CHAPTER XXII. ....- 112 -

CHAPTER XXIII. ....- 118 -

CHAPTER XXIV. ....- 124 -

CHAPTER XXV. ....- 128 -

CHAPTER XXVI. ....- 137 -

CHAPTER XXVII. ....- 140 -

CHAPTER XXVIII. ....- 146 -

CHAPTER XXIX. ....- 148 -

CHAPTER XXX. ....- 155 -

CHAPTER XXXI. ....- 158 -

CHAPTER XXXII. ....- 160 -

CHAPTER XXXIII. ....- 165 -

CHAPTER XXXIV.	- 171 -
CHAPTER XXXV.	- 176 -
CHAPTER XXXVI.	- 178 -
CHAPTER XXXVII.	- 182 -
CHAPTER XXXVIII.	- 185 -
CHAPTER XXXIX.	- 189 -
CHAPTER XL.	- 194 -
CHAPTER XLI.	- 198 -
CHAPTER XLII.	- 200 -
CHAPTER XLIII.	- 204 -
CHAPTER XLIV.	- 206 -
CHAPTER XLV.	- 209 -
CHAPTER XLVI.	- 211 -
CHAPTER XLVII.	- 213 -
CHAPTER XLVIII.	- 216 -
CHAPTER XLIX.	- 218 -
CHAPTER L.	- 221 -

PREFACE
TO JÓKAI'S "RAB RÁBY," IN ENGLISH,
By Dr. Emil Reich.

In "Rab Ráby," the famous Hungarian novelist gives us, in a manner quite his own, a picture of the "old régime" in Hungary in the times of Emperor Joseph II., 1780-1790. The novel, as to its plot and principal persons, is based on facts, and the then manners and institutions of Hungary are faithfully reflected in the various scenes from private, judicial, and political life as it developed under the erroneous policy of Joseph II.

Briefly speaking, "Rab Ráby" is the story of one of those frightful miscarriages of justice which at all times cropped up under the influence of political motives. In our own time we have seen the Dreyfus case, another instance of appalling injustice set in motion for political reasons. "Rab Ráby" is thus very likely to give the English reader a wrong idea of the backward and savage character of Hungarian civilisation towards the end of the eighteenth century, unless he carefully considers the peculiar circumstances of the case. I think I can do the novel no better service than setting it in its right historic frame, which Jókai, writing as he did for Hungarians, did not feel induced to dwell upon.

The Hungarians, alone of all Continental nations, have a political Constitution of their own, the origin of which goes back to an age prior to Magna Charta in England. Outside Hungary, it is generally believed that Hungary is a mere annex of "Austria"; and the average Englishman in particular is much surprised to hear that "Austria" is considerably smaller than Hungary. In fact, "Austria" is merely a conventional phrase. There is no Austria, in technical language. What is conventionally called Austria has in reality a much longer name by which alone it is technically recognised to exist. This name is, "The countries represented in the Reichsrath." On the other hand, there is, conventionally and technically, a Hungary, which has no "home-rule" whatever from Austria, any more than Australia has "home-rule" from England. In fact, Hungary is the equal partner of Austria; and no Austrian official whatever can officially perform the slightest function in Hungary. The person whom the people of "Austria" call "Emperor," the Hungarians accept only as their King. There is not even a common citizenship between Hungarians and Austrians; and a Hungarian to be fully recognised in Austria as, say a lawyer, must first acquire the Austrian rights of naturalisation, just as an Englishman would.

The preceding remarks will enable the reader to see clearly that Hungary never accepted, nor can ever accept Austrian rule in any shape whatever;

and that the entire business of political, judicial, and administrative government in Hungary must legally be done by Hungarian citizens only. The King alone happens to be an official in Austria as well as in Hungary; but according to Hungarian constitutional law he cannot command, nor reform things in Hungary except with the formal consent of the Hungarian authorities, in Parliament and County. In Austria indeed, the "Emperor" was, previous to 1867, quite autocratic; and even at present he has a very large share of autocratic power.

Now, Emperor Joseph II. desired to melt down Hungarian and Austrian manners, laws, and institutions into one homogeneous mass of a Germanised body-politic. With this view he commanded the Hungarians to practically give up their own language, their ancient national constitution, and old County institutions, thinking as he did, that such an unification of the Austro-Hungarian peoples would make the Danubian Monarchy much more powerful and prosperous than it had ever been before. He sincerely believed that his scheme of unification would greatly benefit his peoples; nor did he doubt that they would readily obey his behests to that effect.

However, the Emperor was quite mistaken as to the effect of his imperial policy upon the Hungarians. Far from acquiescing in his plans, the Hungarians at once showed fight in every possible form of passive resistance, rebellion, scorn, or threats. To them their Constitution was, as it still is, dearer by far than all material prosperity.

The Emperor's ordinances were coolly shelved, not even read, and with a few exceptions, all his commands proved abortive. Many Hungarians admitted then, as others do now, that Joseph's reforms were in more than one respect such as to benefit Hungary. Yet no Hungarian wanted to purchase these reforms at the expense of the hoary and holy Constitution of the country. Joseph, in commanding all those reforms, without so much as asking for the consent of the Estates, violated the very fundamental principle of the Hungarian Constitution. This the Hungarians were determined to resist to the uttermost. In the end they vanquished the ruler, who shortly before his death withdrew nearly all his ordinances, and so confessed himself beaten.

It is in the midst of these historic and psychological circumstances that Jókai laid his fascinating novel. A young Hungarian nobleman, indignant at the illegality and injustice of public officials of his native town, who shamefully exploit the poor of the district, approaches the Emperor with a view to get his authorisation for measures destined to put an end to the criminal encroachments of the said officials. The Emperor gives him that authority. But far from strengthening young Ráby's case, the Emperor thereby exposes him to the unforgiving rancour of both guilty and innocent officials who desperately resent the Emperor's unconstitutional procedure.

The novel is the story of the conflict between the young noble and the Emperor on the one hand, and the wretched, but in the nature of the case, more patriotic officials, on the other. As in all such cases, where virtue appears either at the wrong time, or in the wrong shape, the ruin of the virtuous is almost inevitable, while no student of human nature can wholly condemn his otherwise corrupt and despicable enemies. In that conflict lies both the charm of the novel and its tragic character.

As in all his stories, Jókai fills each page with a novel interest, and his inexhaustible good humour and exuberant powers of description throw even over the dark scenes of the story something of the soothing light of mellow hilarity.

EMIL REICH.

London, Nov. 1st, 1909.

INTRODUCTION.

Now it is not because the double name of "Rab Ráby" is merely a pretty bit of alliteration that the author chose it for the title of his story, but rather because the hero of it was, according to contemporary witnesses of his doings, named Ráby, and in consequence of these same doings, earned the epithet "Rab" ("culprit"). How he deserved the appellation will be duly shown in what follows.

A hundred years ago, there was no such thing as a lawyer, in the modern sense, in the city of Buda-Pesth. Attorneys indeed there were, of all sorts, but a lawyer who was at the public service was not to be found, and when a country cousin came to town, to look for someone who should "lie for money," he sought in vain.

Why this demand for lawyers could not be supplied in Buda-Pesth a hundred years back may best be explained by briefly describing the two cities at that epoch.

For two cities they really were, with their respective jurisdictions. The Austrian magistrate persistently called Pesth "Old Buda," and the Rascian city of Buda itself, "Pesth," but the Hungarians recognised "Pestinum Antiqua" as Pesth, and for them, Buda was "the new city."

Pesth itself reaches from the Hatvan to the Waitz Gate. Where Hungary Street now stretches was then to be seen the remains of the old city wall, under which still nestled a few mud dwellings. The ancient Turkish cemetery, to-day displaced by the National Theatre, was yet standing, and further out still, lay kitchen gardens. On the other side, at the end of what is now Franz-Deák Street, on the banks of the Danube, stood the massive Rondell bastion, wherein, as a first sign of civilisation, a theatrical company had pitched its abode, though, needless to say, it was an Austrian one. At that epoch, it was prohibited by statute to elect an Hungarian magistrate, and the law allowed no Hungarians but tailors and boot-makers to be householders.

Of the Leopold City, there was at that time no trace, and the spot where now the Bank stands, was then the haunt of wild-ducks. Where Franz-Deák Street now stretches, ran a marshy dyke, which was surmounted by a rampart of mud. In the Joseph quarter only was there any sign of planning out the area of building-plots and streets; to be sure, the rough outline of the Theresa city was just beginning to show itself in a cluster of houses huddled closely together, and the narrow street which they were then building was called "The Jewry." In this same street, and in this only, was it permitted to the Jews, on one day every week, by an order of the magistrate, to expose for sale those articles which remained in their possession as forfeited pledges. Within the city they were not allowed to have shops, and when outside the Jews' quarter, they were obliged to don a red mantle, with a yellow lappet attached, and any Jew who failed to wear this distinctive garb was fined four deniers. There was little scope for trade. Merchants, shop-keepers and brokers bought and sold for ready-money only; no one might incur debt save in pawning; and if the customer failed to pay up, the pledge was forfeited. Thus there was no call for legal aid. If the citizens had a quarrel, they carried their difference to the magistrate to be adjusted, and both parties had to be satisfied with his decision, no counsel being necessary. Affairs of honour and criminal cases however were referred to the exchequer, with a principal attorney and a vice-attorney for the prosecution and for the defence.

At that time, there was in what is now Grenadier Street, a single-storied house opposite the "hop-garden." This house was the County Assembly House whence the provincial jurisdiction was exercised. It had been the Austrian barracks, till finally, Maria Theresa promoted it to the dignity of a law-court, and caused a huge double eagle with the Hungarian escutcheon in the middle, to be painted thereon; from which time, no soldier dare set foot in its precincts. Here it was only permitted to the civilians and the prisoners confined there to enter. Only the part of the building which faced east was then standing: this wing comprised the officials' rooms and the subterranean dungeons.

The magnates carried on their petty local dissensions, aided by their own legal wisdom alone, yet every Hungarian nobleman was an expert in jurisprudence in his own fashion. There were even women who had proved themselves quite adepts in arranging legal difficulties. The Hungarian constitution allowed the right to the magnate who did not wish the law to take its course, of forcibly staying its execution, and the same prerogative was extended to a woman land-owner. The commonweal also demanded that each one should strive to make as rapid an end as possible to lawsuits. Long legal processes were adjusted so that there should be time for the judge as well as the contending parties to look after building and harvest operations, as well as the vintage and pig-killing. On these occasions lawsuits would be laid aside so as not to interfere with such important business.

But if the tax-paying peasant was at variance with his fellow-toiler, the local magistrate, and the lord of the manor, were arbitrators. So here likewise there was no room for a lawyer.

But when the peasant had ground of complaint against his betters, he had none to take his part. There was, however, one man willing to fill the breach, although he had been up to this time little noticed, and that man was Rab Ráby—or to give him his full title of honour, "Mathias Ráby of Rába and Mura."

He it was who was the first to realise the ambition of becoming on his own account the people's lawyer in the city of Pesth—and this without local suffrages or the active support of powerful patrons—but only at the humble entreaty of those whose individual complaints are unheard, but in unison, become as the noise of thunder.

The representative of this new profession did Ráby aim at being. It was for this men called him "Rab Ráby," though he had, as we shall see, to expiate his boldness most bitterly.

In what follows, the reader will find for the most part, a true history of eighteenth century Pesth. It will be worth his while to read it, in order to understand how the world wagged in the days when there was no lawyer in Pesth and Buda. Moreover, it will perhaps reconcile him to the fact that we have so many of them to-day!

CHAPTER I.

They sit, the worshipful government authorities of Pesth, at the ink-bespattered green table in the council room of the Assembly House, the president himself in the chair; close beside him, the prefect, whom his neighbour, the "overseer of granaries," was doing his best to confuse by his talking. On his left is an empty chair, beside which sits the auditor, busy sketching hussars with a red pencil on the back of a bill. Opposite is the official tax-collector whose neck is already quite stiff with looking up at the clock to see how far it is from dinner-time. The rest of the party are consequential officials who divide their time between discussing fine distinctions in Latinity, and cutting toothpicks for the approaching mid-day meal.

The eighth seat, which remains empty, is destined for the magistrate. But empty it won't be for long.

And indeed it is not empty because its owner is too lazy to fill it, but because he is on official affairs intent in the actual court room, whereof the door stands ajar, so that although he cannot hear all that is going forward, he can have a voice in the discussion when the vote is taken.

From the court itself rises a malodorous steam from the damp sheepskin cloaks, the reek of dirty boots and the pungent fumes of garlic—a combined stench so thick that you could have cut it with a knife. Peasants there are too there in plenty, Magyars, Rascians, and Swabians: all of whom must get their "viginti solidos," otherwise their "twenty strokes with the lash."

For to-day is the fourth session of the local court of criminal appeal. On this day, the serious cases are taken first, and after the death-sentences have been passed, come a succession of lesser peasant offenders for judgment.

Some have broken open granaries, others have been guilty of assaults, but there are three main groups. To one of these belong the settlers from Izbegh who have been convicted of gathering wood in the forests of the nobles. The second section embraces those culprits who were artful enough during the vintage to cover the ripe grapes over with earth, (so that the magnates should be cheated out of their tithes), and to evade the heydukes who kept watch and ward over the vintagers. Thirdly, there were the offenders who had formed a deputation to the chancery court, and dared to pray for a revision of the public accounts for the past twenty-five years, a request at once temerarious and stupid, for twenty-five years is a long time—long enough indeed for accounts to become rotten and worm-eaten.

But that they were in sufficiently good order, the revenue for this particular year, 1783, testified, seeing it amounted to sixty thousand gulden, of which six thousand were paid to the ground landlord, and two thousand towards the internal expenses of the province, with a balance in hand of fifty-two thousand gulden—not an extravagant outlay, surely!

But what remains for the peasant?

Why just those twenty strokes with the lash. These solve the question of "plus" and "minus."

The presiding judge, Mr. Peter Petray, only records his vote through the door, but he himself is doing his official part, for from the window of the adjoining room he superintends the sentences carried out in the improvised court below. There are the prisoners in the dock on whom the vials of justice are being poured forth. They are by no means a contemptible study either for the psychologist or the ethnographer. The Rascians are the defaulters against the vintage rights, and loudly they shriek and curse as the blows are administered, whilst the outragers of the forestry laws are mostly Swabians, who take advantage of the pauses between the lashes roundly to abuse the overseer. But there are many other delinquents besides in that motley crowd, who simply clench their teeth and await their chastisement.

But the eye of the law must itself watch over the execution of judgment, so that nothing in the shape of an understanding between the heyduke and the culprit, tending to mollify the punishment, may be arrived at. Much depends on how the blows are laid on. Not only does the sentence provide that the due number of lashes may be fulfilled, but likewise that the strokes should be heavy. It is for this that the judge, if he sees the heyduke falter in his work, urges him on to harder blows, by calling out "Fortius!"

But Judge Petray knows how to combine duty and pleasure. For Fräulein Fruzsinka, the niece of the prefect, is also in the room, and their whispered confidences and languishing glances show that the judge and the young lady have not met here to discuss simply official questions.

Whilst the notary in the next room is reading the indictment in a loud enough tone for Petray to be able to follow him, this dignitary manages to interpolate various interesting "asides" to his companion amid the fire of cross questions, and only calls out his vote when asked for it.

Only the prefect cannot just now leave his post as assessor, and it is impossible for him to see all that goes on. In the pauses therefore between the blows, the flirtation between these two goes on merrily.

It was just then that Fräulein Fruzsinka whispered something to her lover.

"Willingly," he answers, "but while I do it the Fräulein must take my place at the window, and count the strokes in my stead."

"And remember the heyduke's name is 'Fortius,'" added the judge to his representative.

Fräulein Fruzsinka leaned out of the window still laughing heartily, and began to count as if she were noting a scale of music. The culprit, seeing a girl's smiling face looking down on him, appealed to her for mercy. And the young lady, who was by no means hard-hearted, called out to the heyduke: "Don't beat the poor fellow so pitilessly, Fortius." But that official only flogged all the harder.

At the twelfth stroke, Petray came back and slipped something into the hand of the girl as she leaned out of the window.

This something she pressed to her lips as she withdrew again behind the curtain, hiding it in the great locket she wore on her breast. The judge counted on.

Now it was the turn of a gipsy band, six of whose number had stolen a goose, and were to receive half a dozen lashes apiece in consequence. Later on they will provide the music at dinner, at the command of their prosecutors: "Now we fiddle to you, then you will play to us!"

Fräulein Fruzsinka, with a parting hand-clasp, hastens away to see to the setting of the table, for the silver and glass and table-linen are her special care. The judge raised her hand to his lips as she left.

CHAPTER II.

It was now time for dinner, whereat we may have the honour of making a closer acquaintance with the host and hostess and their four guests.

The prefect, Mr. John Zabváry, with his jaundiced complexion and bleared eyes, is an excellent specimen of the perfect egoist. Whosoever it is that comes to him, whether to ask, or to give something, is equally an enemy in disguise. Does he ask a favour? what is it he wants? Does he bring something? why is there not more of it? With that perpetual dry cough of his, he always seems to be calling attention to the faults of someone or other. He does not even dress like anyone else, but sits at the end of the table in loose shirt-sleeves, his head nearly extinguished by a huge red velvet cap, from which dangles an enormous red tassel, that seems to mock at received Magyar modes. He is a shocking speaker, and when he gets angry, words fail him, and he begins to stammer. He is, however, the uncle and guardian of Fräulein Fruzsinka, which fact perhaps accounts for his short temper.

For Fräulein Fruzsinka, with her pretty face and arch ways, her bright eyes and alluring smile, is none the less a domestic affliction in her way. How the prefect longs for someone to rid him of her! How willingly would he not give her to the first comer.

But it is her own fault that no one marries her, for she flirts desperately with each admirer in turn. You see it even as she sits at the table, keeping up a cross-fire of bread-pellets with the judge in a way that is anything but ladylike. The prefect coughs disapproval and shakes his head each time he glances at his wayward niece, who, on her part, only shrugs her shoulders defiantly.

Yet is Judge Peter Petray a highly distinguished man. The dark Hungarian dolman that he wears suits him admirably. His black curly hair is not powdered in the Austrian mode, nor twisted into a cue, but curls over his forehead in a most attractive fashion, and his short moustache proclaims him a cavalier of the best type.

His neighbour, the president of the court, Mr. Valentine Laskóy, is a good specimen of the Magyar of the old school, with his squat little rotund figure, short red dolman, variegated Hungarian hose, bright yellow belt, and tan boots. The long fair moustache that droops either side of his mouth, seems to vie with the bushy eyebrows half defiantly. Yet it is a face that is always smiling, and the owner has a powerful voice wherewith to express his feelings.

The dinner lasted well into the twilight. How describe it? Everyone knows what an Hungarian dinner implies. With other people, eating is a pleasure, with the Magyar it is a veritable cultus.

The meal was enlivened by anecdotes, and those of the most racy kind, whilst the fragrant fumes of tobacco wrapped the company in a cloud of smoke.

When they at last rose from the table, the judge drew from under his dolman a little note that Fräulein Fruzsinka had slipped into his hand under the table—a missive that an onlooker might have taken perhaps for a love-letter. The judge, however, pushed it over to the president, exclaiming as he did so, "Worshipful friend, will you please verify this little account?"

"What is it? I can't see to read by candle-light." And with that the president pushed the document over to the prefect.

"It's only the statement of accounts," grumbled the host, as he thrust the paper from him, while he growled: "That is my niece's affair and has nothing to do with me!"

"I can't see by candle-light," repeated the president. "I can't make out the letters." For a good Hungarian never puts on spectacles. Whoever has good eyes may read if he will.

His worship, the judge, had good eyes as it happened. But Fräulein Fruzsinka kicked his foot under the table, a hint her admirer well understood.

"Let us hear how much we four have eaten and drunk in four days." Here it is:

12 pounds of coffee.24 pounds of fine sugar.626 loaves of wheaten bread.534 decanters of wine.154 pounds of beef.4 sucking pigs.107 pairs of fowls, turkeys, and geese.54½ gallons of Obers beer.174½ pounds of fish.24½ pounds of almonds.18¼ pounds of raisins.422 eggs.3 hundred weight of finest wheat flour.

Each item was greeted with a roar of laughter from the company. What was here set forth could not have been consumed. Moreover the expenditure was the affair of Fräulein Fruzsinka, who superintended these payments.

It was the judge's cue to be polite under the circumstances. Fräulein Fruzsinka held her table-napkin before her face while it was being read, in order to hide her blushes.

Behind her stood the heyduke with the inkstand, so that the document might be duly signed by the authorities. Happily the item of the ink wherewith it was signed was not put down, else, doubtless, it had amounted to a bucketful! Then they all exchanged the greeting customary at the close of a meal. If anyone had anything further to say, it was about the gipsy musicians who were just beginning to play.

CHAPTER III.

A genuinely welcome guest does not take his leave at nightfall; the prefect's visitors therefore put off their departure till the next day, for the evening before they had sat long at the card-table, whereat the prefect had won back from his guests, and that to the last kreutzer, all that it had cost to entertain them.

Fräulein Fruzsinka had played cards till daylight. She had at first no luck whatever, willing as she was by some slight cheating, to bring it, but since her fellow-players were ready to let a pretty girl have her way, she won at last ten ducats. Mr. Laskóy, however, lost the whole of his salary. But the money would at least be restored to him, for it was the custom that whoever won most must refund the president his lost money, in view of the possible wrath of that important official. The master of the house smuggled the ten ducats through Fräulein Fruzsinka, into the president's hand.

"Take care," laughed the girl, "Gyöngyöm Miska does not rob you on the way."

"I shall hide it where no one can find it, in the lining of my cap. There it will be safe enough. Besides, Gyöngyöm Miska is just now prowling about the county of Somogy. Captain Lievenkopp himself, with all his dragoons, would hardly succeed in driving him into our neighbourhood."

"Ah, well, I only say, look after your gold pieces!"

The president laughed contemptuously. Lievenkopp was, it was well known, one of Fräulein Fruzsinka's admirers.

The president and the judge drove together as far as the next post station, where their ways parted, and meantime chatted amicably.

"Isn't our hostess a charming person?" began the president as they left the inn.

"I don't say she isn't."

"I must admit you certainly show your good taste in that quarter."

"Surely only like any other?"

"Come, come, what avails evasion? When I look into the fair lady's eyes I don't see the expression there, you do. Can you deny it?"

"Well, and if I have looked into her eyes, what of it?"

"Oh, we know all about that. Everyone knows that you and the lady of the house were carrying on a flirtation whilst the sessions were going on."

"Did I flirt?"

"Most emphatically you did. I know everything. Last night, when I went to my room, I heard voices through the door of our hostess' boudoir. I waited in order to listen, and sure enough it was the prefect who was holding forth angrily about you against a shrill high-pitched voice, which was obviously that of your Fräulein Fruzsinka. Thereupon, the lady retorted that there was an understanding between you, and that the affair was quite serious."

"Bah! As if I meant to marry every girl to whom I have made a declaration," laughed the judge.

"Aha, that would be quite as difficult to bring about as if Fräulein Fruzsinka wished to marry all those who had courted her. It cuts both ways. Yet she is a charming girl! If she could only find some good man who would marry her. Why not you, eh?"

"Most certainly not. For if someone else marries her, I am certain that she will be true to me. But if I, and not anyone else, wed her, then sure enough she'll deceive me every day."

"But if you don't mean to, then it were surely a great mistake, besides a mere quibble of words, to leave in the fair lady's hands a pledge that could be legally produced as argument for the plaintiff."

"What do you mean?"

"Tut, tut. I haven't presided twenty years for nothing in criminal law; I understand what tokens mean. What happened in the little ante-room? What has the defendant to urge on his behalf?"

"Why, I only superintended the carrying out of the law from the window."

"And in the intervals taught your hostess how to conjugate the verb amo, to love, eh?"

"Stated but not proven—but if it were so?"

"Consequently, the lady may be justified in urging: 'If he really and truly loves me, let him give me a love token, a lock of his hair.'"

"Why not?"

"Exactly—now you stand convicted! Need I remind you that you only sought a pair of scissors to cut off a curl of your hair, and while you did that, your lady-love registered the blows for you as your locum tenens. Yet you were giving the most dangerous blow of all to the guileless loving heart which beat under your gift, for Fräulein Fruzsinka hid the curl in her locket, and when we came away, I noted how she leaned out of the window and kissed the locket over and over again. Is the impeachment sufficient?"

"No, I won't admit it is. It's based on a false premise. Up to the time when I went for the scissors, I grant you it was a sound one, but here the facts alter. As I stood before the looking-glass, with the scissors in my hand, who should come in but the Fräulein's' little black poodle, and as usual he put out his fore paws caressingly. Thereupon, a brilliant idea struck me. The hair curled as well round the poodle's neck as it did on my head. No sooner said than done. The Fräulein wasn't looking; she was too busy with the sessions, so quickly nipping off a superfluous curl from the dog's neck, I slipped it into my lady's soft hand; into her locket it goes forthwith. But don't betray me! For if the Fräulein knew it, she would poison us all at the next dinner."

Mr. Valentine Laskóy was not given to groundless merriment, but he could not fail to see the point of this jest; first that one of the dog's curly locks had been transferred to the locket, and secondly, that it had been kissed with transport by the owner. And thereupon he burst into such a guffaw of laughter that the horses thought it was a volcanic eruption, and began to shy and rear accordingly, so that the coachman and the heyduke with him could not bring them to a standstill on the bridge before the post-house, and the passengers were all but sent flying from their seats. But at this point Mr. Laskóy had to get out to await the companions he had left behind, who were coming on in the coach.

"But don't say a word to anyone," was the judge's parting injunction to his companion.

"Trust me! But, all the same, whenever I see a black poodle I shall laugh at the thought."

And off went the judge, for his time was up.

At the bridge, where the roads branched off, Laskóy waited for the coach to come up.

But what a time the coach was coming, to be sure! He could not imagine what had happened to it. It was past mid-day, his ever-growing hunger made the delay of the diligence all the more wearisome. But in spite of it all, he waited patiently.

At last the famous vehicle came in sight, but only slowly, although the road was quite good. What could have happened?

CHAPTER IV.

Now what had really happened to the coach was that it had lost one of the big screws out of the hind wheel, so that the latter had come off. For a whole hour had they hunted for the screw without success, and then they tried to get on without it, but that was a difficult business. If a peasant loses a wheel-nail, he can easily find a substitute; the screw of a coach, however, is not so easily replaced. What straps and ropes they had to hand were knotted and wound round the axle, but the quickly rotating nave had in a few minutes torn all to shreds, and would not go round properly, much to the detriment of the horses who now had to drag the lumbering conveyance with a wheel that would not work, through the tough, sticky morass, which made the way much more toilsome.

Not that this affected the merry mood of the president as he took his place inside. Every now and again he whistled for sheer lightness of heart.

"Fire away, there!" he cried to the driver.

But the driver was not equal to the task, as he urged his steeds over the morass through which the four slow old hacks dragged the rickety vehicle with its broken-down wheel.

Meanwhile, on a hillock which rose tolerably steep from the roadside, waited a horseman mounted on a strong wiry beast, that stood with his muzzle snuffing the ground like a setter scenting the trail, with watchful eyes and pricked ears, but so still that he did not even brush off the flies that settled on his withers and flanks. The man himself in the saddle was equally motionless; he was dark and hawk-eyed, with curly hair, and a tapering pointed moustache. He wore a peasant's garb that was scrupulously fine of its kind, his countryman's cloak being richly embroidered, and his sleeves frilled with wide lace. In his cap he wore a cluster of locks of women's hair and a knot of artificial flowers; at his girdle gleamed a pair of silver inlaid Turkish pistols, while from the pommel of his saddle hung another, double-barrelled, and in his right hand he carried an axe. An alder-bush had hidden the stranger up till now, so that he could not be seen by the coaching party till he himself hailed them.

"Now you traitor, you knave, are you going to stop or not?"

Was the coachman going to stop? Yes indeed, he sprang down from his box in terror, promptly crawled under the coach, and whimpered, "Alack, your honour, it's Gyöngyöm Miska himself, it is indeed!"

The mounted cavalier pranced up to the coach, the noble charger tossing his proud head to and fro, so that the harness-fringe flew round him.

"Now we've got something to laugh at and no mistake," growled the coachman. Yet he laughed too in spite of himself.

The highwayman himself began to laugh as he accosted the president.

"So you've recognised me, have you, for the celebrated Gyöngyöm Miska?"

"How pray did you become Gyöngyöm Miska?"

"Don't you remember me by that name? You yourself gave it me. Have you forgotten how when, years ago, in the County Assembly, I had begun a speech, you called out to me in the middle of it, 'Ay, Gyöngyöm (my jewel), hold your peace; you understand no more of these things than half a dozen oxen put together,' so that I could not get any 'forrader,' for people laughing at me. Since those days the name has stuck to me. Everywhere I go I am received with the greeting, 'Here's Gyöngyöm Miska, worse luck!' So then, I say to myself, 'I'll be a Gyöngyöm Miska,' and show them such things as no one else can. And people talk about me, don't they?"

"But you won't rob me, will you?" implored his victim. "Do you want my horses?"

"Make your mind easy. I rob nobody. I only take what is given me, and carry off what the possessor does not value, and as for such wretched nags as you drive, I tell you plainly I wouldn't have them at a gift. I am pretty hard to please in horseflesh, I can tell you. So don't let's waste time in talking. I ask for nothing that people have not got. I know too that you are in a hurry. So just give me ten gold pieces, and then you can drive on."

The president did not wish to understand the hint, as he said sulkily, "What do you mean?"

"Only those ten Kremnitz ducats that you drew as salary for your work on the Bench."

"True enough, friend, that I have received them, but the prefect won them from me at cards last night, and I haven't one left. He did not give me back the money he had won. Turn out my pockets, search me if you will, and if you find there anything but a bad groschen, it shall be yours. Here's my sword-pouch. See, there's nothing inside. And if you like, you can take my boots off, but you'll find no gold there, I warn you."

The highwayman pressed his axe between his fingers, and tapped quite gently with the butt end of it on the crown of the president's head, where the velvet lining of his fur cap hung out. What was jingling inside?

The smile vanished from the lips of his victim. His round face became suddenly square with astonishment.

Now there must be something wrong about that. Who had betrayed him? No man knew it but one.

Gyöngyöm Miska did not let him waste time in further consideration. With a pickpocket's dexterity he drew from under his cloak his hunting knife from its sheath, ripped out the velvet lining, and possessed himself of the ducats in a trice. Then, with a pressure of his knees, he turned his horse round, and in the twinkling of an eye, horse and rider were over the marsh. Only then did he turn round to utter as a parting greeting the formula of the law courts: "I commend to you, my lord, my official services," and disappeared through the poplar-trees.

"It is a stupid business," grumbled the president, whose good humour had been torn away with that cut into his cap-lining.

And a stupid, not to say absurd business it certainly was.

But Gyöngyöm Miska, cracking his hunting whip merrily, bounded away over the sedge.

It was already evening. The autumn sun cast long shadows over the level plain. At the edge of a wood burned a herdsman's fire. By it sat a girl in riding-gear, her head supported on her hands, at her feet two greyhounds lay stretched out, her horse was tethered to the stem of a poplar. At the cracking of the whip she sprang from her resting-place, threw a bundle of dry faggots on the fire, mounted her horse, snatched up her whip, and cracked it as a counter signal. Across the plain, starred with wild anemones, the two met; bending down from the saddle, they embraced and kissed each other, and were off once more, the one eastwards, the other to the west.

Meanwhile, scarcely had the guests withdrawn from the Assembly House than an official courier rode up the Old Buda Street into Pesth. A courier of this kind was so unusual a sight, that everyone hastened to his front door to see him. He wore a red frock coat, leather gaiters over his boots which reached up to the knee, and a cocked hat with a tuft of red feathers. Every postmaster is bound to provide him with a fresh mount does he need it, and a blast from his horn will compel every peasant to hold at his service as many oxen or horses as he possesses. The sound of his horn is a well-known one, and as the courier gallops up the street, the children, blowing through their hands, mimic the blast, and the elders crane their necks to see what may be his errand. It was for the prefecture he was bound.

"Très-humble serviteur, Mamselle Oefrosine!" Thus the courier greeted Fräulein Fruzsinka de Zabváry. "Postage not paid, but I ask three kronen, because I've ridden well, to say nothing of having to go back! There are a thousand gulden inside."

It was the courier's way to recommend the letters he handed in as containing a thousand gulden. So he was paid the fee; but there was nothing like a thousand gulden in the letter thus sent to Fräulein Fruzsinka, for it was from the captain of dragoons, Heinrich Lievenkopp, and why there was nothing of the kind in the letter, may now be told.

Fräulein Fruzsinka paid the courier, but ordered him to wait at the prefecture so that she might give him the answer to take back. It was likewise to the interest of the postman to urge the despatching of a reply. Then she broke the seal and read the letter in question, written in the stilted affected style just then so much in vogue, with mythological phraseology mixed up with barrack slang. It ran as follows:

"My most adored Lady,

"By the winged feet of Mercury himself, do I address a message, surely very agreeable to your grace. God Mars has taken it into his head to complete the heroic labours of Hercules. That scoundrel of a highwayman, 'Gyöngyöm Miska,' has, after escaping our annihilating force on this side of the river, retreated across the Danube, and has taken refuge in the Ráczkeve Island—protected by Neptune and Hermes, those divinities of the robber. Meantime, must we patiently wait on the shore till we get a ferry to carry us across. The wretched fellow was playing us off, since he swam across the other arm of the Danube and reached the farther side. Thereupon, the Viennese civilians who were with us, declared, forsooth, that we might not pursue him, because it would be crossing the border of another county!

"So we had to return to Pesth till the county of Pesth should supersede the county of Weissenburg in its strategic co-operation. But rumour has it that the redoubtable robber has come back from Weissenburg county to that of Pesth, and is haunting the Vörösvár woods. Therefore have I received new marching orders from the commander-in-chief to march with my squadron on to Vörösvár. To-morrow, at the first streak of dawn shall we start on an expedition which brings me on the wings of the Hours to the charmed circle of my adorable Calypso in the beauteous Vörösvár Vale of Tempe.

"There is, however, a small but fatal incident that must be recorded, that has much disquieted me, which I will set forth to the Fräulein. Last week I was amusing myself with Mr. Justice Petray (a good fellow by the way), in dallying with Fortune's painted cards, on which occasion a thousand dancing sprites turned the wheel very unluckily for me, so that I lost twenty ducats to the justice, and had to give him my parole as an officer that I would pay him to-morrow. Item, he insists on my redeeming my word, because to-morrow there is to be an enquiry into the accounts, and among other things will be missing the twenty ducats from the treasury. But owing to the incredibly bad state of the roads the allowance my aunt sends me has not arrived, nor do I know how I can settle the affair. And so for me there remains nothing but to take my leave of the world with a pistol-shot, and embark in the boat of Charon, or else to take refuge under the protection of my good genius, and call her to my aid. I humbly suggest that she might, for just this once, be an intermediary with her rich uncle for me, and borrow the above-mentioned sum on my behalf, which I pledge my word, as a cavalier, gratefully to reimburse directly I get my aunt's allowance.

"May the Fräulein accept the most humble homage of Heinrich von Lievenkopp."

Off went Fräulein Fruzsinka, when she had read this letter, to her uncle, the prefect.

"I say, uncle, dear, will you advance me ten ducats out of my allowance?"

"Oho, my dear," answered Mr. Zabváry in a tone which suggested the melancholy whine of a dog. "What's the matter? I really can't advance any more money, for my account at the bank is already in danger of being overdrawn. But what did you so suddenly want ducats for? Is the captain of dragoons in difficulties? That seems to be a chronic ailment with him. Yes, indeed, I know, he wants more pecuniary aid, that's it! Otherwise he'll blow his brains out? Heaven grant he may! If he'd only do it once for all! What does a dragoon captain matter to me? A man who never means to marry, but just scares away the eligible suitors. I wish the devil had taken him to Silesia. And, pray, if he means to marry, am I to keep him? I should think not, indeed, considering he's got his old aunt. But even if he has, it will fall upon me in the end. Just write him the right sort of answer in proper Latin: 'Centurio' = Captain, 'pecunia' = money, 'non est' = is there none; 'si valves valeas' = if there's no wine, then drink water!"

"Very good, if you won't give me any, I'll ask someone else," said Fräulein Fruzsinka defiantly, banging the door after her as she went out.

Mr. Zabváry did not think much of that, for it was quite customary for Fräulein Fruzsinka to raise loans on all sides; from the overseer, from the chief herdsman, nay, from the shepherd's man she would borrow, and they never dared to ask the prefect for repayment, but probably then and there reckoned—as the saying goes—that "discretion was the better part of valour" in such a case (which is a wise conclusion if you can but come thereto). Fräulein Fruzsinka, however, left all these possible creditors unexploited, and calling for her horse, and her riding whip, and two pet dogs, she went off on a hunting expedition into the open country.

She did not, certainly, appear to be troubling about game, but seemed much more concerned to reach the wood; once there, she paced along the side of the brook till she came to the thicket.

There she took a path which led through it, till she reached a picturesque circular glade on whose edge six armed men in their coloured cloaks, lay encamped by a herdsman's fire. When the most gorgeously garbed one among them perceived the Fräulein, he sprang forward to meet her, and as she approached he hastened up to her, lifted the young lady from her horse, and kissed her on both cheeks. Both the dogs appeared to recognise the cavalier, for they sniffed at him in a decidedly friendly way. Then, with their arms round each other's necks, they paced along the flower-decked turf, speaking together in a low voice. And the end of it was that the lordly cavalier, after whispering to the Fräulein, mounted his horse, shouldered his weapons, and trotted off, with all his accoutrements, in company with the young lady herself in the direction of the high road.

What then happened we have already seen.

Fräulein Fruzsinka had her ducats when she came back. She put them with the other ten, enclosed them in an envelope, gave them to the waiting postman, and the red-coated courier was before nightfall on his return journey, blowing the while the lustiest blast on his horn.

And thus had Fräulein Fruzsinka, at one blow, accomplished three, to her, eminently desirable ends.

First she had made her adorer, Gyöngyöm Miska, aware on what side danger threatened him; at the same time she had procured the ten ducats which her other admirer needed to redeem his word and avoid the fatal shot; in the third place, she had helped her third suitor, the judge, to verify the municipal accounts and make them balance.

But those ten ducats must have truly been bewitched, since they were fated, in twenty-four hours, to pass through many pairs of hands, to disappear, be stolen, disappear again, and again be stolen, and only then to come to a stand-still.

That Fräulein Fruzsinka had put all her admirers in a good temper, however, and benefited all three, can we duly testify.

CHAPTER V.

In the Szent-Endre and the adjoining Izbegh vineyards the vintage was in full swing. It was an excellent harvest, the wine promised to be unusually good, and all the vineyards were filled with joyous labourers.

But from the vineyards the new wine was conveyed away by one road only, in great casks, while heydukes, armed with pikes and muskets, guarded the route. For all that grows in the vineyard must first pay the requisite tithes.

At the entrance of the one open road four huts were erected, and before each stood a huge vat. The first belonged to the Bishop of the diocese. As the cart, laden with the casks of "must," or new wine, passes, the episcopal steward takes out his tithe. Then the cart proceeds to the second hut, where the court chamberlain deducts his share. Thence it arrives in front of the two huts which, facing each other, bound the narrow road, so none may pass unchallenged. No matter whether the owner is hailed in German or Magyar, the sacristan of the parish acting for the Catholic priest, appropriates his own tithe from the cask, or if he speaks Rascian, it is for the Greek "pope," he takes his share.

Only then can the convoy proceed. Yes, indeed, so it might, if there were not a fifth hut in the way, where two heydukes seize the horses' bridles, and on right and left the owner is hailed by officials who want to know why he has broken the "portion" rule. (For thus in their simplicity have the peasants abbreviated the word "proportion.")

Such is the method in which the taxes are extorted.

Whoever is in a position to do it, holds himself in readiness to compound for the "Harács," as it was called in Hungary, from a Turkish word, by opening his purse and paying up the arrears of the tithe in groschen, which settled the matter, for to pay the tax in silver was illegal. Consequently, on the table of the fifth hut fell many a well-stuffed bag of copper coins, which the officials had squeezed out of the vintagers. There were, however, many who were not well enough provided with small change to satisfy this crowd of creditors, and so had to pay up the arrears in kind. That is why the great vats stand there in the road.

But the "red Jew" carries his casks into the small Slovak carts that take it down to the Danube, and ships it to Vienna, and pays, too, his tax of two Rhenish gulden for his wine.

It can well be imagined how to the overtaxed peasant wine-grower who has run out of money, this same "red Jew" is a friend in need, quite ready to help him out of his difficulty, for he will pay for his wine at the rate of two gulden a kilderkin. But this did not happen in well-regulated communities. Only the municipality had the privilege of selling wine, and to it the citizen only dare retail his vintage. And the price which he received for it was fixed by the law at one gulden.

So the wine-grower pours likewise into the great vat his "deputy-tax," wherein he reckons a gulden for a kilderkin, and the "red Jew" draws it out again at two gulden a kilderkin.

Thus it befalls that the owner of the vineyard brings the bottles which he has brought with him empty to the vineyard, empty home again. And yet that is called a first-rate vintage! But it was hard for the good man himself to esteem it so, and no wonder he was doubtful!

And thus the vintage went on till nightfall. Then the gates of the vineyards were shut, and the judicial vintagers paused in their work, yet not to betake themselves to rest, but to carry on further business within doors.

The judge and his deputy, the notary and the jurymen, all conferred together, the notary being auditor and controller in one, whereby it may be gathered that he was a very clever fellow.

The Jew Abraham was likewise called into the council, in order to assist in the money-changing.

For at that epoch all kinds of money were current in the country, which only came into evidence as they passed in daily exchange. To dispose of them was not easy, so the Jew was bidden to give proper money in exchange for them. When he got back to Vienna he could in his turn get rid of it.

During the money-reckoning transaction, Abraham appeared with the accounts giving the amount of money taken over, the price of the wine, and the bad money left behind.

"Can't you buy this bad money too, father Abraham?" queried the notary.

"No indeed, my lord, for if I change false money they will lock me up, but you will quietly put it away in the cash-box, and pay out with it, your servants' wages, your heydukes, messengers, and foresters. In due time, these coins will again be in circulation at the tradesman's stall, or the inn, and the public will be fingering it once more for fees and fines, and so the bad money comes round again, just as the sun goes round the earth, for it is not by any means lost."

Everyone laughed at the Jew's explanation.

Then Abraham stated how much he would give in gold for the small change he had taken, and the business was settled without further ado.

"But now, Mr. notary," proceeded the Jew, "just make me out a receipt to attest that I have changed the money, and that we are quits, but write it in Latin, not Rascian."

"All right, Rothesel."

"Also, I would ask you not to write my name 'Rothesel,' but 'Rotheisel,' with an 'i' if it is just as easy to you."

"But everybody calls you 'Rothesel'?"

"You may call me what you like, but in writing at any rate, I am 'Rotheisel.' I had this favour granted me in Vienna, from the Kaiser himself—that I might write it with an 'i.'"

"And a nice round sum that very 'i' cost you in Vienna, Abraham, or I'm much mistaken! Confess frankly, it did!"

"Pray why should I confess anything about it? What does it matter whether this 'i' cost me but a single heller, or a hundred thousand gulden—you, not I, pay them, after all is said."

When the Jew had gone, the notary packed up the ducats in stacks, and placed them beside him round the inkstand, while the president began: "Well, now the outsiders are off home, only the privileged councillors and the members of the council remain, in order to be present at the opening of the great coffer."

Now it is not permitted to every official to glance at the contents of the mysterious coffer. As the privy council alone remained, the notary fetched out from the cupboard, as many night-caps as there were men, and each one drew the covering thus provided over his head, so that only the tip of his nose was visible. This was done so that none might see where he was going. When all were thus blindfolded, the notary alone excepted, the latter took a light from the table, and gave the end of his stick into the judge's hand; the judge in his turn reaching the end of his to the juryman behind him, and so on, till the chain of blindfolded men were ready to start. Where? Ah, that was the notary's secret, for he it was who directed their progress.

"Now there come steps," he cried, "one, two, three," and so on, till he had counted ten. Then a key creaked in an iron lock. "Stoop down so you don't hurt your heads," came the word of command, and they passed through a low door. "Here we are," cried their leader, "now you can look."

The jurymen had often been in this place before. It was a low-pitched cellar, with a massive, vaulted arched roof, and in a corner of it, there stood an iron coffer made fast to the wall.

Beside this iron chest stood a Rascian "pope," whose hand they could reverentially kiss if they wished. How he came there no one knew.

The "pope" produced a large, curiously wrought key, and the notary a second one like it.

"These are the keys, open it who can!"

Three or four times some jurymen made the attempt, yet without success; in vain did the keys press right and left in the wards, but it opened not.

"We are wasting time," cried the "pope." "Do you try, Mr. notary, you understand it."

Whereupon the notary turned the keys, and the coffer was opened.

Everyone wanted to see inside.

There were nothing but ducats there: ducats, indeed, by hundreds, in fine transparent bladder bags, through which the yellow metal gleamed seductively. The sacks stood as in battle array, like so many soldiers close to each other. There must be a fabulous lot of gold there! Now another row was to be added to it. Then from a side compartment of the chest, a small book was fetched out wherein the notary entered all kinds of accounts. And strange entries might those be, judging from the frequent exclamations of the jurymen, which showed that the budget he examined was a notable one.

"Tut, tut," cried the notary interrupting, "you don't want it published to all the world."

"But if it has to be, eh?"

After which, certain accounts were duly registered in the little book, and the great coffer was again closed. Then the "pope" spoke.

"I see well enough that you have again husbanded your funds carefully, and that the money has increased, but where does the blessing of Heaven come in? You never give a thought to the Church! You promised to buy a new church bell, to gild the church roof, and to build a house for the parish priest. There's no money for all these things, but the coffer gets fuller and fuller."

"Make yourself easy, your reverence," answered the notary, "all that may come next year, if we are spared. For that the small cash-box will suffice."

"So you think it will, do you? What has ruined the hospital? The poor sick folk nearly perish of hunger in summer, and are nigh frozen in winter, whilst you carry off the timber by cart-loads as presents to Pesth, and then think of the amount of smoked sturgeon and caviare and wine you send thither, and all for the magnates, but nothing for the sick and needy!"

"Let it be, your reverence, there's nothing so advantageous for the sick as fresh air, and nothing so harmful as overloading their stomachs. But it's far better that we should give firing for the magnates, than that they should make it hot for us!"

"And the poor-house which our revered Queen, Maria Theresa, endowed, is it not still empty? What are we about that we do not find inmates for it? But you find none."

"The devil we do! Don't the blind and the lame stand each Sunday before the church door, but if we want to befriend them, we've only to say: 'Come you, poor wretches, we'll show you the way into the poor-house,' and off they run in a fright, so great a horror have they of the bread of the State."

"You children of the devil! And what of the poor Izbeghers whose forty houses were burned down? The Emperor allowed them as much from the treasury as the worth of the houses amounted to, but you raised the rents of the remaining houses and then dunned them for the money."

"That's natural enough, seeing the Emperor let the State annex the burned part in order to pay so much the less to the ground-landlord. If Peter has nothing, then pay Paul, that is the rule."

"A godless rule too! Amend your ways, I say, for if next year as many complaints reach my ear as have this, I'll denounce your coffer to the Treasury."

These words only provoked laughter.

"Your reverence is not such a bad sort," ventured the judge in a conciliatory tone.

Thereupon, the keys were withdrawn, the night-caps again donned, and the notary led his blind men again to the ground-floor of the council chamber, where they congratulated one another on the risks run.

"Only yon priest should not have it all his own way with his maledictions," grumbled the judge. "But they are all like that. Each one of them thinks that hardly earned money should be wasted on churches and hospitals."

"I also think, my lord, that it would be better that such an unreasonably big sum of money should be divided to each one as he has need," suggested a juryman bolder than the rest.

The speaker might, from the assenting murmur which greeted his speech, take it for granted that he had a good many on his side, but the eloquence of the notary soon crushed such sympathy.

"Ay, my dear friend, that would kill the goose which lays the golden eggs. This coffer is our pledge of power, our shield of protection, our bond of union. As long as it exists are we rulers in this city and in all its dependencies. As long as this coffer answers for us, so long can we get the laws made in our favour. As long as we have our money, they won't take our sons for military service, or ask us for accounts, and if a meadow or a plot of land is to be divided, we look after the allotment. It is we who direct public works. It is we who fell the timber in the forest, who cast the net into the Danube, and limit the vintage; we buy and sell; and fix the tithes. As long as the key of that coffer is in our hands, we must needs be great powers in the city, like Kaiser Joseph in his palace at Vienna. At the end of that key we whistle a tune to which all men must dance."

"Quite right, quite right!" shouted the whole assembly.

And who could contradict them?

CHAPTER VI.

The Jew Abraham was the father of twelve children, all sons, and all red-haired. And each one equally resembled his father.

Yet it will be well to explain matters from the beginning.

Up till the Emperor Joseph's time, the Jews had been devoid of any family names, as once in the Promised Land.

But when Joseph II. admitted the Jews to the rights of citizens, he stipulated that they should render military service if called upon, and that they should choose a surname—and that a German one.

To this end, royal commissions were despatched on all sides which should provide the Jews with surnames. And a nice business it was! Whoever had a well-filled purse had a free choice, if it so pleased him, but woe to him who set about it empty handed, for the nickname wherewith his mocking neighbours had christened him, stuck to him pitilessly.

Because Abraham had not sufficiently opened his purse-strings, he still had to go by his nickname of "Rothesel," wherewith he was known among his neighbours.

The epithet "roth" (red), he had received from the colour of his beard, but he had been qualified as "esel" (ass), because he had done nothing more enterprising with his wife's dowry of two hundred thalers, than buy up wine with it. On this account everyone had decided he must be an ass. And everyone, on the face of it, was right. For what could a Jew want with wine? He dared not retail it, for the trading rights belonged only to the communes, to say nothing of the difficulty of transporting it over the frontier. Whence could he carry it? for in Hungary the law forbade any Jew to trade in such wares.

So that when his neighbours called Abraham an ass for laying out his money in wine when he began life, they were not far out, for he hardly earned salt to his bread by such a business.

But Abraham was in his way a student of the times. Looking ahead, he saw under the rule of the later Hapsburgs that many ancient laws, though still unrepealed, had nevertheless fallen into desuetude, and consequently that the statute forbidding Jews the commerce in wine, might follow suit. Consequently, Abraham found means of transporting his Hungarian vintages to Vienna. And as he was the first in the field his enterprise was crowned with success. Nor did he deceive the customer as to the difficulties of the Hungarian wine trade.

In spite of all this, he did not part with his wealth too readily. The commission had expected that he would come out with ducats by the thousand, but he produced nothing more than a cellar full of wine. In retaliation for this they left him his nickname of "Rothesel."

What did it matter to him, for what is a name after all? The name of the creditor is always a good one, that of the debtor as surely a disgraceful one.

But his own family did not share his views on the subject. If it was indifferent to the father what men called him, his wife and children took a different view of "Rothesel," and, owing to their urgent representations, Abraham determined to rid himself of this incubus, yet without paying too dearly for it.

He reckoned two hundred ducats would cover it, and with this sum off he went to Vienna, ostensibly, on a question of his wine trade.

Arrived there, he began to think out how best he could forward the affair without getting too much fleeced in the process.

He began at the beginning, that is to say, at the chancery court, where all such problems have to be conciliated. And a long list it was! The expediting of such business is a serious matter.

But to the Jew there suddenly came a brilliant idea. He bethought him of an acquaintance at Court. The title of this acquaintance was doubtful, for he was only a young man, and whether to address him as a chancery clerk or as chancellor, he knew not. He was the nephew of the postmaster of Szent-Endre, Mr. John Leányfalvy. This worthy had adopted the orphan son of his sister, while yet a child, and had sent him to Vienna that he might carve out a career for himself in the imperial city. Each time that Abraham had made his business visits there, he had spoken to the postmaster and asked him if he had any message for "young Matyi." And when the uncle had taken this opportunity of sending his nephew a gift of country produce, Abraham always carried out these commissions faithfully, and was duly welcomed by "Mr. Matyi."

The latter was quite at home at Court, and had employment in the palace itself. What he did there, whether he had a voice in the Kaiser's councils, or brushed his coat, Abraham did not know, perhaps the latter was the likeliest supposition; in this case, he would be a patron to be prized, for servants are worth propitiating.

Consequently, the crafty Jew had determined to seek out the postmaster's nephew at headquarters. And in order he might not appear empty-handed, he took a pear with him. At that time there was a rage for pears carved out of wood, whereof one half formed a musical box, being filled with a mechanism which enabled him who put it to his mouth to produce quite a respectable tune. Such a pear did Abraham buy in a shop at Nürnberg, but he stuffed the hollow half of the pear with two hundred ducats. This pear he had destined for the young man if he prospered his petition with the Emperor. The said petition was drawn up neither by agent nor attorney, but as concocted by Abraham, ran thus: "Your Imperial Majesty, the high commissioners insisted on calling me 'Rothesel,' I only beg permission to insert a humble little 'i' in the middle of my name."

Furnished with this formula, Abraham set out for the palace. The entrée there proved much easier than he had imagined. For was there not a standing order that no petitioner should be denied admittance? So he was allowed to enter the great corridor, where already many people were assembled.

Abraham had what you might call prodigious luck at the very outset. The first person he met in the ante-chamber was "Mr. Matyi" himself. His appearance was that of a refined handsome youth of about four-and-twenty, with a red and white complexion like a girl's; he wore his hair powdered, a pea-green silk coat turned up with red, an embroidered waistcoat, a lace-frilled vest, with knee-breeches of cherry-coloured velvet, silk stockings, and buckled shoes. At his side hung an Italian rapier, and from his waistcoat pocket dangled a watch-chain laden with all kinds of trinkets. Under his arm he carried the tri-cornered hat of the period.

Moreover, this elegant young dandy was not ashamed to recognise his old acquaintance in the crowd; no sooner had he caught sight of his red mantle than he went up to him, asked him how he fared, and how it was with his uncle, and when he heard Abraham's errand, exclaimed, "Why that's a mere trifle." Thereupon, taking his hand, he led the Jew through three or four rooms in succession, which they traversed without knocking, till they came to a fifth, where he hung his hat up on a peg, as a sign that they had reached the presence-chamber, and told the Jew to wait while he should announce him to the Emperor. Abraham's knees nearly failed under him when he knew that only those folding doors divided him from the Kaiser. Yet his friend could enter freely; he must then be some kind of chamberlain.

In half a minute the latter was back again.

"You can enter, Abraham."

And thereupon he pushed the Jew, with his petition in his hand, through the door.

Abraham saw indeed little more of the Emperor than his boots, but these, he noted, had not certainly been blacked for a week; if "Mr. Matyi" was really his servant, he didn't know his duties that was plain.

Back came Abraham again into the ante-room.

"Mr. Matyi" was busy at a writing-table; he seemed to have some important correspondence to transact there.

The Jew was radiant with delight; he hardly knew where to begin: "It's right enough; the Emperor himself has countersigned the petition with his 'fiat.' Here is his name! He himself has put in the 'i,' praised be the Lord!"

But suddenly he broke off in his thanksgiving as he regarded the document. "Ay, woe's me!"

"What is the matter, friend?"

"Why, his Majesty has clean forgotten to put the dot over the 'i,' and without this, the 'i' looks exactly like an 'e,' and it only means from being a short ass, I shall now be but a long one! Alas, I am a dead man. I beseech you to be so very kind as to put the necessary little dot in for me, so that it may be done with the same ink. You have the pen in your hand ready."

"What are you thinking of?" cried "Mr. Matyi" indignantly, "to correct the imperial hand-writing, why, it would be a rank forgery! Give me the petition, I'll take it back to the Emperor, so he may put it in."

And thereupon, off he went through the folding doors with the paper.

Abraham breathed freely, he had attained his end, and this without laying out thousands of ducats; he had managed it for two hundred. He fumbled in the money compartment of the musical pear, and laid the ducats on the writing-table of "Mr. Matyi," so that the latter should not fail to see them when he returned to his correspondence.

The young man was soon back again.

"Here you are! God be with you! Greet my uncle for me, and tell him I have much to do, that I want for nothing, and send my good wishes, and a happy journey to you!"

Abraham put the petition in his pocket, crying over it like a child.

"Mr. Matyi" accompanied his protégé to the next room, thence he trusted him to find his way out.

While the Jew was struggling with the door-handle, back came "Mr. Matyi," red with rage, seized Abraham by the collar of his mantle, and with the other thrust the pear under his nose, asking angrily: "What do you mean by leaving this on my table?"

Abraham took it as a jest.

"Well now, I have only brought you some pears as usual."

"But the ducats?"

"They were for the gracious favour which the young gentleman has been so kind as to show me."

"I have shown you no kind of favour. You wanted justice and you have obtained it. Take back your gold!"

"Why should I take it back? Hasn't the young gentleman deserved it for all his trouble? Did he not get the dot put on the 'i'?"

"I will not accept a handful of gold for a dot over an 'i.'"

"But it's worth it to me? It's not a bit too much. The young gentleman needn't take offence. He can pay his debts with it."

"I have no debts."

"Oh, you have no debts, do you say? Don't tell me a Viennese dandy has no debts. You owe neither the tailor nor the host anything? What, don't you want to make your sweetheart a present?"

"I have none."

"Who could ever believe it? How you blush. Well, take it, make merry with it, gamble it away with good comrades. For I won't have it back."

"I drink no wine, I don't gamble, I have no good comrades; this money you will take, for it hurts me to receive it. Those I serve pay me for what I do. He who does such work as mine asks for no reward but his master's, and can take no bribe from another. Take your gold back."

"As you will, Mr. Ráby," said the Jew, and he put the ducats in his pocket.

CHAPTER VII.

"Very good then, Mr. Ráby," pursued the Jew. (He no longer thought of him as "young Mr. Matyi.") "But before I leave this place, nay, before you send me packing, I must needs have three words with you."

"All right, out with them!"

"Now the first is this: since I first weathered winter's snow and summer's dust on this good Mother Earth of ours, I never before met a man who was frightened at money. I see him for the first time to-day. You were positively averse to keeping my gold. Nay, I believe that you wanted to break my head on account of it. And now I find you have no sweetheart, you neither drink nor gamble; you fraternise with no one. That again is something quite unheard-of. And finally, a man will not dot the 'i' of another person's writing, that also is something out of the common, let me tell you."

"Well for one word I think that is long enough—what else?"

"The second concerns myself. As truly as that I yesterday was 'Rothesel,' and to-day am 'Rotheisel,' so surely is it that Rotheisel won't neglect a treasure which Rothesel has discovered. I know of a treasure, in fine, for the carrying off of which, as in the fairy tales, only clean hands can avail."

"I don't understand what you are talking about."

"Well, I do. There is a treasure lying buried in a certain place, a solid heap of more than a hundred thousand ducats, on the track of which I would set a champion."

"I still do not understand. To whom does this goodly hoard belong?"

"This money has been wrung from the sweat and blood of the poor and the oppressed, nay, squeezed out of ragged and hunger-bitten wretches, moistened by the tears of widows and orphans, purloined, and concealed from the Crown. It is the people of your native town, good sir, whose misery has augmented this treasure, and who starve and complain for the lack of it, while beggars swarm throughout the country. If this sort of thing goes on, the whole State must go to the dogs. I know what I am talking about, and will gladly lead you to the hoard. When you are in a position to rescue it from the dragon's clutches, two-thirds of it will go back to the poor wretched folk it was wrung from, and a third to enrich the man who restores it."

"But if you know all this, why not do it yourself?" questioned his listener.

"Tut, tut, my most respected sir, have you then studied to such little purpose as not to know the laws of your native land? Does it not stand written that the plaintiff must be a Christian? The Jew can do nothing. And, moreover, were I as good a Christian as the zealous old sacristan who opens the church every morning single-handed and shuts it at nightfall, I should not be the man for this business. For it is just such a man as you is wanted, my respected sir, a man who, once he has set his hand to the work, will not allow himself to be beaten out of the field. For as long as the seven-headed dragon that guards the treasure sees that no one attempts to raise it, he'll wag his seven heads more boldly than ever. As soon as the delegates who are told off to take charge of it, notice that by chance ten or twenty heaps of ducats have been left perhaps on the table, they go back and verify that all is in good order. They will resent the adventurous knight's interference, and will give him his quietus if he is not wary. He must press on against all foes, even if help fail him. How should a poor insignificant mortal like myself be fitted for such an undertaking? For such a quest, a powerful chivalrous man is needed, who has the entrée at Court, who is likewise a noble himself, and can wield the pen as well as the sword, in fine, one who has a heart open to the cry of the poor and oppressed, and the faculty of sympathising with the people. They are not my people—I am only a foreigner here, but it goes to my heart when I see how the harrow tears and the clods are broken, how for others is the sowing that these may reap. Then I thank God that He has not given me a portion in this land, but that I am a stranger here. Believe me, Mr. Ráby, the nobles always know how to oppress the vassals. The Turkish pacha at most, has shorn his subjects: the Magyar landlord has fairly plucked his, but the Szent-Endre council flay their victims of hide and hair alike. So that's my third word!"

"All right, just give me more precise details over all this, and come and look me up at my lodgings; there we can talk it over; I shall be at home the whole evening."

So at the appointed time, Abraham went to discuss matters with Ráby, and did not get home till morning. He literally talked the whole night long.

Yet when he at last took leave, he bound his friend on his honour:

"That you never betray how you knew all these things. The Spanish Inquisition was mere child's play compared to what those good people would do to me, if they knew that it was I who had made it so hot for them."

CHAPTER VIII.

Mr. John Leányfalvy was a narrow-minded man. He was the postmaster of Szent-Endre. He neither paid nor received visits; he had but one hobby, and that was gardening. This he rode with a persistency worthy of a Dutchman. He grew flowers of which no one had ever heard before—exotic blooms almost extinct, but for the fostering shelter his garden walls afforded.

He was specially celebrated for his melons. At the time of the melon-harvest, two great mastiffs guarded the melon-plot over which his bedroom window looked. In this garden all his spare time was spent. He was so busy one afternoon over his melon-beds, that he did not observe how his mastiff, who by day was chained up, was growling at a man who stood before the garden gate. He only became aware of the new-comer when the latter wished him good day. He looked round and saw a stranger dressed in the latest modish costume of Vienna, and finally, he recognised in the apparition his nephew, young Matyi.

"Why bless me if it isn't my nephew Matyi. I hardly recognised you in this fashionable coat, I declare. But very welcome you are all the same."

And the old man embraced his nephew heartily.

"Ay, but you've become a man since I saw you last. You only want a moustache," and he looked at Ráby's smooth-shaven face critically. "But you are not in a hurry to be back in Vienna, I hope?"

"Well, unless you want to send me away, I needn't be in a hurry to go back, as I could stay here all the winter," answered Ráby.

"Well, don't talk to me about sending you off. I know well enough you are under someone else's orders."

"Yes, uncle, under orders to stay here for some time."

"Oh! I take it, you are here then for the taxation commission?"

It was an office which had at that time but an unenviable reputation in Hungary.

"More pressing business still," answered the young man with a smile, as he whispered something in the old gentleman's ear, which was evidently an important disclosure.

The features of the old man relaxed.

"Now that's something like; that's capital! Now I can reckon you a man. Only don't neglect the work."

"Trust me!"

"And then don't begin among the lesser folk, but get hold of the great people. Go straight to the prefect himself; he's the one to tackle. Ay, I could give you some good advice. Hear all, see all, and hold your tongue, as the saying goes. But you know all about that, and have no need of a plaster over your mouth."

"Yet if I find the guilty, I shall not spare them, I warn you, whoever they be."

"You will see, my boy," said the old gentleman, rubbing his hands, "if you tackle the prefect properly, you will be court judge of Visegrád, year in and year out." And he clapped his nephew on the shoulder.

"What kind of a berth is it in Visegrád?"

"Ay, my boy, that's the fattest plum in the neighbourhood; it's worth more than a hundred county court magistracies, and it happens to be just vacant."

"How could I hope to get it?"

"What a stiff-necked man it is to be sure! Didn't you get to Vienna? You don't surely reckon yourself among those people who let themselves be cajoled by the gift of a fine horse or a roll of ducats: a man like you is worthy a bigger bribe."

The young man became suddenly crimson.

"But, my uncle, I don't come for that—for the sake of a horse or money, or even a court magistracy, not to be bribed by the great, but rather to redress the grievances of the folk who are oppressed, and to rectify abuses."

At this speech Mr. Leányfalvy shifted his zouave from the left to the right shoulder.

"Don't you know, my dear boy, that out of the mouth of the poor, complaints are not heard. There must be a God who hears them, nevertheless. Yet the government is a power against which one man can avail nothing. How can you protect the sown fields from the marmots? Man is just such a marmot. Dismiss him who is now in office, and put another in his place; you only change for the worse. As long as there are fools and knaves in the world, so long will the one always rob the other."

"Now if you reckon abuses of office among social ills, I can but tell you that if you have a will, you can amend them. And this will have I."

"Yes, but have you likewise the power? 'Whoso is wanting in strength is powerless in wrath.' Besides, who stands behind you?"

"The Emperor himself."

"And who else?"

"Isn't he enough?"

"That doesn't suffice; you must have the presiding judge as a patron, or the lord chancellor, or at least the district commissioner. If you can only ensure the Emperor's favour, that doesn't go far. What can you say to our Emperor, except 'May it please his Majesty,' and that he is lampooned daily. Every day there come some such scurrilous pamphlets to my notice."

"The Kaiser believes in unlimited freedom of opinion."

"Hang freedom of opinion! If I were Emperor, and anyone printed such things about me, I would take my axe and play such a tune on the writer's head with it, that he would not ask for a second one. And then if the Hungarians see that the Austrians dare thus to insult the Kaiser, what liberties will the Hungarian not allow himself?"

"Yes, indeed. All those who are shocked at his novelties, murmur against him. They abuse him because the freedom hitherto only accorded to a certain class and creed, will now be extended to all his subjects indiscriminately."

"Let us talk about the melons, my dear boy. Look at this one with the mottled rind. When it's ready you can eat it without harm. But take a bite, before it is ripe, and you get a horribly sore mouth. Now it's just the same with liberty. When it is ripe, the grower can present it to the people on a pewter plate. But cut it before it is ready, and the melon and he who eats it, alike are done for. I know you will maintain that one can force the melon to get ripe, if you have hot-beds and green-houses. Now you and your friends, the philosophers and philanthropists, are just such growers at the present time. Who could get enough hot-beds and forcing-houses for the whole world? Wait till the dog-days come, and the heat of the sun will let each one ripen in its proper measure."

"Good, uncle. I accept the melon allegory, and will answer you in your own gardening terms: If you want melons, you must sow the seeds. Some sprout, others lay dormant. Then comes the worm to devour them, and the mildew and the frosts to blast the young shoots, yet, in spite of all, your true gardener tends them to the end. Such a sower am I, who plant what is entrusted to me in the ground, that others may reap the harvest."

The simile pleased the old gentleman much; he stroked his moustache thoughtfully.

"You are the right sort, my boy. And if you feel equal to the task, undertake it. But I fear you won't succeed! But you have not come here to stir up a hornet's nest, have you?"

"No, uncle. First of all, I shall procure the actual facts of the case, and till I get them, I shall not say a word to anyone."

"That's well and good. But how will you get those facts?"

"I have reckoned for all that. I mean to settle down and buy myself a house, with a field and vineyard. As an inhabitant of the city, I shall have the right to mix myself up in local affairs."

"That sounds like business. For that matter, I can recommend you a house that belonged to the notary's brother. It's a fine property, with garden, vineyard, and meadow attached. The owner is a drunken good-for-nothing, and over head and ears in debt, but can, by realising the property, pay his debts, and still have something left. Leave the contract to me."

"Agreed then, uncle. The money question can soon be settled, as I have what will be necessary."

"So far, so good. But after, when you have your facts, who is going to be prosecutor?"

"I myself will be."

The old gentleman stroked his moustache doubtfully.

"Oho, my boy, that's a dangerous game. Do you know that the law won't allow you to do it anonymously? The prosecutor must act in his own name."

"I shall lodge my complaint openly so that the guilty can recognise me."

"Then be sure they will try and get rid of you."

"That is the fortune of war."

The old man smiled slily.

"It has just occurred to me you can't be prosecutor."

"Why not?"

"Why, pray, have you not studied law in Vienna? Docs not the decree of St. Stephen lay it down that the prosecutor must be a married man? If you are single, you are not qualified to make the depositions."

"All right, I'll marry."

His hearer fairly shook with laughter.

"My boy, I've heard many motives suggested for matrimony, but never one like yours. You are going to marry to help the people to their rights! Remember that—

"'He who takes himself a wife, Does but heap up care and strife.'"

"But, uncle, what can you, who were never married, have to urge against matrimony?"

"Oh, I've nothing against your marrying. Leave that also to me. I have found you a house; now I'll find you a wife."

"It is very good of you, I'm sure."

"I'm not joking. I know of a right suitable maiden for you. You remember when you were still a lawyer's clerk, pretty little Mariska, the notary's daughter. Well, she has become a fine girl. Since her mother's death she manages the household entirely, and nowhere is there one so well ordered as Tárhalmy's. She spends no money beyond what she gives to the poor, and knows how to save as well. She's none of your frilled and furbelowed fine ladies, and does not frizz her hair in the latest fashion, but just dresses like a modest Magyar maid; and when you talk to her, you hardly know what colour her eyes are, so modestly are they cast down. Nor does she waste time in chatter, but gives you a plain answer to a plain question, with the prettiest blush imaginable. That's the wife for you, my boy, and a right comely one, I promise you."

"All right, uncle. When I've bought the house, and had time to look round a little, I'll go and see her."

And with that, Ráby took his leave.

CHAPTER IX.

The postmaster did exactly as he had promised, and he did it promptly.

"Now I have got the house, you've got to set up housekeeping, but don't buy much furniture, the wife will see to that. Till you get a wife, I'll lend you my maid-servant to keep house; she's also a good hand at milking, for a cow you must have; and your cooking will have to be done at home, for there is no café or hotel here, as at Vienna. And don't trust your wine-cellar key to anyone else!"

Mathias Ráby took this good advice, and arranged his new house as if he were settling down for good in it. He had his fields sown with crops, his vineyards overhauled, and laid in a stock of winter provisions. But he encouraged no gossips, took no interest in outsiders, and was reserved with acquaintances to the verge of taciturnity.

But general rumour had it that the gentleman who had thus settled among them, had been sent by the Kaiser himself to investigate matters of state in Szent-Endre.

Soon after this, Ráby made an excuse for going to Pesth so as to call on the Tárhalmys.

Tárhalmy was the county notary, and lived in the Assembly House assigned him. Ráby knew it well, for when he was a clerk, he used to go there every day. When he reached the door, the heyduke who stood sentry, barred his way, with his musket under his arm, one foot crossed over the other, and his shoulder against the door.

"Tell me, my friend," for thus did Ráby accost the old heyduke, "is the worshipful pronotary at home?"

The man answered, his worship had just gone out, but his lady-daughter was within, and would be delighted to see the honourable gentleman.

Ráby hastened up the familiar wooden stairs, that were so well worn down the middle.

Our hero needed no guide through these rooms. He knew all the nooks and corners of the house, and likewise the time at which callers might come—between the hours of three and four in the afternoon. First he betook himself to the ante-room, where he laid aside his sword and hat. But there was no lackey there to announce him, he had to knock therefore at the first door, to hear a "come in," before he ventured to enter without further preamble.

It was the familiar dining-room, where the women-folk were used to betake themselves to their spinning-wheels.

They sat there now, the Fräulein and the two maids. The spinning-wheel was to our grandmothers what the cycle is to the women of to-day; nay, it took also the place of the pianoforte itself.

Mariska had certainly grown very pretty since Ráby had last seen her, although, as Mr. Leányfalvy had remarked, she was quite simply dressed, and did not curl her hair. He was also quite right about her blushing when she was spoken to. In this instance, words indeed were not needed to bring the colour into her cheeks, she no sooner saw the visitor, than she crimsoned to the roots of her hair. The young girl rose respectfully from the spinning-wheel, glanced shyly at the intruder, and ere he could forbid it, had made him a childish curtsey and kissed his hand.

Ráby was very nearly being angry.

"But, Mariska, do you not recognise me?"

"How should I help recognising you, Matyi?"

"Why then do you kiss my hand?"

"Ah, you have become a great man since those days."

"Were I ever so great a man, I would not allow my hand to be kissed by a lady."

"But I am no lady, you see."

"Nor am I a great man. And now please give me your hands that I may kiss them."

But the girl put both hands behind her back.

"No, for then should I be a lady indeed. Please be seated."

She motioned Ráby to the leather-covered sofa, and sat down again by the spinning-wheel, as she deftly began afresh to twist the flax into fine silky threads, so that they could talk if they wanted to.

The two maid-servants did not leave the room, but just listened to all that their mistress and her visitor said; it was but proper, they thought.

Ráby was meanwhile thinking how to baffle the maids. To this end he asked in German what she was doing?

The young girl gazed at him with her great blue eyes full of sorrowful amazement. Fancy expecting that in the household of the pronotary of Pesth, that stronghold of Magyar freedom, that anyone, much more the daughter of the house, should speak German! She lowered her eyes, and whispered timidly, "I do not understand German."

"You do not understand German? Why, whatever would you do if you went to a ball here in Pesth, and could not speak to your partners?"

"I never go to any balls; I can't even dance," murmured the girl.

"You mean to say, you don't dance? Well then, however do you amuse yourself?"

"When I have time for it, I read."

"And what in the world do you read, if you only know Hungarian?" asked Ráby.

"Father has a fine library, and so he chooses books for me."

"And how do you spend the whole day?"

"Oh! I have a small garden in the courtyard; I love flowers!"

Tho two were silent, and Ráby looked around him.

The whole room was eloquent to him of the past. There, by the work-table, was still the little box containing thread, scissors, and thimble, which he himself had made when he was a clerk. There over the couch, hung a withered wreath of dried flowers which he recognised. Nothing was lost; all had been carefully preserved, even the pen which he had used for the last time in the office, rested still behind the mirror with his name inscribed upon the holder.

And yet they had not expected him; all these souvenirs had not been spread out at the news of his coming. They were, everyone, abiding witnesses to the way in which his memory was cherished in a guileless maiden's heart which loves, while it yet hardly knows what love is.

Mathias Ráby was surely strangely ungrateful to the fate which had preserved such a treasure for him. But it is the way of youth, so unregardful is it of the treasures true love spreads for its unheeding eyes, to be its own for the asking.

But his meditations were interrupted by the entrance of Miska, the heyduke, who came to announce that his worship, the notary, was ready to see Mr. Ráby if he would wait upon him in the bureau.

Ráby rose from his seat, and took leave of his hostess, who accompanied him to the door.

There they exchanged the usual farewell greetings, and she laid her little hand in his shyly, as if fearing the ceremonial kiss. As Ráby took the small soft fingers in his, a magnetic shock, as it were, thrilled his being, so that he would fain have asked the question which was on his lips, the question the girl would have seen in his eyes, had she but raised her own.

And Mariska, too, yearned to ask him, "How long do you stay?" How gladly would she have heard the answer that it was for some time, how naturally would the invitation have risen to her lips to Ráby to come again often and see them.

But instead of all this, they did but hold each other's hands a moment half-fearfully, as if each were afraid of the other's kiss.

This once, at any rate, did Ráby have the chance of grasping that invisible golden thread which runs once through the life of every mortal. Well for him who seizes it, for it will lead him safely through all perils, but woe to him who lets it go! He cannot pick it up again.

Ráby did not seize the thread.

"Good-bye!" they murmured. And a right good word it is this "God be with you!" Yet what if man refuses the blessing the good God proffers him?

CHAPTER X.

When Ráby went into the office, the clerk told him that the chief was expecting him in the "state-room" as it was called, in which distinguished guests were received. This apartment was much more richly furnished than the rest; it was therefore intended as a compliment to Ráby, that the pronotary should receive him there, rather than in his bureau.

The pronotary was a fine-looking man of distinguished bearing. His thick grey hair was combed straight back from his brows, and except for his short moustache, he was clean-shaven. His short embroidered dolman reached to his hips, and was confined by a costly girdle, wherefrom depended a little pouch containing pen and ink, while his watch-chain dangled from his breeches' pocket.

Ráby was rather doubtful as to what sort of greeting he should venture on. The French style exacted a solemn posturing with sundry bows and curtseys; the German fashion demanded you should shake your neighbour's hand as lustily as possible, but old-fashioned Hungarian etiquette prescribed that the younger should kiss the hand of the elder. Ráby bethought him of the kiss he had received in coming thither, and that decided him. He would pay it back now to the father. The face of the old gentleman brightened at this greeting.

"Look you, my friend," he exclaimed in a clear deep voice, "in former times, I would have patted you on the head, but I cannot do that now for fear of dishevelling the coiffure your friseur has arranged. Don't you regret, by the way, wasting so much flour?"

His guest was glad to catch the old man in such a good temper, and determined to profit by it, so he kept up the jest.

"Yet it is far better surely, that I should tumble into flour than bran?"

"I think not, my boy, besides you are not so far from tumbling into bran as you seem to think."

Ráby looked at him with astonishment.

Tárhalmy's face became suddenly grave.

"I know well enough why you are here!"

(How could he know why he had come? wondered his guest.)

"Not at my house, but why you are in this country. And if you will permit me, I will tell you what I think about your mission."

"Oh pray do!" exclaimed Ráby.

"Well, my young friend, you know I have always loved you as my own son. I recognised all your capabilities, and always said 'that boy will some day do great things!' A better brought-up, better disposed youth than you were, with a higher sense of honour, could not be found. I would not hesitate to entrust you with untold millions—or an innocent maiden. But I warn you, if you persist in the way you have marked out for yourself, you will soon be rotting in one of our prisons; and I shall hear your chains clanking, without being able to stir a finger to set you free."

"And all that because I am a friend of the people?"

"Rather an enemy of the nation, say!"

"Are not the people and the nation one and the same?"

"No, not at all: the nation is the state. You idealists cannot see the wood for the trees; you cannot see the nation for the people. Only make the people believe that they fare better under a despotism than under a constitution, and you are the right side of the hedge."

"So you think it's a choice of being ruled by one tyrant or five hundred thousand."

"Wait, young man, the five hundred thousand are the defenders of the country on the field of battle, judges, commanders, pastors of souls and teachers."

"Yes, it was like that formerly. But time does not stand still, even if conditions remain the same. The new age demands a better system of defence, a more enlightened code of justice and government, as well as better methods of instruction."

"But you can't get all that in Hungary by just speaking the word! Nor anywhere else, for that matter. We defend our much abused Asiatic traditions, only through passive resistance."

"Yet the question which once was asked of old from the oracle of Dodona, is still the pressing problem for us: which is the most desirable, a flourishing Hungarian nation according to the ancient idea of it, or popular freedom?"

At these words, the pronotary shook the young man cordially by the hand.

"That was a pertinent question. I honour you for your candour. So many proselytes of the Emperor that I have come across so far, will insist on it that between these two antagonistic ideals a compromise is possible: that, after the abolition of the privileges of the nobles, with an equalisation of taxes, and a mutual obligation to bear the common burden, the country can remain the same as it was. But you openly admit there are only two alternatives, in the face of which we must needs choose. You have chosen your part, I too have made up my mind. I believe that in our part of the world it is more necessary for the constitutional, patriotic Hungarian nation to endure, than for the peasants to have one day a week more for idling; that it is better for the aristocracy to give orders to the mob, than that the mob should give orders to the aristocracy."

The young man laughed aloud.

"No, no, my honoured friend, I do not come here with the intention of touching our hereditary constitution with my little finger. In this does my whole mission consist—in rectifying abuses which cry aloud to Heaven for redress in the Court of the County Assembly."

"And pray who entrusts you with it?"

"Firstly the Emperor, and then the oppressed people themselves."

"That's just where the fault lies: neither the Emperor nor the people have the right to lay such a duty on you. That right belongs alone to the Pesth Assembly."

"But the Crown has the right to demand that such a right be exercised."

"Very likely. The Assembly will do whatever it be called upon to do."

"And if the Assembly acquit itself badly? For its own officials are guilty of the misery of the people."

"Oh, that is no secret. Our officials are in a body quite ready to fleece the folk in the very way that has aroused your indignation. But up till now, we have elected these officials ourselves, and we would rather have them over us, even if they were stained with the seven capital sins, than have the Emperor's nominees, were they angels from heaven. This is no legal quibble, but a question of actual conditions. Whatever the people suffer, they will recover sooner or later; if a man dies, another is born in his place; but the constitution can neither suffer nor die. You stand for the Emperor, I stand for the voice of the nation. Both are mortal. We shall see which of the two survives. But I warn you to reckon on no one's support in the work you have undertaken, for everyone will regard you as an enemy."

"Thank you," said Ráby. "Also, there is a satisfaction in remembering that there is at least one man I can reckon on who won't desert me."

"And who is that, pray?" asked Tárhalmy smiling rather grimly, for he thought it was the Emperor he meant.

"Why myself."

The pronotary embraced him, exclaiming tenderly as he did so: "Poor fellow, poor fellow!" Then he said gently: "Farewell, in case I never see you again!"

And Mathias Ráby went away without mentioning even a word of Mariska. What a horrible thing these politics are, to be sure!

CHAPTER XI.

Ráby had scarcely left, than pretty Mariska put her little head in at the opposite door which led from the reception-room to the dining-parlour. Mr. von Tárhalmy was striding up and down the apartment as if perturbed.

"Did you call me, dear father?" asked the girl.

"No, no, child; but come in."

"You are not vexed, father?"

"Not a bit of it, my dear."

"I thought you were quarrelling with someone."

"Nothing of the sort. We have only been discussing some business matters. So just come in."

The girl nestled up to her father's side affectionately.

"I quite thought you called me," she murmured, "and that you said, we have a guest coming to-morrow, Mariska."

"Aha, you are right enough," smiled Tárhalmy. "Of course I said so. Your cousin Matyi will dine with us to-morrow. Bless me, if I hadn't quite forgotten all about it."

"And it's well I should know it in good time."

"Yes, indeed, and see you have his favourite dishes for him. Have you plenty of stores, or must any be procured?"

"No, indeed, I have everything I want in the house."

And therewith, Mariska kissed her father's hand, nay both of them, and danced back into the next room as light-hearted as a bird.

And the two maids at the spinning-wheel must be up and doing; one to pound almonds in the mortar; the other to sift fine flour for fritters. The Fräulein herself set about peeling lemons, seeing she was going to make some of Matyi's favourite cakes, such as no Vienna pastry-cook could turn out. And through the whole household there was the sound of singing, for Mariska too could sing on occasion—and this was one.

But the pronotary himself sent his heyduke to go and find Mr. Mathias Ráby, and tell him, with his compliments, that he would expect him to dinner the next day.

Ráby was meantime interviewing some of the high officials of Pesth.

The first one he visited was the lord-lieutenant of the city.

For this visit he had to put on court dress, as that official was a direct representative of the Emperor.

His Excellency was an unpopular person, disliked by everyone. He was a hard man whom nothing softened. He sympathized with no one, and he was in nobody's good graces. Yet he was a personality everyone had to reckon with.

His very appearance bespoke the man. The copper-coloured complexion and ill-shaven face, with its deep frowning eyebrows, heightened the natural defect of his neck, which was twisted towards the right shoulder. His hair was lank and reddish; his dress a cross between the Hungarian and Austrian mode, slovenly and dirty, and stained with snuff, while the order of St. Stephen, which he wore round his neck, was defaced and half torn away. His voice had a repellent snarl about it. He spoke German with everybody, but it was a vile patois.

When Ráby was ushered into his presence, his Excellency was drinking his coffee, and his visitor had to stand till he had finished.

When he had set his cup down, he got up, and turning abruptly to Ráby, asked him if he were a count?

His visitor could not imagine what prompted this question, but he answered that he was only an untitled gentleman of good family.

Thereupon his Excellency pointed to Ráby's silk vest, and snapped:

"Well, then, what do you mean by this? According to the prescription of the 'dress regulations,' no one under the rank of a count may wear embroidery."

And in fact there was at this time a "dress regulation" in force to this effect. Kaiser Joseph carried his paternal interest in his subjects so far as to lay down rules as to how they should dress. Fashions and ornaments which were permitted to the count, were not allowed the baron. In this way, you could specify at first sight what rank a man held, for even his hat revealed it. Only for princes and princesses was it permitted to wear both black and white feathers; counts wore white alone, barons black, and so forth down the scale. These sumptuary laws even affected walking-sticks which had their mountings differentiated according to the rank of the possessor.

That was why Ráby had offended the lord-lieutenant. As a simple gentleman, he had no right to either gold or silver embroidery.

"This is the dress usually worn by the secretary of the imperial cabinet," was the only explanation Ráby offered.

"Ah, that is another thing. But I don't approve of these concessions being allowed to those who are not men of rank."

He scanned his caller mistrustfully from head to foot, and then went on stiffly. "But I already have your credentials. Discharge your duty, but take care what you are about, for you will find no one here to help you out of a difficulty. So I have the honour to be your very humble servant."

But Ráby did not mean to let himself be dismissed in this fashion.

"I too, am your Excellency's very humble servant," he answered. "But I have a special mission to your Excellency which concerns both of us: my duty is to speak, as it is likewise to present you with the imperial warrant."

The determined tone of the speaker levelled at once all distinctions of age and rank. His Excellency vainly took refuge in walking up and down the room, for Ráby kept pace with him, and he poured forth his whole story into his ear, for he was determined that in such a high quarter, the right side should be known.

When he had finished his explanations, he raised his cocked hat with an elaborate bow, bent his knee ceremoniously to the proper degree, and withdrew, with the three paces prescribed by correct etiquette, to the door.

Mathias Ráby now hastened to the dwelling of the district commissioner, who lived alone in an old house at Buda. Before it stood a sentry, and at the entrance was also a porter who rang the bell if a visitor came in a sedan-chair—the favourite means of locomotion. You could, if you wished, have a carriage, but it was not so comfortable. Nor was it advisable to go on foot, for in the covered ways which led round the water-city, it was dark enough to cause ordinary pedestrians to dread being robbed—as indeed they easily could have been.

Ráby hastened up the steps of the district commissioner's house with renewed confidence, for the commissioner had been one of his Vienna acquaintances, and so when the lackey announced the visitor, ordered Ráby to be admitted at once, though he had not finished his toilet.

At that epoch, dress was no light matter even for a man. The friseur was occupied in shaving his client; then from one box he took out some white cosmetic, from another some red colouring, to apply them to the proper place on the cheeks, for, at that era, not only women, but also men of fashion painted their faces. Then the eyebrows were darkened, and blue streaks were faintly outlined on the temples with a paint-brush dipped in ultramarine; finally, a patch was applied with artful dexterity on the right spot above the reddened lips. Only when all this was done, could the final operation be carried out—that of powdering the curled and twisted hair, the patient holding meanwhile a kind of paper bag before his face, whilst the barber powdered the coiffure with a large brush.

"How are you, my friend?" was his host's greeting, as Ráby entered. "I'll be done in a few minutes; meanwhile, sit down and read."

On the writing-table, to which he motioned Ráby, lay some of the latest pamphlets and pasquinades of the moment, mostly directed against the Emperor.

Ráby turned them over. "I've seen these before," he remarked.

"And is not his Majesty very angry at them?" asked the commissioner.

"Not a bit of it; he sends for the pamphlets, and not only does he make me read them to him, but he is heartily amused."

"Otherwise the author might find himself fastened to the wheel, eh!"

"Joseph has thought of a more sensible punishment. A writer sold his pasquinades at thirty kreutzers apiece, and built a house with his profits. But recently the Kaiser, as soon as one of these productions appeared, had it reprinted and sold for eight kreutzers. The result was that the writer had the whole edition left on his hands, while everyone bought that issued by the Kaiser. The proceeds were given to charity."

"Not a very seemly trade for an Emperor, eh? It were far more becoming to a prince to have the fellow's head off."

"Yes, the Kaiser has distinctly plebeian ideas, it must be owned."

"What too did he mean by putting in the pillory an officer of the Guard? Only think of it, just for misappropriating from the treasury sixty-six thousand gulden. And it was only to build an alchymist's laboratory. Could he help it because it turned out a failure?"

"Ah, well, now the ice is broken."

Meantime the friseur had finished his work and gone, so it was easy for Ráby to broach his errand, with such an opening:

"The Emperor visits with extreme severity the embezzlement of public funds; it is for this very purpose that he has sent me to bring to light certain abuses connected with the Szent-Endre municipality."

"I know, I know," said his Excellency, as he poured some eau de Cologne over his hands, "it has come to my ears. But you will be a long time finding your way out of that tangle, once you get into it; let me warn you. By the way, is there a new opera company at the Vienna theatre?"

"Ah, my good friend, I've no time to run after plays and players. I've dramas of my own to look after, and they deal with the picking of other people's pockets."

"The deuce take your dramas! Does one still see pretty women at Vienna? Where do you have your evening gatherings during the winter?"

"We go to 'The Good Woman.' The sign-board is a woman without a head."

"What does the hostess say to that, pray?"

"I shall have no chance of asking her, seeing that I shall spend the winter here, and pass my time in verifying accounts."

"Stuff and nonsense! Cut it short, sir, and get back to Vienna as soon as you can. Say you have found nothing. By the way, have you been in Pozsony? They say they pay their theatrical companies far better than we do; isn't it a shame?"

"May I venture to ask if his Excellency will deign to listen to my representations about the Szent-Endre affair?"

"My dear fellow, just tell me everything. I am wholly at your service. And don't mind my interruptions. I shall hear all. Have the officials really so oppressed the poor? It's unheard-of! And the Rascian 'pope' might well speak out. He's a good sort! Just such another as some of our priests in Vienna. Did you ever hear how—oh, yes, I'm listening right enough. I see quite well that you've discovered some sort of roguery. The story of the hidden coffer sounds just like a play, doesn't it? 'The Hidden Treasure,' or 'The Forty Thieves.' Go on! I declare that notary ought to be placed in Dante's Inferno. What was that celebrated forgery case, by the way, when some count or other, of high family, was put in prison surely? You can't be too severe with that kind of thing. Yes, the small fry, like your notary, don't get out of the net, but the man with a handle to his name, gets clean off! We ought to make some examples in high places."

Ráby longed to express to his Excellency his conviction that the Szent-Endre culprits would also elude justice; but it seemed wiser to be silent till his loquacious friend had had his say.

And now indeed the district commissioner, who was really a good sort of fellow, showed that he had quite understood the whole business.

"You leave it to me, my friend; I'll follow it up. You may reckon on my help. If the councillors show themselves recalcitrant, we will know how to make them dance! But now it's time for the theatre, my friend. What do you say to coming with me? I have a box. You will be able to see all the pretty girls of Pesth and Buda together."

"Much beholden to you, but I regret I can't take advantage of your offer," answered Ráby; "I must hasten homewards to send in my report to the Emperor."

"Oh, what's the good of drawing up reports? Take my advice and don't send him any. And if you won't come to the theatre with me, then come and dine to-morrow and we can talk things over."

But Ráby went home to draw up his report.

Meantime, the lord-lieutenant was demanding of his secretary:

"Which is the Statute that treats of nobilis cum rusticis tumultuans?"

The secretary was a walking legal code. He not only knew that the law in question was article thirty-three, of the year 1514, but could quote the passage word for word: "Noblemen who take part in any risings of the peasantry shall be banished, and shall forfeit the whole of their estates."

His Excellency uttered a growl of discontent; evidently the citation was not an apt one.

"What about that other statute of Nota Conjurationis?"

"Article forty of 1536 pronounces sedition to be high-treason. See Nota Infidelitatis."

His Excellency shook his head.

"And that of Calumniator Consiliariorum?"

"Article of the year 1588 runs as follows:—Whosoever shall calumniate and unjustly attaint any of the Empire's councillors, shall be condemned to lose his head and forfeit all his goods."

"That is better. You can go."

The speaker was obviously contented this time.

But immediately afterwards he recalled the secretary.

"Which article is it that treats of the Portatores Causarum?"

"Article sixty-three, of the year 1498. Whosoever shall bring his cause before a tribunal other than that of his own country, shall be arrested and imprisoned in the Dark Tower."

"Now you can retire."

His worship, the district commissioner, who during Ráby's relation had appeared to pay not the slightest attention to the Szent-Endre story, had no sooner got to his box at the theatre, than he sent immediately for pen, ink, and paper, and, quite oblivious of the play, hurriedly drew up a missive to the prefect, wherein he set forth Mathias Ráby's mission, and how he had been directly authorised by the Emperor to revise the finances, pointing out that he was well informed as to everything, even to the contents of the strong box. He would further suggest that it would be wise for the prefect to go and look into things for himself, otherwise disagreeable consequences might ensue.

This note he sent by a special messenger to ensure its speedy delivery.

Tárhalmy's heyduke came back late in the evening with Ráby's refusal. He could not come, because he was already pledged to dine with the district commissioner.

"You need not trouble about the almond-cakes, Mariska," said the pronotary to his daughter, "Cousin Matyi will not be with us to-morrow, he is flying higher game."

And all at once the sound of singing ceased in the house.

CHAPTER XII.

Hardly had Mathias Ráby returned to Szent-Endre than he realised that everyone was aware of his mission. Gifts of all kinds poured in, and his servant told him that in his absence two casks of wine had arrived—she knew not from whom. In the courtyard, big stacks of firewood had already been piled up—the gift of some anonymous donor, while the poultry-yard was full of feathered stock which seemed to have flown down from the skies.

It was a pity the recipient did not appreciate them. Yet he knew the time would come when all those who now plied him with gifts, would be ready to deprive him of everything, if he ventured to set foot in their streets. He forbade the maid to touch any of them under pain of instant dismissal. The poor girl was quite dumbfounded with surprise, for what could one have better than such presents?

On the day of his return, two well-known citizens appeared at his door with a smart coach and four beautiful horses. One of them was Mr. Peter Paprika; in former times he had himself fulfilled a term of office as magistrate six years, so he understood the situation. The two had come to wish Mr. Ráby good day, Peter Paprika adding that, as his worship must have so many journeys to make in so many different directions, he was sure he could not exist without a carriage and horses. For Ráby, moreover, the price of the whole equipage, including horses, would only be forty gulden! Nor need he be surprised at this abnormally cheap price, for they were not stolen. The four horses were from the stud of the State, the carriage was the best the local builder could turn out.

Mathias Ráby thanked them for the offer, but refused to buy the equipage, even at this price.

However, they still pressed their bid, adding that fodder for the horses would be provided gratis, whereupon Ráby told them point blank that their bribes would not in the least avail to turn him from his purpose.

Mr. Paprika returned dejectedly to the town council where his colleagues waited to learn the result of his mission.

"I'm afraid," he announced to his fellow-councillors, "it won't avail us to dip in the little chest for this. We have a difficult customer to deal with. We must dive into the big one."

They talked the matter over, and determined that if necessary, they would sacrifice half the common wealth, and for this, bleed the treasure itself, to such an end. And Peter Paprika was entrusted to find out a new opportunity for proffering the bribe.

So the next day they sought out Ráby, and put the whole thing before him. They hinted broadly enough that you did not muzzle the ox that trod out the corn, and that he who cut up a goose was justified in keeping the best bit for himself, and other like arguments, and finally laid on his table the sum of three thousand ducats.

Even to-day three thousand ducats are not a sum to be despised: in those days, indeed, they represented a respectable fortune. But Ráby nearly drubbed the envoy who brought them out of the room. He was righteously indignant, and angrily showed the messenger the door.

"I never saw a man so angry," growled Peter Paprika, "I've heard men often enough refuse money in so many words, but they contrived to pocket the ducats discreetly, directly they have the chance." So they thought it might happen this time. A week elapsed, and people already began to smile knowingly at Ráby when they met him in the street, saying to themselves, "He only wants a little bigger net, but he'll be caught in the end."

How greatly was popular opinion disconcerted, when in all the churches the following Sunday, a "command" from the Emperor was read to the effect "that the three thousand ducats which the worshipful town council had given to Mr. Mathias Ráby for benevolent purposes, were to be divided among the inhabitants whose homes the preceding year had been destroyed by fire, and that each one would receive seventy-five gulden apiece."

What a procession it was that took its way to Ráby's house. The unfortunate victims of the conflagration came with their children and chattels to thank their benefactor and to kiss his hand. The homes of many of them had still to be made good, and the help could not have come at a more seasonable time. But it set the officials against Ráby. They could not tell the recipients of this bounty what had really happened. But the latter guessed immediately that the town council had given Mr. Ráby three thousand ducats, not for any charitable ends, but in order to bribe him, and that he was making over to them these ill-gotten gains. Well might the poor regard him as their deliverer!

Nevertheless, the councillors began to shake in their shoes. Judge, notary, and old Paprika hastened to the prefect, and announced with anxiety and horror that a dragon had been set on to them, who would not be pacified with the treasure itself.

"Well, we'll just fetch out a bigger one still to satisfy him."

What that greater treasure was, we shall in the course of events now learn.

CHAPTER XIII.

For some days the great circuit had been in full swing in the city. It was a new institution, inaugurated by the Emperor Joseph, whereby the lord-lieutenant or his representative, annually had to make a tour through the county to procure information of all kinds, and refer the same to the district commissioner, of whom there were ten in all throughout the country.

The business was easily settled in some counties. But in that of Pesth, which is as large as a German kingdom, the number of official entertainments was so great that it demanded an ostrich's digestion. These municipal officials, like the lord-lieutenant himself, must eat and drink hard three or four days running, while, at the end, the whole burden of the work fell on the substitute, the eldest and best qualified magistrate. No one answered to this demand better than our old friend, Mr. Laskóy.

When the circuit came to Szent-Endre, it was naturally the turn of the prefect to give an entertainment. To this the imperial court secretary, Mr. Mathias Ráby of Rába and Mura, received a formal invitation in due course.

As it was so great an official gathering, he put on his Viennese dress, and arrived at the prefecture by twelve o'clock, the hour appointed.

He was received by a lordly looking lackey, who discreetly gave him to understand that he was somewhat early, that the gentry were still in council, but that till dinner-time, he might, if he would, go into the garden where he would find Mademoiselle, the prefect's niece.

Ráby instantly conceived a high opinion of the lady of the house, who, thus immediately preceding a great banquet, could find leisure to walk in the garden. She could not be wholly wrapped up in her housewifery.

But how find a garden he had never seen and seek out a lady who was a complete stranger to him? However, help was nigh. Just as if it had scented him, a black poodle came running down the corridor wagging his tail, as welcoming the guest, and finally took the end of Ráby's cane between his teeth and drew him to the door that led into the garden. Ráby, seeing the dog wanted to play with the cane, let him have it, whereupon the cunning little beast seized it in the middle and preceded Ráby down the garden path where Fräulein Fruzsinka was to be found. The garden was laid out in the prevalent mode, in a maze composed of trees, among which one had vainly sought for an outlet. There, indeed, Ráby had never found the lady on his own account, for she had ensconced herself in the innermost recess and was reading, seated on the mossy bank.

She was no longer the Hungarian amazon who had worn the riding gear we met her in, earlier in this story. She was now the Viennese "élégante," whose toilette proclaimed her the lady of fashion, with her walking-stick, her elaborate coiffure, and lace ruffles, all irreproachably correct. Nor were cosmetics and patches wanting that the mode demanded, and she answered Ráby's greeting with the prescribed German formula: "Your servant, sir."

The poodle broke the ice, by running up with his cane and laying it at his mistress' feet.

But Fräulein Fruzsinka picked it up gently and gave it back to Ráby. She held a richly bound book, Wieland's "Oberon," which she showed to her guest.

Now with ladies who read Wieland you can talk of something else besides ordinary themes. And in the first quarter of an hour of his conversation with her, Mathias Ráby discovered that his hostess was a highly cultivated woman who could discuss the French philosophers as an ordinary provincial belle might the latest fashion in head dresses, and speak German fluently.

And her eyes, how marvellous they were!

They came out of the maze pursuing the talk on literature, and bent their steps towards the flower garden. Passing the flower-beds, Fräulein Fruzsinka betrayed also her knowledge of that "language of flowers" which just then was the rage in Vienna. The young lady broke off a twig of evergreen, and gave it to Ráby, who well recollected the couplet which set forth its symbolism:

"The evergreen is always green, although it blossoms never,So may the friendship 'twixt a man and woman last for ever."

But there was nothing of the coquette about her; she made no advances whatever.

The sound of the dinner-gong here breaking off their talk, his hostess accompanied Ráby back to the house, where the company were impatiently awaiting them. The dinner was already on the table.

The Fräulein presented Ráby to the other guests who all greeted him warmly.

The meal threatened to be interminable, as course succeeded course, till at last someone threw out a hint to the effect that a little exercise would be good for the diners, who had a game of skittles awaiting them.

"Skittles," indeed, was as it were the word of dismissal, and the suggestion nearly spoiled the proposal made by another guest that after dinner they should have a song from Fräulein Fruzsinka on the clavichord.

But the skittle players were in the majority though there was a keen opposition.

Finally matters were compromised by settling that they should have their hostess' song first, and then the skittles. At first a few of the guests loitered round the clavichord, at which Fräulein Fruzsinka, with her really sweet voice, was commencing a ditty. But you could not well smoke there, so one by one they stole out into the garden where the skittles were already in full swing.

Meanwhile, Fräulein Fruzsinka remained at the clavichord alone with Mathias Ráby, who from his knowledge of music could turn over for her at the right moment.

The singer soon shut the music book, and rose impatiently from the instrument.

"What people these are!" she exclaimed with a little irritated gesture of her hands. "Not a lofty idea, not a noble aspiration among them, as far as one can judge. And that is our world!"

Ráby, who had the instincts of a courtier, sought to excuse his fellow guests.

"Their own official concerns fill their minds entirely."

"Their official concerns indeed! Yes, I should think so! Did you hear the anecdotes with which they regaled each other at table? Quite frankly, with the most shameless cynicism. Yet they were all true. Among such people as ours, ignorance, idleness and greed counter-balance one another. Not one of them knows his business: each neglects his duty. But see if there is anything to be got out of any official function, and everyone is ready to seize it for himself."

Ráby held a brief for the accused.

"With us, offices of that kind are ill-paid. The official's salary is scant; he has, too, a house and family to keep up."

Fruzsinka laughed aloud. "There is not a married man among all of them. They are all a penniless lot who come to pay their court to me. Each of them would marry me, were they not all afraid of me!"

"Afraid of the Fräulein? You must make a strange impression on them."

"Yes, think of it! Can you believe that anyone is frightened at me because I wear a fashionable gown, read novels, am clever at music, but indifferent to kitchen and cellar; thereat the wooer shudders. He says to himself, 'he cannot possibly tolerate that,' and takes himself off forthwith."

"On the contrary, dainty toilettes and culture bespeak wealth, and that alone should be one more spur for the suitors, surely."

"Oh certainly, if they were sure that my uncle, who is rich, were going to leave me his money. But that is a secret no one knows. There are two things my wooer cannot find out, whether my uncle really loves me, and whether I know how to flatter him well enough, so as not to forfeit his affection. And truly I do not quite know myself."

"And that surely is not difficult to decide. For your beautiful toilettes and good education witness sufficiently to his affection for you."

"Ah, as far as my education goes, I have only to thank the gracious Empress Maria Theresa, for I was educated at her Elizabeth Institute in Buda, and my education cost no one a heller. And as regards my dress, my uncle insists on my dressing well, in order to captivate each new-comer. If it is an aristocratic cavalier who appears on the scene, forthwith I must don my pearl-embroidered bodice and lace stomacher and the plumed hat, but if it be an ordinary townsman, I wear the provincial dress of the simple country girl. Yes, would you know everything at this, our first meeting? And, indeed, as it is the first, so will it be the last. But would you hear how that must be, come with me into my own sitting-room, for here someone will overhear us."

Ráby was already under the spell of the sorceress, and he followed her willingly into her boudoir.

"You are not the first, dear Ráby," pursued his hostess, "who has come into this town vowing vengeance on us, to demand that justice be done. I say 'us,' for as you see, I too am leagued with this confederacy. And each of such emissaries in turn have I seen withdraw after a time, his anger appeased. Now, once more, they hear that a man of iron has come to set his foot down with inexorable rigour; he distributes the vast bribe which has been offered him, among the poor, while to win him over, even the great coffer is ransacked, but in vain. Thereupon, the authorities bethink them of another treasure still, the prefect's niece. And they trick her out as a fashionable lady, and leave her alone with the incorruptible. You see I am quite frank! Do you not blush for me? I do for myself, I can assure you. Take my advice, and fly from this place!"

"But, Fräulein, all you tell me does but make me still more determined to pursue the purpose for which I came hither."

"I see you to-day for the first time; I know nothing of you but what I have heard from your opponents; but what I have heard of you only makes me take your side. You are no ordinary man. Go, I tell you, and save yourself; flee from this place!"

"I save myself?"

"Yes, indeed! You cannot imagine how evilly disposed to you are those among whom you find yourself. Indeed, they have threatened to take your life."

What does she mean? Will she scare him away from the field of his labours, so that intimidated by her words, he returns to Vienna? Or has she measured her man, and seen that he is to be best caught by seeking to divert him from his purpose? And does she know that for such a one, the most powerful enticement of all will be to seek to turn him from his goal?

Ráby responded to the signal that his hostess made him, to come closer; nay, he took the fan she held, and fanned her and himself with it.

"That is splendid; why it will make my stay here quite a romantic experience," he said.

"You will rue it, however, and expose yourself to a thousand dangers which you have not the power to withstand. I see you are confident of your strength. But if you had to fight with someone, would it not disquiet you to know your adversary was an excellent shot. Suppose the moment you entered the field, someone whispered to you: 'Be on your guard; your second is in league with your opponent, he has placed no bullets in your pistol.' Would you not, in such a case, refuse to fight?"

"But the case is quite unthinkable."

"So you deem it. But to prove to you, that I am not seeking, as your enemies would have me do, to try and entangle you in my net, I will tear asunder the snare already closing round you, and show you something which shall enlighten you once and for all."

She went to her writing-table and took out of a drawer a letter.

"Say, do you know this handwriting?"

"Very well, it is that of the district commissioner."

"The note was addressed to me, in order to awaken no suspicion. Please read it."

It was the letter which the district commissioner had written at the theatre.

As he read it, Ráby fairly crimsoned with wrath. He was thunderstruck to find that his official chief, who had promised to support his mission, should have a secret understanding with those whom he was pledged to punish. Whom should he trust, if this was the state of things?

"Now will you not fly?" said Fräulein Fruzsinka. Her words urged him to go, but her eyes held him back.

"No, indeed! now will I remain," cried Ráby impetuously, as he rose to go. And as if to prove that he had determined to do and dare all, he hastily seized her hand and raised it passionately to his lips.

And she did not withdraw hers, but vehemently returned its pressure, as if to say: "This is the man I have long been looking for!"

"Leave me now," she whispered; but her eyes seemed to say, "Come again, soon!"

Mathias Ráby knew now that fate had led him to a kindred soul at last!

CHAPTER XIV.

Were this story a romance pure and simple, it would suffice to tell that Fräulein Fruzsinka had fire in her eyes, and Mr. Mathias but a heart of wax, that, consequently, when they met, the one melted the other.

But since this history is, in the main, a true narrative, we do not think it should be supposed that such was the case. Mathias Ráby being a diplomatist as well as a philosopher, did not seek in the lady of his dreams a Venus Anadyomene, but rather a fully equipped Minerva, and he thought that he had before him a high-minded woman, whose insight penetrated the evil intentions of his enemies, and whose hands should serve to set him free from the snares their wickedness had woven around him. To save such a woman from a degrading position was in itself surely a knightly and a noble deed. And what a splendid help would it not be to him, in the struggle that lay before him, to choose such a companion, who could circumvent the designs of his enemies, and be to him a guardian angel as well as a helpmate.

So it came about that one day Mathias Ráby sought out his uncle, Mr. Leányfalvy, with this request.

"I have come, my dear uncle, to remind you of your promise. I need a 'best man.'"

"A 'best man'? All right, my boy, I'm ready; let's have the horses put to."

"It won't be necessary; it is only at the other end of the city. It is to the prefecture I want to go."

"It's the Fruzsinka, then," exclaimed the old gentleman, and he began to scratch his head in deep perplexity. Finally, he blurted out, "Listen to me, my boy, take my advice and choose anyone else."

"Uncle, I forbid you to speak thus! She is my betrothed."

"I will not say anything against the woman of your choice. I will only say this: your father and mother were worthy God-fearing folk. If there had been twenty commandments to keep instead of ten, they would have observed them all scrupulously. And they loved each other so dearly, that when your father died, your mother followed him the very next day. And so it can be said to your own credit, that you are neither a murderer nor a robber. Therefore, I want to know how it is that, since neither you nor your parents have ever committed mortal sin, such a punishment should be destined for you, as marrying Fräulein Fruzsinka?"

"Uncle, I forbid you——"

"If you only knew the woman she is!"

"I know quite well, she herself has told me all."

"All, has she, what sort of an 'all' is it?"

Mathias Ráby shrugged his shoulders as one who does not understand grammatical subtleties. "Oh, with women, the world is an everyday matter."

"But these are not everyday matters."

"Well, I will hear no evil of her."

"May Heaven forgive me if I make a mistake! But what does it concern me after all? Yet I found for you a nice, well-brought up girl to whom the other one cannot hold a candle! What are the black gipsy eyes of the one compared to the innocent blue ones of the other? But if such a wife pleases you, there is nothing more to be said. Only you will have a wife and no mistake, I'll warrant you!"

"Now, dear uncle, I beg of you to come and accompany me in my wooing."

Mr. Leányfalvy began to see that he must play a part in this pantomime after all.

"I've no clothes to go in," he explained. "In these I could not enter such grand company."

"I will bring you a new coat from Pesth."

"It's no use, nephew. Among such grand folks a simple gentleman like me, who am a mere nobody, has no business. Take the district commissioner with you; he is a great man, and can write worshipful before his name."

"I don't want any great men. I'd rather have you!"

Now the postmaster came out with his true meaning.

"I don't want to be your 'best man!'" he said bluntly.

"You don't, and why not?"

"Because I am exceedingly angry, and I should quarrel with you. I am seriously vexed with you, not because you insist on marrying Fruzsinka—you can be angry with yourself for that—but because you are leaving that sweet, pretty, innocent child, to eat her heart out in disappointment. I do not want to have anything more to do with you; you are nothing to me. Now go, and take your grand friend with you!"

"Very well, I won't take anyone. I'll go alone and ask for her myself."

Thereupon, Ráby turned away and went. It would be indeed absurd that a man, in such a high position, who had been educated at the Theresianum, and was the trusted confidant of the Emperor himself, should let himself be dissuaded from his purpose by a simple unlearned rustic.

The contradiction only strengthened him in his determination.

And then—those glorious eyes!

Ráby was one of those men who, once having set themselves an end in view, pursue it unflinchingly. He went straight away to the prefect, stated plainly his errand, and asked for the hand of his niece.

The prefect, however, pushed his cap back a little off his brows, and demanded somewhat abruptly if his visitor understood Hungarian?

Ráby was a little disconcerted by the question.

"Yes, I can speak Hungarian," he answered shortly.

"But, my friend, to speak Hungarian and to understand it are two very different things, as we shall see directly. I ask you, what is it you want? Do you want to take my niece Fruzsinka as your wife, or do you wish to be the husband of my niece Fruzsinka?"

"Surely that is one and the same thing," said the suitor.

"Not a bit of it; they are quite distinct. Let's put it plainly. For instance, you elect to be my niece's husband. In this case you come and live here at the prefecture, and you get thrown in as a marriage settlement, a coach and four, a coachman and lackey, and will have in fact all the money you need. If you are tired of the chancery work in Vienna, we can get you elected administrator of Visegrád, which post happens to be vacant. You only need walk into it, or if you would prefer to do so, you can easily keep your appointment at Court, and a deputy will look after the Visegrád affairs for you, perhaps better than you could yourself. All you have to do is to spend the income, if you come to live here. This is one alternative. The other is that you take my niece as your wife, and make your own little home for her, and the rest is your concern, not mine. Now I have spoken plainly, do you understand me?"

"Perfectly, and I am also ready with my answer. I ask for no prefecture, no coach and four, no administratorship; I only ask for Fräulein Fruzsinka, whom I love; I ask for the lady, not for the property."

"Well, go and have a talk with her. If she is agreeable to the proposal, I won't raise any objection."

Thereupon, he sent the wooer to Fräulein Fruzsinka, who had previously suggested to Ráby that he should come on this particular day and formally propose for her hand.

"You come without a 'best man,'" said Fruzsinka, as Ráby entered. "You have found no one who would undertake the office, that is it. Each of the friends you asked refused, and tried to set you against me?"

"I assure you, Fräulein, that there is no man living from whom I would listen to the slightest word against you, not even my own father. I will tell you truthfully how the matter stands. I have one good old friend in this world whom you know well, my uncle Leányfalvy. I begged him to bear me company, but he refused solely, however, on this ground, that he had already chosen a bride for me, a playmate of my childhood, and had so set his heart on my having her, that he is angered at my making another choice."

"And why not marry the playmate of your childhood?"

"That too will I tell you, and be as candid with you as you were with me. This girl is a dear, gentle, little creature, whose life it were a shame to link with my own stormy career. Why, I should have to transform myself to marry her. If I were a man who simply swims with the stream, and troubles not as to what passes outside his own house, then could I woo such a bride indeed. But I am possessed by a demon of unrest that will let me have no peace; the misery of the people is constantly before me, urging me unceasingly to champion their cause against their oppressors. Nothing shall stop my mouth from pleading their rights. My life will be a perpetual struggle, I see that clearly. And can I fetter to such a destiny, a mere child whose only strength is her inexhaustible patience and gentleness? Every moment would it not be a torment to me, that each woe I drew down upon my head would fall likewise upon that of a guiltless and innocent being with a hundredfold weight. No, Fräulein, when I reckoned up the obstacles to the career I had set before me, I determined to ask no woman to share it. Till fate threw me across your path, I had never thought of marriage. But at the first glance, I said to myself, 'There is the complement of my own being; there is a woman whose soul is consumed like mine with a restless consciousness of the world's woes. No one can understand her as I do.' What shocks others in you is just what attracts me. My destiny can only be shared by one who has plenty of ambition and no dread of danger. If you are truly mine, give me your answer."

Fräulein Fruzsinka's only response was to throw herself on Ráby's breast and take his face between her hands.

Three weeks later, the marriage ceremony took place. When the wedding was over, the worthy prefect rubbed his hands and murmured, "Now thank Heaven, Mathias Ráby has already the yoke round his neck. That is something to be thankful for."

CHAPTER XV.

Wonder of wonders! Fruzsinka had become domesticated. Since her marriage, she had been a different being. Her former rich dress was now exchanged for a simple homespun gown, and she wore only the national dress of the Hungarian woman. She rarely even looked in a book, for the young matron was now wholly occupied with the things of the household.

She made an ideal housewife, superintending everything herself, and never parting with her keys. She kneaded the dough for the fritters which no hand must touch but hers; she skimmed too the milk, and roasted the coffee. She even had a spinning-wheel brought in and sat at it, though the yarn spun did not amount to much, only the spinning-wheel indeed knew whether it went backwards or forwards.

But on her lord and master, Fruzsinka lavished the most passionate devotion. Never did she allow him to leave the house without her buttoning his coat for him, and had he the least ailment she made no end of ado.

She never dreamed of going out without him, and was, as a matter of fact, jealous of every pretty woman, but Ráby liked to think that her watchfulness had regard rather to the designs of his enemies than from any other cause. He began to see that all women who love their husbands are alike, and that those stories of the wives of heroes who themselves spur their spouses on to fight and place the sword in their grasp, belong to the domain of myth, not to that of reality.

For the rest, Ráby's business seemed as if it was going to settle itself smoothly. The municipality gave orders to the district commissioner who, in his turn, forwarded directions to various subordinate officials, and a deputation, which was entrusted with full judicial powers, was elected to audit the accounts. All was ready for taking active steps, Ráby only needed to come forward with the formal impeachment, for he now held the threads of the business in his own hands.

The various officials concerned strongly suspected that they themselves were mixed up in the affair, but consoled themselves with the thought that the commissioner would himself preside.

But the district commissioner was very easy-going, had they known it, and that was his failing. He did not like seeing his friends set by the ears, therefore he betrayed the inimical intentions of each one to the other, in order to frustrate strife. They should leave one another alone; why quarrel, when you might live at peace with your neighbour, was his philosophy.

At last the important day dawned when the commission was to sit for the investigation of the Szent-Endre accounts. The district commissioner did not keep them long waiting. His impartiality was shown by his accepting an invitation to the prefect's to dinner, and by inviting himself to Ráby's to supper, for he too had been an old flame of Fruzsinka's.

They assembled for the great work in the Town Hall, and had unearthed accounts of years' standing—and nice models of book-keeping they were, full of erasures and corrections, just where the most important entries could be expected. Under such circumstances, the commissioner divided the work up, so that each one might do his share of it without being overlooked by the others. Ráby could have burst with indignation when he regarded the commission's irregularities as to procedure.

With the most unblushing impudence, all sorts of frauds, corruptions, and tyrannical methods were simply ignored in the investigation.

"Fiddlesticks!" exclaimed the commissioner to the protesting Ráby, "that happens everywhere."

And finally, when the worshipful commission of burghers who understood about as much of finance as a hen does of the alphabet, summed up the results of the revision, they gave out, that in spite of all efforts to make them balance, there was a deficit amounting to eighty-six thousand gulden, for which it was impossible to account.

"Fiddlesticks," cried the commissioner again, "let's go on!"

"No, no, we cannot possibly pass that over, and we will not go on," cried the indignant Ráby. "Does not your worship recollect that on account of just such a deficit, a captain of the guard had, but a while back, to stand in the pillory with a black board round his neck. Shall an officer of the imperial body guard be thus punished, and these who have hidden the gold, go free? These things are no trifles. Will you be pleased to order that the secret treasure-chest be produced."

The reference to the captain of the guard was not, it seemed, without its effect on the commissioner. He struck the table with his long cane as if to threaten the company, as he spoke.

"Hear, you people! This business passes all bearing. In the Emperor's name, I herewith order you to fetch out yon secret treasure-chest, in which the embezzled money is stored. And if it is not here by two o'clock this afternoon, at which hour we have to be ready with our report, I shall have you all clapped into the Dark Tower. So look you to it! Now we'll go to dinner!"

Ráby did not appear at the prefect's banquet; he never allowed his wife to have her meals alone. It seemed a long while till two o'clock, the hour named for the continuation of the investigation, when they promised to let him know. And he remembered the question of the timber had not been touched on. This must be worked in somehow.

At last it was time to go to the Town Hall. The councillors sat round the long table waiting for him.

"Now, you gentlemen," ordered the district commissioner, "out with your secret chest."

The notary rose obediently from his seat, and went into the adjoining room, whence he came back with a small iron casket about the size of a lady's workbox, which he brought and set down on the table.

"Here, your lordship, is our secret chest, here too is the key; be pleased to open it for yourself."

The district commissioner looked in, and found inside the sum of two gulden and forty-five kreutzers all told.

"This is our treasure," cried the notary dejectedly. Everyone burst out laughing, and even Ráby himself could not forbear joining in, though it was no matter for jest.

When the laugh had subsided, Ráby was the first to speak: "Now then, you gentlemen of the council, that was a pleasant jest, but permit me to remind you that it was a question not of this cash-box, but of the great chest, the secret way to which only the notary knows how to find."

"I know of a secret way?" exclaimed the notary. "Who dares say that of me? I beg the commission to search the Town Hall thoroughly, to see whether anyone can discover a secret passage there. If you find one, well, there is my head, ready to lie on the block!"

"I know well enough," said Ráby, "there is such a place: to brick it up perhaps is not difficult. But there is another entrance. The Rascian 'pope' knows it, and will be able to show us where the entrance to this stolen treasure is. I would suggest that he be cited."

To this the district commissioner had an objection.

"The Rascian 'pope' is an ecclesiastic, so cannot be summoned before a secular tribunal. He is under the immediate jurisdiction of the Patriarch of Carlovitz. The Patriarch will not understand the procedure of the

Hungarian commissioners, but is only responsible to the Croatian and Slavonic tribunals. The Szent-Endre municipality can address a memorial to the Archbishop of Carlovitz to cite the Greek pastor of Szent-Endre at their tribunal, if he does not mind giving the information."

So this was settled.

Ráby looked at the clock.

"We had other circumstances to consider. There is still the question of the timber. My indictment charges the municipality with aiding and abetting great devastation in the woods. Whilst the poor are not allowed to pick even dry brushwood in winter, and the sick in the hospital are dying of cold, the overseers are allowed to sell timber, and to give away hundreds of stacks as bribes. This cannot be gainsaid. There are the felled trees to witness to it."

"What do you mean, Mr. Ráby? That is all very well, but it may, or may not be true. You just let us manage our own affairs," said the notary.

The district commissioner here remarked that the thing must be looked into, and if proven, this alone would be cause enough to bar all those concerned from holding office. He thereupon ordered a carriage should come round directly, so that they could examine the wood while it was yet daylight.

Whilst they were waiting to start, suddenly a man rushed in white with terror.

"For Heaven's sake, come quickly, gentlemen, the wood is on fire!"

All sprang up from the table, for sure enough the wood was on fire. In vain did Ráby try to appease them, the conflagration could only have just broken out, and it would be easy in the damp winter weather to master it. No one listened to him; it was all up with the commission and its enquiry.

All made for the street, shouting "Fire!" and clamouring for ladders and buckets to extinguish the flames. At last they produced the only watering-cart the city possessed, but a hind wheel was off, and how to get it along no one knew. Helpless confusion reigned. Crowds of distracted citizens ran up and down the streets; the men shouted, the women screamed. Amid the barking of the dogs, the cackling of hens, and the ringing of bells, the townspeople tore hither and thither as if possessed, while the dragoons galloped about trying to keep order.

"Come along, my dear fellow," said the district commissioner to Ráby. "Let's go to your poor wife, she will be distracted with fear and anxiety: it's time you consoled her."

And really it was the wisest thing Ráby could do.

And sure enough, there was Fruzsinka awaiting them at the gate, and it was touching to see how she fell on Ráby's neck, sobbing her heart out, for she had feared some harm had come to him. Nor did she recover herself, but the whole evening trembled every time the alarm bell rang, and was inattentive to their distinguished guest's choicest anecdotes which he told for their benefit during supper.

Before he left, the news came that the wood was quite destroyed by the fire.

"It is all your fault," he cried to Ráby. "Had you never raised that unlucky question about the timber, no one would have thought of setting fire to the wood, and this enormous damage might have been avoided."

Only the presence of his wife prevented Ráby coming to blows with the district commissioner.

CHAPTER XVI.

Ráby had said nothing to Fruzsinka of what had happened at the commission. But when the guest had gone, he brought out his travelling bag and began to pack up as if for a journey.

"Is it possible you are going on a journey?" asked Fruzsinka reproachfully, "without telling me? Don't you know that the wife packs for her husband?"

Ráby did not want his wife to guess whither he was bound. So he made her believe he was only going as far as Tyrnau to take the official depositions regarding the Szent-Endre affair; though since the commission had reduced the whole business to such a farce, how to produce his proofs and, as prosecutor, lay the matter before them at head-quarters, he hardly knew himself. So he told her he could not take her with him, because he would have to travel by diligence or in a peasant's cart, and such a jaunt would be too trying in winter for a delicate woman.

"Now if I were you, I would not go to Tyrnau; I would rather go straight to Vienna, and tell the Emperor himself what roguery is going forward here."

Ráby was astounded. This was precisely what he had intended to do, and the journey to Tyrnau had only been a pretext.

"I would lay the whole plot before him," went on Fruzsinka, "and would say, 'Sire, send a man in my place who may bring these conspirators to book, and make an end to their intrigues.'"

Ráby began to understand. Then he said aloud: "But I don't know of any man who would take on such an unthankful business."

"Is it possible that you mean then to go on with the struggle?" asked Fruzsinka plaintively. "Dearest, I beseech you, think of our position. We are living among enemies. Those who were not ashamed to set fire to the wood, to wipe out the proof of their guilt, will not shrink from burning our own house over our heads. I tremble each time you go out, and have no peace till I see you again. Every night I dream they have murdered you. O Ráby, the very thought of living among these people makes me shudder, there are surely no other such vindictive folk on the face of the earth. Come away from this place. Let us go to Vienna! There your career is made. Leave this thankless, malevolent people to their fate!"

Mathias Ráby's heart grew suddenly heavy, and a dark misgiving gripped him in its clutches.

"You would be the first to despise me," he exclaimed, "were I to be weakened by your words, and quit my post to fly to another country."

"Do you mean then to continue the struggle?"

"It is no question of struggle, but rather of right and wrong and just punishment," he answered gloomily.

"Ah, well! I suppose it is only womanly weakness that gets the best of me. Yet I, too, have thought out the whole affair. You mean that the embezzlements which you have brought to light shall be avenged?"

"Yes, that is what I do mean!"

"Now, has it ever occurred to you that if anyone investigates this affair, at least a part of the odium which it incurs, may fall on your wife?"

"How can that be, Fruzsinka?"

"You remember that absurd housekeeping account, don't you?"

"Yes, indeed, the one we all laughed at so heartily. But how would your name be mentioned in connection with such a business? The items were set down by the head cook, and the prefect settled the account."

"But everyone knows that it was to my advantage. Now suppose I was confronted with the prefect and the cook, in the case of a formal inquiry? Would not it be a disgrace for you?"

"And pray would it not be a disgrace," returned Ráby, "if your husband had to make this confession to the Emperor who sent him: 'Sire, I am no better than all the others you have sent to right your subjects' wrongs, and here I have come back to tell you that everywhere in this world roguery reigns triumphant.' And if he answered me never a word but just looked at me with those keen eyes of his, what shame should I not feel? You shrink at being confronted with the prefect, because the least morsel of the pitch which sticks to him may perchance darken the tip of your little finger, but you do not blush that I may stand before the Emperor and say: 'Sire, here is my wife, with whose paint I have daubed the prefect white.'"

Frau Fruzsinka at this changed her point of attack.

"Remember," she urged, "that if we fly in the face of my uncle, we risk losing a considerable property."

Now it was Ráby's turn.

"You fear the prospect of losing the property, but I tremble at the chance of your possessing it."

"I do not understand," faltered his wife.

"I quite believe you," returned Ráby bitterly.

Fruzsinka dared not pursue this tack further, it was time to try another. She threw herself on her husband's neck, and gazed with those wonderful eyes of hers straight into his.

"Ráby, did we swear that we would make the people, or ourselves happy, which was it, dear?"

At those words, and that glance, Ráby's heart softened.

What can one advance to those most unanswerable of arguments?

Who will blame Mathias Ráby if he weakly gave way then, as many a strong man had done before him, and threw his half-packed bag into a corner.

And as the temptress had gone so far, now she proceeded still further:

"Now I'll unpack for you," she cried merrily.

Thereupon, she took the hunting-pouch from the wall and carefully filled it with savoury spiced meat and flaky white bread; then she deftly replenished the flask with wine, and cried: "Now go and enjoy yourself! Don't stay mewed up in the house. You are bothered; well, go and get some sport, and let the fresh air blow the cobwebs away."

And so saying, she helped him on with his shooting coat, and handed him his gun, and so it fell out that Ráby hung up his sword and knapsack, and went neither to Tyrnau nor to Vienna, but just into the copse to try and shoot hares. He heard behind him, as he left the house, the merry song his wife was warbling to herself.

As he sauntered along the street, it occurred to him that up till now he had not met one of his former acquaintances in the town, nor seen a single one of his old schoolmates.

But just then, he ran on to a townsman, whose wasted bent frame and dejected air did not prevent Ráby from recognising him as one of his old contemporaries. The man wore a leathern apron, and carried carpenters' tools. He returned Ráby's greeting politely and was about to shuffle past him. But the latter stopped him.

"Dacsó Marczi! Is it possible? Are you really Marczi? And won't you just wait that we may have a word together; it is so long since we have met."

And he seized the limp hand of the stranger and held it fast.

"Oh, I am indeed glad to see your worship again," returned his new-found friend.

"Never mind 'my worship,' you can leave him out of it," said Ráby. "Didn't we sit beside each other at school, and you would pass me without a word? Tell me how things are going with you?"

The man looked round to left and right, and in his eyes there lurked a nameless fear.

"Well, as far as that goes," he began, "but don't let us talk here, it is not wise to discuss these things in the street."

Ráby dropped his hand. "Ah, you are afraid suspicion may rest on you if you are seen talking to me!"

"It is not that. But I fear, on the contrary, that it might be unpleasant for you, if you were seen talking to a mere carpenter. I am just going to look after my mates in the lower town who are putting new joists to the burned houses. May Heaven bless your efforts to help the poor people!" added the man in a lower voice.

"Good, I'll go with you," said Ráby, "it's all the same to me which way I take."

"But don't let yourself be drawn into talk with them. They are always ready to complain, and there are always people ready to repeat all that is said."

So they walked together down the street—the dapper sportsman, and the working-man in his leather apron.

Ráby well remembered the houses they passed, and their owners, and asked after the latter.

"Yes, they all live there still, but the houses no longer belong to them. The magistrate has bought one, the notary another, and Peter Paprika a third. The original owners are only there as tenants, and now they have put an execution in the houses."

"And wherefore?"

"For what was owing for tithes."

"And is old Sajtós still there, who used to be so good to us boys when we came home from school?"

"Yes, indeed, you may see her any Sunday at the church door begging."

"Sajtós begging? Why she was quite a well-to-do woman. What has happened to her?"

"Oh, the old story, 'bad times.' There are many more who have come to beggary in the same way. Just go any Sunday morning past the door of the

Catholic church, where the beggars congregate, and you will see plenty of your old acquaintances," said Marczi sorrowfully.

"But what has brought them to it?"

And Marczi told him many a sad record of oppression and misery that wrung Ráby's heart as he listened.

But now they had arrived at the lower town, where the ruins of the forty houses burned out in the great fire still stood. The streets hereabouts were nearly a morass and all but impassable.

The men who were commencing to put the roofs on, greeted Ráby timidly, as if half afraid, and they quickly drove indoors the women who stood furtively about in the surrounding courts. Ráby's questions they only answered with the greatest caution, fencing with his enquiries as to why the work of restoration had been so long delayed. Marczi drew him away.

"They will never tell you where the shoe pinches," he said, "whatever bait you offer; they know too well what the end for them would be. You would listen to their grievance and then retail it to the Emperor. He would send to the town council to know why his subjects' wrongs were not redressed? Thereupon the complainants would be arrested, get twenty strokes with the lash, and the Kaiser would be told the grievances of his subjects were amended. Oh, our people know better than to complain! At no price would they confess why their houses are yet unfinished, or how much of the compensation is still owing."

"Surely their wrongs cry aloud to Heaven," said Ráby indignantly. "I only wish I could get documentary evidence of it!"

"Well, they won't give it to you, but if you really wish it, I could get you many such testimonies by to-morrow, and bring them to your house."

"And are you not afraid of the authorities being angry with you?"

"I? What does their anger matter to me, I don't need them, but they can't do without me. I've got them too much in my power. Listen, for you are an honest man, to no other would I venture to say it. One day they summoned me to bring my masons' tools to the Town Hall. No sooner had I arrived, than they bid me go to the secret passage with the notary, which only he and I know of; the aperture was made during the Turkish rule, and except the notary and the Rascian 'pope,' no one knows the whereabouts. I had to wall up the opening."

"So you know the entrance to the room which contains the secret treasure?"

"Yes, indeed, I know it; I have so managed it that no one save the notary shall ever be able to find it again."

"And would you be willing to take me to it?" Ráby ventured to ask.

"No, for they have bound me by a terrible oath never, except at the bidding of the notary, to break open the walled-up passage. What I have sworn, I hold sacred, but this much will I say, that you can still manage to get there."

"Through the 'pope' who knows the other entrance, eh?"

"Mark well, not through the first. It is as much as his life is worth to betray that secret. But there is another way yet. If you can gain the ear of the Emperor, persuade him to order the election of new representatives in the council, then there would be neither the judge, nor the notary, nor any at present in office to reckon with. If we get a new notary, I could show him the secret passage without any difficulty, since my oath compels me only to 'open it at the notary's bidding.'"

"That is a good idea, Marczi, I will try and follow it out."

"You too care for the rights of our poor oppressed folk. May the good God reward you! But I will tell you where our greatest danger lies; it is in the surveying of the land that the Emperor has ordered. The whole work the surveyor performs is a sham. The best fields under his survey become ownerless, and the municipality takes possession of them. The common folk have to be satisfied with sterile, marshy waste land, and the peasants have to sell their last cow, because they have no pasture for it. Come with me a little way, and I will show you."

So Ráby sauntered the livelong day with his old school-fellow through the fields, and saw much. If the new surveying measures were taken, four-fifths of the peasants' property was ruined, the remaining fifth was devoured by their oppressors, and the owner became houseless and a serf.

Towards evening, Ráby turned homewards with an empty game-bag and a heavy heart.

His mood surely had not escaped Fruzsinka, for she welcomed him with more than ordinary tenderness. She had prepared for his supper some of his favourite dumplings, but somehow even these delicacies failed to satisfy him, and he only wanted to go to bed.

The next morning, Marczi was there quite early. He brought what he had promised, a whole hoard of documents. Ráby took them into his study, and was the whole day long deciphering them.

Marczi, meantime, went about his own business.

As he came out towards the market-place, at the end of the long street, he heard the tones of a bagpipe, and the strains of a violin fell on his ear. But when he came up with the music, he saw what was going forward. The recruiting officers were coming down the street.

So the Emperor wanted soldiers, that was evident enough.

And a right merry affair it was, this recruiting!

They chose out from among the hussars the finest looking fellow, and he was sent from town to town with a dozen comrades to enlist recruits.

They played and sang some such song as this as they went:

"Merry is the game we play,See, our uniforms so gay,And the ensign that we bear,'Twas our sweethearts placed it there!"

They each carried a bottle of good wine in their hands, and every citizen they met was promptly treated to a cup, till he noticed that they wore the hussar uniform. But no human power, once he had tasted the wine, could then free him, and he belonged thenceforth to the recruiting sergeants.

The recruiters reaped the best harvest in the market-place, where they led a riotous dance. It was a regular Magyar measure, a wild, capricious "Csardas," with a dash in it of defiant pride, every movement and gesture suggesting reckless abandon. The clapping of hands, the clinking of spurs, the stamping of feet, all helped towards it, and when the last movement came, foot and heel vied with each other, as the tall figures swayed hither and thither, with the sabre swinging jauntily at their sides, and the "csákó" on their heads. No wonder that with a dozen such warriors dancing in a row, the women's eyes sparkled as they watched, and they beckoned to the tallest men in the crowd to come and join in.

The recruiters had finished their dance, and were coming along the street where Marczi was walking.

In front was the recruiting-sergeant, and he seemed in a right merry mood. Behind him came the piper, taking wild leaps and bounds as he played an accompaniment to the dancers on his bagpipes; then followed the rest, strutting along like peacocks, offering the bottle to all they met.

Marczi did not look at them; he was in too much of a hurry. But the recruiting-sergeant stopped him.

"Halloa, comrade, won't you stop for a word? Anyone would think you had stolen something by the way you run."

"I am in a hurry. I have a job I want to finish. You have done your work, I see?"

"Don't be a fool, man, we can only live once. Have a drink!"

"The deuce take your drink. Don't you see that to-day I've carpentering business on hand. It won't do for me to get giddy when I'm on the ladder."

"Well, a gulp of wine wouldn't do you any harm. You don't go any further till you've had a swallow from my bottle, I tell you."

"Oh, very well," and Marczi took the proffered drink.

"Here's to our true friendship, comrade!" said the other as he followed suit.

Marczi was turning away, having thus gratified his interlocutor, when the latter called him back.

"Marczi, Marczi!" he called, "here's something for you. Here, hold out your hand!"

And the recruiting-sergeant pulled out a thaler from his coat-pocket, and forced it into Marczi's hand, shaking it as he did so.

This time the carpenter would have gone off in earnest, but the other called him back in quite a peremptory tone.

"Dacsó Marczi," he shouted, "you must stay, you can't go now. You have drunk of the soldier's wine, and accepted the press-money, now there is no drawing back, so off you march with the rest!"

The carpenter stood dumbfounded whilst they pressed an hussar's "csákó" on his head. He felt for the handle of his saw in the belt of his apron. For one instant he had a wild impulse to fall upon the sergeant; but then he reflected, it was all his own fault. So he resigned himself to his fate. What had he to regret, indeed, in leaving this town? There was no one there who would weep for him. So he quietly took off his apron.

"If I am to be a soldier, let us see where the wine bottle is. Piper, play my favourite song, 'A soldier's life for me!'"

"The Danube waters long shall flow'Ere thou again my face shalt know."

"Now, Mr. Corporal, are you ready? Off we go, and walk and talk till morning."

And the newly-made soldier drank with the recruiters to his new profession.

On the morrow, the recruiting-sergeant went with the ex-carpenter to his old home, so that he might arrange his affairs there before leaving. He had an old aunt to whom he could safely entrust his belongings. Besides, ten years after all, are not an eternity. They pass before one can look round.

The good old soul was busy tying up her nephew's bundle, when a messenger appeared with an official air, and the order:

"Dacsó Marczi, it is settled at head-quarters that the recruiters are to stay a week here; during that time you are to stop here and not attempt to go anywhere else; but you are to put your three horses to, and drive to-day with relays to Pesth."

Marczi was inclined to rebel, but it availed nothing.

The sergeant only laughed.

"It's no jest, Marczi. They reckon on you for the relays. A gulden for every horse and each station, besides money for the driver, and for drinks."

"But why should I go with relays, when there are plenty of carriage owners who have nothing better to do than to chatter with jackanapes?"

"My dear fellow, this is why, so you shall not think we are getting the best of you. You know that the surveyor has finished his work and is to leave the town to-day. You know, too, how angry the mob are with him. They will pelt him with stones. But if they see that you, whom they all like, are the coachman, they won't do it for fear of hitting you."

In half an hour from that time, a light carriage, drawn by three good horses, stood at the gate of the prefect's residence, where the surveyor was staying. On the box sat Dacsó Marczi himself. The orderlies carried out the surveyor's documents, done up in large bundles, to lay them under the leather covering of the back seat. The surveyor himself was well guarded against the cold, having on a seasonable fur coat and warm overshoes, while the lappets of his fur cap were fastened well under his chin.

"Now, Marczi, if you drive well, we'll drink to-day to any amount," he cried.

"Ay, that we will," agreed the driver as they dashed off.

Mathias Ráby was again pressed by his wife to go and get some shooting. Perhaps he might be more lucky to-day, and bring home a hare.

His spouse was all affection and anxiety. So he went.

But the things Ráby had heard lately he could not get out of his head.

Therefore he did not go far into the country, but turned back in the direction of Pesth. There, he saw a mob of men, women, and children, who all seemed to be waiting for someone.

He would not ask for whom, for he knew they would not tell him.

But hardly had Ráby gone a few hundred paces past them, than he noted a carriage drawn by three horses, coming from the prefecture at a quick gallop, whereupon the whole crowd of people, till now silent, burst forth with loud cries, and placed themselves on either side of the road.

The passenger inside the carriage he did not recognise; neither could he make out what it was the mob were shouting to him. But their tone was sufficiently menacing. As the equipage dashed between the rows of people, the yells became still louder, whilst fists were raised and sticks were brandished threateningly. The carriage did not stop, but cleared the mob till it had left it far behind.

When the carriage reached Ráby, he saw the surveyor cowering on the back seat. Now he gathered what the people's cries had meant. But he did not understand what it was till the carriage pulled up close to him, and he recognised in the driver, Dacsó Marczi.

"Your very humble servant," exclaimed the surveyor to Ráby. "Did you hear the infernal row they made? That's the way they receive me everywhere. If Marczi had not been my coachman, I should have had stones thrown at my head."

"Your worship," cried Marczi, in a voice already thick with wine; "is there still some brandy in the flask?"

"Yes, Marczi, here you are, drink!"

The coachman took the bottle and emptied it.

"Marczi, you will do yourself harm!" objected Ráby.

"Not a bit of it," stammered the driver, whilst he set down the flask, and with that he whipped up the horses, and off they flew, so that the wheels scattered the mud on all sides.

At one spot where the high road nears the Danube, a side-path winds in the direction of the river towards the ferry. When Marczi's carriage had reached this point, the coachman turned the horses and urged them with the whip along the path. Then all at once the carriage dashed from the steep bank into the river below.

"Help, help!" yelled the driver, waving his hat; but horses and carriage were already struggling against the strong tide of the river, now swollen by its spring flood.

But no help was forthcoming, and Ráby only saw a man muffled up in a fur coat, struggling desperately to free himself from the sinking carriage, but the heavy garment dragged him helplessly down. Soon the vehicle with its passenger began to sink, and at last the horses' heads disappeared in the stream. Coachman, surveyor, and documents all had gone to the bottom of the Danube. Nor was any trace of them ever found.

Mathias Ráby stood horror-stricken on the highway, while around him the wintry wind swept over the stubble fields, and carried it with the sound as of a howling of many voices that echoed afar off like the laughter of despair.

END OF THE FIRST VOLUME.

CHAPTER XVII.

This catastrophe was destined to affect Ráby's mood in a fateful way. When he went home he told his wife all that had happened, and she quickly guessed the sequel.

"Now you will be more intent than ever on pursuing your mad enterprise," she said.

"And shall I let myself be shamed into abandoning it by the fate of an ignorant boor, who, little idea as he had of the higher virtues, was ready to sacrifice his life in order to save his fellow-citizens from beggary?"

"You will drive me to exasperation," cried Fruzsinka.

"I would rather have your anger than your contempt, dearest."

"And is our love nothing to you at all?"

"Better that the whole world hate me for my determination, than to earn your love through cowardice. I know that your very opposition to my work is a proof of your love, and therefore, I pray you, my angel, Fruzsinka, listen to me. If I leave this place, I shut every door to a future career. It is now or never, I must go to Vienna. If I write and tell the Emperor that the struggle is of no avail, he will dismiss me at once from my post."

But Fruzsinka answered nothing, she only wept.

That meant of course that Ráby ought to have stayed at home, for only a heart of stone could leave a weeping woman and refuse to comfort her. But Mathias Ráby had just that heart of stone, and he was quite prepared to leave his wife in tears, so to Vienna he went. For you could travel there quickly enough, as there was a famous diligence which carried its passengers in a day to the Austrian capital.

Moreover, no one except Fruzsinka knew he had gone to Vienna.

There he showed himself nowhere. He knew that the Emperor was accustomed to walk every morning in the so-called "meadow garden," where, clad in a simple short coat and plain hat, he was often taken for one of his own equerries. There Ráby could speak to him, and tell him how matters stood in Hungary.

The Kaiser commended what Ráby had already done and encouraged him to go on and prosper. He gave him every aid in his power to help him, including a special pass, wherein all to whom he showed it, were adjured to respect the bearer's person. But he advised Ráby only to show this letter in a case of extreme necessity, and begged him not to tell anyone of the interview he had just had.

Then Ráby hastened homewards, feeling he had ordered his affairs for the best.

On the return journey he arranged to reach Pesth in time to attend the meeting of the County Assembly.

First, he proceeded to the Assembly House to look out certain documents.

The first person he met was the pronotary, Tárhalmy.

Tárhalmy was more friendly, yet more gruff than ever. He called Ráby into his room, and when they were alone, exclaimed:

"You come at the right time, my friend, for we have already cited you as a 'runaway noble,' as the legal phrase has it."

"Cited me! What in the world for, I should like to know?"

"Yes, my friend, you are impeached. And guess wherefore! They say you are Gyöngyöm Miska himself, and actually dare to accuse you of robbing the Jew Rotheisel three days ago in the Styrian forest."

Ráby hardly knew whether to laugh or to be indignant at such a charge.

"But surely that is a very poor joke!" he protested.

"I quite agree that it is. But they have only just brought the accusation, and you can easily get out of it by proving an alibi."

Ráby reddened in spite of himself.

"But I cannot lower myself so far as to disprove so preposterous an allegation," he said. "Besides, you have only to call Abraham Rotheisel to give testimony that it was not I who robbed him. I shall prove no alibi."

"My dear fellow, I know you won't. Simply, because you won't own up to where you have been for three days past, and the person who could prove your alibi could not be called as a witness. I shall not be the judge: you know that the chief notary only acts as referee of the tribunal in such cases. You will naturally never confess where you have been these last three days. But there are people who want to know, and that is the serious side of the jest."

"Rotheisel will be quite ready to disprove it; he knows me well enough."

"I know it. But the testimony of a Jew only counts in our law when he is sworn."

"Won't Rotheisel swear?"

"I am not so sure. The Jew very rarely takes an oath if he can help it. The Talmud makes it very difficult for him. But you can depend upon it, Abraham Rotheisel will be as anxious as possible to clear you from such an absurd accusation, directly he hears of it."

"He is a good kind of man," said Ráby, "and I am certain that he will swear."

"I hope he may. But anyhow, it will be decided to-day, as the tribunal is sitting even now."

"And shall I have to stand in the dock?" said Ráby anxiously.

"Yes, I am afraid you must. So I advise you to stay here and see the business through."

"With your permission I will first write a letter."

"Pardon me, dear friend, but in this room you may neither write nor despatch a letter."

"Am I then a prisoner already?"

"Not exactly, but you are accused, so that I cannot officially be a party to any correspondence you carry on. Meanwhile, I would suggest you just go upstairs to my own private rooms, where you will find my daughter who will give you pen, ink, and paper, wherewith to write; moreover, she will gladly carry it to the post herself. Then, seeing that the business will be prolonged till evening, you will, I hope, share our homely dinner with us."

A blow in the face could hardly have hurt Ráby more than this kindly proposal. For would it not mean meeting Mariska again?

But Ráby had a ready excuse for not accepting Tárhalmy's hospitable offer.

"I am grateful indeed for your kind invitation, but I am being strictly dieted just now for a nervous complaint, and hardly dare eat anything but dry bread."

"Nervous complaint, eh? Why, what does that mean?"

"Well, for one thing, I cannot sleep at night."

Tárhalmy was just going to give him some good advice, when the tension was broken by the entry of a heyduke coming to announce the arrival of the Jew, who had to be carried in a litter to the court, as he was still weak from the wounds he had received, and could not stand.

At the announcement that Abraham was ready to give his testimony on oath, the tribunal formally cited the defendant to appear before them.

Ráby recognised a good many of his acquaintances sitting round the table. The tribunal was presided over by Mr. von Laskóy, whose usually merry mood had become serious for awhile. He asked the parties implicated their creed and calling, and all the customary questions.

Then a young man, in whom Ráby recognised an old school-fellow, rose, and read out the formal indictment in which Mr. Mathias Ráby of Rába and Mura, gentleman, and an inhabitant of Szent-Endre, was accused of disguising himself as a highwayman named Gyöngyöm Miska, and of robbing peaceable travellers. How on a particular day he had waylaid the Jew, Abraham Rothesel alias Rotheisel, in the Styrian wood, had stunned him with a blow on the head, and had stolen from him the sum of five thousand gulden. The proof whereof being that whilst the said Mathias Ráby was in the neighbourhood without anyone knowing his exact whereabouts, the depredations of the redoubtable robber had been going on. Moreover, it was known to all, that, though Mathias Ráby had inherited no great wealth from his parents, he had, nevertheless, scattered money lavishly on all sides—which fact greatly strengthened suspicion against him. But the most convincing testimony of all would be furnished by the Jew's own driver, who would swear to the identity of the accused with Gyöngyöm Miska. The prosecutors now asked for the witnesses to be sworn, and demanded that the said Mathias Ráby, if convicted, might be hanged, or if his rank forbade that, beheaded.

The reading of this impeachment was received by all present with the seriousness befitting the situation. The president then turned to Ráby.

"Will the accused deny this impeachment by proving an alibi?"

"I abstain from making such a defence," answered Ráby, "and only ask to be confronted with my accuser."

The first witness for the prosecution stepped forward in the person of the coachman, whose appearance betokened him to be a rogue of the first water, and obviously ready to swear to anything, provided he were well paid for it.

According to the customary formula, he was questioned as to his antecedents, and owned up unconcernedly to having himself been nine times in prison.

When asked if he recognised in Ráby the robber who had waylaid the Jew Rotheisel, he answered promptly:

"Recognise him again, I should just think so! There can be no question of their not being one and the same. Only then he happened to be wearing a black wig, and a curly moustache, with a peasant's cloak over his shoulder. But I knew it was Mr. Ráby directly I heard his voice."

Ráby, addressing the court, now spoke in Latin, knowing that the peasants were ignorant of that language,

"I protest against the evidence of this witness; I know him for the coachman who drove the official who came to bribe me. This witness therefore is not impartial."

The prosecutor replied that this could not be proven, but Ráby interrupted him whilst he turned to the witness and said to him in Magyar,

"Pray how could you have recognised my voice since I have never spoken to you in all my life?"

"Ay, does not the worshipful gentleman remember that I drove Mr. Paprika into his courtyard in the new coach and four. The gentleman talked so loudly then, that the deafest man must have heard him."

And thereby the case against Ráby fell to the ground.

It must in fairness be admitted that on this, as on later occasions, many upright and honourable men sat in the jury who were quite ready to take Ráby's part, though they were in a minority. One such here protested against such a witness being heard on oath, and the coachman was consequently discharged.

Now, however, old Abraham, supported by his two sons, entered the room, his head still bound up on account of his wound, his legs trembling visibly under him.

"Abraham Rotheisel," said the president, "tell us plainly, how was the attack on you made?"

"I tell nothing of the kind," retorted the Jew. "I have not come here to lay a complaint. Gyöngyöm Miska is not here. You have summoned me simply to bear witness that it was not Mr. Ráby who robbed me, and that I willingly do."

"Think of what you are doing, Abraham! It was dark, you could not see your assailant's face, remember."

"Ay, if it had been but Egyptian darkness, and if I had been as blind as Tobit, nay, if the highwayman and Mr. Ráby had been as like to one another as two peas, yet I will swear it was not Mathias Ráby, whom I have known from his childhood, ever since he was a baby. Moreover, neither his face nor figure resembled in the least those of the man who robbed me."

Here the Jew was questioned as to his assailant's appearance, but persisted that in no wise did the robber resemble Ráby. The "worshipful gentleman" who robbed him was, he said, very different looking.

"Why do you call him a 'worshipful gentleman,'" asked the president.

"How do I know he might not have been one? I have seen highwaymen and gentlemen very much alike indeed," answered the Jew, "and in time may see still more. But I keep my convictions to myself."

Ráby's counsel here observed that one witness contradicted another, and thus tended to invalidate the evidence.

"Naturally," returned Laskóy, "only kindly remember that according to our laws, the testimony of a Jew against that of a Christian can only be accepted on oath."

At the sound of the word "oath," Abraham's two sons began to tear their garments, and throwing themselves at the feet of the magistrate, they implored him not to allow their father to be sworn, as it was contrary to the Talmud.

"I fear I cannot help you in this matter," answered Laskóy. "I must carry out the law regarding Jews witnessing against Christians. If you would free your father from the need of swearing, you must ask Mr. Ráby; one word from him obviates the necessity of an oath. He has only to prove an alibi, and the case is immediately dismissed."

Whereupon the two young Jews dashed across to Ráby, fell on their knees before him, and begged and implored him with might and main, to set up this alibi—it was only a matter of speaking one word.

But old Abraham flew into a mighty rage.

"Get up both of you, and be off directly, and leave a brave man in peace. Who called you to come hither, running after me as the foals after the mare? Hold your miserable cackle, and away with you! Be kind enough, Mr. heyduke, to turn these two noisy fellows out of the court. Go home at once, you boys, I don't need your support, or your teaching in this matter. And I beg pardon, gentlemen, for the behaviour of these two good-for-nothings. Now I am ready to be sworn."

So after the two young Jews had been turned out, Abraham was sworn, though he took the oath in Hebrew, so that none present could follow the formula.

When it was over, Abraham prepared to leave the court, for Mathias Ráby was free. This time at least had he escaped the dungeon his enemies had prepared for him.

CHAPTER XVIII.

Ráby could hardly bear the delay in getting home. When the open verdict was pronounced, a coach was already at the door of the Assembly House, to bear him on his way: he threw himself into it, while the sparks flew under the swift hoofs of his horses.

Szent-Endre was not, after all, the other side of the world, but the distance seemed endless. On the way, he racked his brains as to how he would find Fruzsinka. Yet he could not have possibly dreamed of what his actual home-coming would be.

As he sprang from the vehicle, to knock at his house-door, he found the summons of the court nailed under the knocker, with all the misdemeanours and crimes whereof he had been falsely accused before the tribunal, set forth at length. As is well known, these kind of summonses were fixed to the house-door, were there no means of presenting them to the person cited.

Rage drove every other thought from Ráby's mind when he found this disgraceful document fluttering over his door. He tore it down indignantly, and beat with hand and foot at the entrance to gain admission.

Poor Böske, the maid-servant, at last opened it, looking white and frightened. "Why had they allowed this thing to be fastened to the door," he inquired angrily.

"I humbly beg pardon," stammered the girl, "the gentleman who brought it nailed it there with a hammer, and said if I tore it down I should be hanged."

"Why did your mistress not do it?"

"The gracious lady-mistress?"

"Yes, my wife, where is she then?"

"Ah, my dear kind master, how shall I tell you? Please don't kill me for it! The gracious lady-mistress has left home."

"Stuff and nonsense! She has only probably gone to pay a visit."

"Ah, no indeed, she has not done that, she has, oh how shall I say it, run away. The very day the gracious master went, the lady-mistress wrote a letter and gave it to the gipsy Csicsa to carry. She did not wait for an answer, but packed up, called a coach, loaded it with her luggage, and drove off without saying a word about the dinner."

"Perhaps she has gone to her uncle's at the prefecture?"

"No, indeed, she went in the other direction; I watched her from the street-door down the road, as far as I could see."

Ráby went into the parlour. The girl had spoken the truth, that was evident. All the chests stood open; Fruzsinka had packed up all her own belongings when she went; she had not even left a single souvenir behind.

Ráby was completely nonplussed; it was indeed a horrible situation for a man who hastens home on the wings of love to find his house destitute of all that made it home for him. He could think of nothing better than to seek out his uncle, the old postmaster, from whom, since his marriage, he had been somewhat estranged.

Ráby entered the old man's room without speaking a word, where he sat down and stretched out his legs in gloomy silence. He shrewdly suspected that his host knew what had happened, and why he was there. How should he not, considering everyone in Szent-Endre knew by this time. The old gentleman shrugged first one, and then the other shoulder expressively, whilst he coughed and cleared his throat in visible embarrassment.

"H'm, h'm!" he said, significantly, "these fashionable ladies have not much feeling. Besides, you can never take them seriously. Therefore you must not let the grass grow under your feet."

"If I did but know where she has gone to?" sighed Ráby.

"Now just wait! I fancy I can help you to find out. For two days past a letter has been lying here addressed to your wife. There—take it and read it." And he handed Ráby a sealed missive.

"I, how can I open a letter which is directed to my wife?" he asked anxiously.

"Yes, indeed, why not? Are not man and wife according to the Hungarian law one flesh? A letter addressed for the one can legally be opened by the other, and I would do it, if I incurred the galleys for it, my friend, if I were in your place. Just read it, and I will be the guarantee that I delivered it into your hands."

Ráby opened the note with trembling fingers.

It was in the handwriting of the judge, Petray, and though short, was quite intelligible.

"My darling Fruzsinka,

"From your own letter I see that you find it impossible to put up with your tyrant any longer. I thought as much long since. You do quite right in leaving him, and the sooner you get away from him the better; the man will come to no good. My house, as you know, will ever be a safe asylum for you. I await you with open arms.

"Your devoted friend,

"Petray."

Ráby's eyes were no longer glazed and staring as heretofore; they shot sparks now.

"Read it, my friend," he said, as he handed it to Mr. Leányfalvy.

"Well, at any rate, now you know where you are."

"Know it, indeed I do," answered Ráby, as he grimly folded up the note, and placed it in his coat pocket.

"And pray what do you mean to do?"

"First, I would have a four-horse coach."

"You shall have it sure enough. And then———?"

"Then I'll go home and fetch my pistols and sword; look for a second, and then—either he or I are dead men."

"That's it! It's the only way. Only see to it that you think it out accurately. Suppose your opponent wants to fight with swords? Perhaps he's an out-and-out swordsman."

"What does that matter? The sword will satisfy equally the duelling regulations, and will merely prove which of us can fence the better."

"Good! But take this much warning. The judge is a very cunning man; you will have to be on your guard. Be careful not to be the first to draw the sword, else he'll be hanging round your neck an attainder in pursuance of an antiquated law which rules that 'he who first draws the sword shall be held to incur blood-guiltiness.'"

"Many thanks, I'll remember your good advice."

"Ah! if you had always done so! Yet I am right glad that you don't look askance at me any longer. You are another man since you made up your mind to fight! How a wife demoralises a man to be sure! There is nothing wanting now, except a sword and a pair of pistols. You need not go home for those. I have a rare old blade which was used at the storming of Buda, and will cut through iron itself; it is worth a good deal more than your parade-sword. And here are my pistols, each is loaded with three bullets; if you understand what shooting straight means, you can kill three enemies at once. So good luck, my young friend, I am glad you are going."

The old gentleman embraced his nephew as if he were going to face the enemy, and had his best horses put in for him, and they brought Ráby to the judge's house in less than an hour.

The uninvited guest just caught the judge going out.

"Come back with me to the house," said his visitor, "I want to have a word with you."

Petray guessed from the speaker's tone that it was on no friendly business that he had come, though he affected not to perceive it, and treated Ráby with his accustomed familiarity.

When they had come into Petray's parlour, Ráby drew the letter out of his pocket and held it before his host's face.

"Do you recognise this writing?"

Petray drew himself up.

"What presumption is this, pray? To open a letter directed to someone else, it is unheard of!"

"It is perfectly legal," said Ráby. "Your protest is useless. In the eyes of the law, a letter written to my wife is a letter written to me."

"It is, I say, a great piece of presumption, to attack a man like this in his own house."

"You need not make such a noise! You may see I carry pistols in my belt." Then adopting a more familiar tone, Ráby added, "It comes to this, either you take one of these two pistols, and we fire according to the prescribed rules, or if you refuse me the satisfaction of a man of honour, I shoot you dead without further ado, as I would a wolf who attacks me on the highway."

The cowardly bully grew pale with fear. To look at him, you would have deemed him a powerful foe to be reckoned with, but he was a very coward at heart, like the braggart that he was.

"All right, I'm not afraid of you, or of anybody else, for that matter. But all this is idle talk! A gentleman does not fight with pistols. That kind of duel exacts no skill. A schoolboy can fire off a pistol. I only fight with swords; so with my sword I am at your service to have it out in proper fashion. Out with yours, and we'll see who is the best man of the two."

"Very well, with swords, so be it," said Ráby quietly, replacing his pistols again in his belt.

"And now you had better make your will, for you don't leave this place alive."

"That our weapons will decide. I have nothing further to say," answered Ráby.

"So, you will venture to draw your sword on me, will you, you silly fellow?"

"With you, or after you. I would not have it said that I drew my sword on an unarmed man," answered his antagonist.

"Don't provoke me, Ráby! I tell you we will have it out here."

"Well, draw then!"

Petray thus urged, endeavoured to draw his sword in earnest from his belt, but that otherwise excellent weapon had never been used since the last Prussian war, and stuck so fast in its sheath that the most powerful tugs quite failed to move it.

Come out it would not. Mr. Petray pulled and tugged to no avail; the blade would not yield an inch.

"Good heavens," cried Ráby impatiently, "hand it over to me, I will make it come out."

And hereupon the two opponents pulled away with might and main at the refractory weapon; Ráby seizing the sheath, and Petray the handle, indulged in a very tug-of-war, but to no purpose; the sword stuck where it was, and did not budge, while the two adversaries were bathed in perspiration with their unavailing efforts.

Had anyone ever seen such an absurd struggle?

Petray was foaming with rage.

"Deuce take the thing! If you want to come to grips, let's fight it out with our fists! There I can be sure of my resources. I'll smash you up, I promise you, so there won't be anything left of you."

"All right," retorted Ráby, and lifting up the sleeve of his dolman, he put himself into a boxer's attitude, and struck Petray two ringing blows with his bare muscular arm, that sent his opponent fairly reeling from sheer astonishment.

Now the judge set great store by his appearance. He therefore reflected that by such methods as these, his enraged antagonist might end in breaking his nose, or knocking out his teeth, and these were both contingencies to be avoided.

"Ah, leave me in peace," he cried piteously. "I am no boxer, I am a judge, a man of the law. If you have anything to bring against me, let it be at the tribunal, I'll meet you there fast enough. But I will neither fence, nor shoot, nor box on your wife's account. If you think I am the first whom your wife has fooled, I am not, by a long way. If you want to fight, look up Captain Lievenkopp—he lives out yonder at Zsámbék. You have a bigger score to settle with him than with me, if you did but know it. He's ready for either swords or pistols. As judge, it's my duty to hinder a fight, not to promote it by myself taking part in one. Go to the tribunal, and I'll give you satisfaction there fast enough."

He spoke rapidly, but Ráby did not wait to hear the end. He clapped his hat on, and jumped into his coach, and cried to the driver to drive to Zsámbék.

CHAPTER XIX.

Ráby only reached Zsámbék the next morning. The dragoon-captain's house he found without any difficulty, for it stood close to the post-station.

There were two other officers with the captain, and three horses stood ready saddled in the courtyard. They were evidently on the point of starting for some expedition, though there was no sign of soldiers going with them.

"Aha, who is this?" cried Lievenkopp as Ráby entered. "Why, bless me, it's Mathias Ráby!"

"Yes, indeed, captain. Perhaps you can guess my errand here?"

"Truly, I cannot do any such thing."

"Well, my wife has run away from me."

"The deuce she has! What already? I did not think she would have gone quite so soon."

"I went first of all to Judge Petray to demand satisfaction of him. He would not give it me, but referred me to you."

"That was very kind of him."

"Now you know why I come."

"I know it, comrade, you want to fight me, sure enough? Very good; just choose one of these gentlemen as your second, and we will decide with him on the weapons. Only one thing delays our immediate meeting, and that is, I have to fight Gyöngyöm Miska."

Ráby was electrified as he heard the name.

"Can't you leave him till later? You will never succeed in catching him."

"Aha, I've got him this time though; I am going at this very hour to fight a duel with him."

"Do you know who this Gyöngyöm Miska really is?" asked Ráby.

"Why he lives at Szent-Torony, two hours' journey from here, where he owns an estate, and is called Karcsatáji Miska. He is the notorious robber, and no other. This is why he is never to be caught red-handed. When he is everywhere driven into a corner, he goes quietly back home, throws off the highwayman's gear, and whoever seeks him there, finds instead of the fierce robber with lank locks and drooping moustaches, a harmless country gentleman, with his powdered hair done in a neat cue, whom twelve witnesses can swear to not having left home for weeks. No one will ever succeed in convicting him. But this once I've caught my gentleman nicely. Listen to how I did it. This very day when we had planned our attack upon the band of Gyöngyöm Miska, we observed a suspicious-looking fellow trying to get in between our railings. We arrested him, searched him, and found sewn into the sole of his sandal, this letter to Mr. Michael Karcsatáji. You probably will know the handwriting."

Ráby recognised the writing of his wife.

"Yes, you can read it, you will understand it better than we do."

The letter ran thus:

"Dear Miska,—Don't have any scruples about the affair in the Styrian wood. The whole suspicion falls on someone who will not be able to prove an alibi. Thine own one."

Ráby's arms fell helplessly at his side. It was as if he had suddenly been stung by a cobra.

His own wife was the traitor who had betrayed him to his enemies! A dagger-thrust in the dark does not hurt one so much as such a discovery.

Ráby distrusted his senses; he would not, could not believe it; he thought he must be dreaming.

"Sit down, comrade," said the captain. "You are a bit upset, and small wonder too. The bolt didn't strike me quite so nearly, yet I too was fairly staggered when I read the letter. Then I called up my two comrades here, and sent my challenge over to Szent-Torony, where Mr. Michael von Karcsatáji was in the courtyard, engaged in marking his newly born lambs. In such a harmless fashion is he wont to spend his leisure! My second presented him with my message: 'This letter which we have intercepted proves that you have an intrigue with a lady to whom Captain Lievenkopp is also paying court. Captain Lievenkopp will not tolerate this sort of thing, and calls upon you to meet him to-morrow at nine o'clock, by the ruined church of Zsámbék, to settle the matter there in proper fashion.'

"The highwayman did not deny that between us there lay ground for quarrel, and he would be at the rendezvous at the time appointed. It is now eight o'clock. We can get to the ruins in half an hour, and there await my opponent. You, my friend, can remain here in my lodgings for an hour longer, and follow on after us. From nine to ten I am at Mr. Karcsatáji's service. As soon as I have finished with him, we two will fire at each other till only one of us remains to tell the tale. But if the highwayman kill me, then you and Karcsatáji will fight till one or the other is a dead man. Is that in order?"

"Perfectly," cried the seconds; "it could not be better arranged!"

Ráby had nothing against this settlement. When the captain had gone he stretched himself on his host's camp-bed, and was fast asleep in a few minutes, completely exhausted by his recent experiences.

The Zsámbék ruins are a remarkable relic of the Gothic period. The nave of the church, thickly over-grown by juniper-bushes, is an admirable place for a duel, where two men, unseen by any outsider, can fire at one another to their hearts' content.

The officers tethered their steeds to a birch stem, and withdrew inside the ruins so that their presence should not be remarked by the people working in the fields.

Meantime, Ráby had awakened and was making his way to the ruins. Nor did he need a guide, for they had been well known to him since his boyhood.

It was yet half an hour to the promised rendezvous, so he just wandered round through the brushwood, which surrounded the church, listening for shots. Perhaps the masonry dulled the sound, but surely he would see the smoke, yet he could neither see nor hear anything.

At last the remaining five minutes were up, and he strode into the ruins. So well had he calculated time and distance, that the hand of his watch pointed close on ten, as he pushed aside the juniper-bushes which hid the entrance to the ruins, and went in.

"Karcsatáji has not yet appeared," said Lievenkopp. "Punctuality is not his strong point."

"I fancy he doesn't mean to come."

"Surely that is not thinkable! In that case we will just go for him in his own house."

"Now, meantime, what do you propose doing?"

"Well, I think that we might get on with our own business and not wait for him. By delay he has lost his right of precedence, and must take the second place. I propose, gentlemen, therefore, that we take the second appointment first."

After a short discussion, the seconds agreed, and since the nature of the quarrel barred all idea of reconciliation, they staked out the barriers, and placed the opponents against the two opposite walls.

The weapons which the seconds handed to them, were a pair of rough old riding pistols, which were so constructed that the bullets fired into a group of ten men, would have probably perforated the cloak of one of the party, provided he had one on. The combatants shot at first at five-and-twenty paces; they were honestly bent on hitting one another, yet neither succeeded. At the second attempt they took aim at twenty paces, again without result.

"Wretched weapons, these pistols!" growled the captain, "if I haven't brought down the vulture's nest in that wild pear-tree."

"Perhaps mine are better," suggested Ráby. "My uncle Leányfalvy gave them to me, and they are already loaded."

So the seconds accepted Ráby's weapons. One of them remarked, however, that the pistols were loaded to the muzzle, so that both of them, in this case, would do well to stand behind a pillar, seeing if one exploded, they would all be dead men, combatants and seconds alike.

"It's quite safe," said Ráby, "the powder is good, and the charge is not too strong; there are only three bullets in each charge."

"Now then, fire! One, two, three."

At "three" Ráby's pistols cracked.

Pistols loaded with three bullets have very often this peculiarity of not hitting the man they are fired at.

After the two first terrible detonations everyone looked round extremely amazed that he and the rest were still alive.

"Re-load your pistols," cried one of the seconds, and they did so. But when they were ready, an idea struck the other second.

"Gentlemen, you have fired three times, and such being the case, honour is entirely satisfied. It is my duty to suggest a reconciliation."

The two antagonists looked at each other.

Was it worth while to fight to the death over this matter? So without more ado, they shook each other by the hand, and were friends.

Now it would be Gyöngyöm Miska's turn, and he would have to reckon with two adversaries instead of one.

So they waited on; yet he came not. What could be the reasons of his delay? Had a wheel come off? Could he not find the ruins?

But these were a landmark, and even if he had gone astray, he must have heard the shots.

"He surely cannot be a coward," muttered Ráby between his teeth, for his national pride was piqued by sundry contemptuous remarks the Austrian officers began to let fall.

At last they heard the trotting of horses' hoofs. He was coming then!

The men rose from the sward whereon they had been lying, and listened expectantly.

The trotting stopped at the ruined wall, and it was obvious that it belonged to one horse only.

Was it possible he would come alone, without seconds, thinking to find them here in the village?

After awhile there was the sound as of several horses' hoofs, but these seemed as if they were going away, rather than nearing the ruins.

"Friends," shouted Lievenkopp, "someone is stealing our horses!"

And all four dashed out of the ruins.

The captain had guessed rightly, their horses had been stolen.

And the thief was Gyöngyöm Miska himself, who, mounted on his own fiery courser, was driving before him the officers' three horses tethered together by their bridles.

"Stop you scoundrel," cried the captain and Ráby in unison.

But he evidently had not the intention to run away. Fifty paces ahead he pulled up and let his horse caracole.

His two grim adversaries subjected him now to a cross fire, for each of them had two pistols. First on one side, and then from the other they fired, but not one of the shots so much as grazed the robber, for his horse pranced about and turned round and round in such a bewildering way while his master was being aimed at, that all four shots missed their mark.

When the firing ceased the horse remained standing at a sound from his rider, as if cast in bronze.

Then Gyöngyöm Miska, raising his musket with one hand to his face, took aim at both, and one bullet whistled through the captain's helmet and the other sent Ráby's cap flying from his head. Whereupon the highwayman raised his tufted hat and cried, "So fights Gyöngyöm Miska!"

And with that he switched his whip, cracking it right and left over the tethered horses, and galloped away with his prey.

CHAPTER XX.

When Mathias Ráby recounted this story to his uncle, the old gentleman declared he had never read or heard any stranger. Then they had a consultation as to what was to be done. It was evident that it was a matter for a lawsuit.

The ancient laws against a breach of the marriage vow were very stringent; and even allowed a husband to put to death an unfaithful wife. But Mathias Ráby found no consolation in such statutes. He did not want to lose the woman still so dear to him for all the grievous injury she had done him, and he was even ready to take her back again, and to pardon her threefold treachery.

"By the law," said his uncle, interrupting Ráby's meditations, "a wife who runs away from her husband shall be restored to him. Now if there be such a thing as justice on this earth of ours, you shall get her back. But what are we to do with the seducer, Petray?"

"We can accuse him on the ground of seduction." And the old gentleman proceeded to quote to Ráby a law dating from the year 1522 which provided for the decapitation of such misdemeanants. So it was plain that Ráby might obtain the condemnation of Petray, and succeed in having Fruzsinka restored to him. But the legal proceedings were very complicated, and it was difficult to determine to which court the case should be taken.

At last they came to the conclusion it would be wise to carry it before the higher court, since it was a question of a capital crime, though much care would have to be exercised in quoting the law under which they prosecuted, as the least difference in the wording might upset their case.

When the eventful day arrived for instituting the suit before the higher court, Ráby was punctually in his place. Petray was also present, but Fruzsinka was only represented by counsel.

Ráby determined he would have no mercy on Petray. If the severe Hungarian law prescribed that the man who seduced the wife of another should lose his head, it should be satisfied.

Petray, the defendant, heard the impeachment out to the end, without once turning pale. He followed with his defence.

He began by quoting old formularies and attacking certain technical defects in the indictment, which, he maintained, should have been carried to the spiritual consistory, as the tribunal for matrimonial disputes. Also he maintained that the action of the plaintiff was not valid, seeing that he demanded the restitution of his runaway wife, and the punishment of the man who had given her an asylum, yet was himself open to the charge of bigamy, since he now had three wives alive.

"What in the world do you mean?" cried Ráby indignantly.

"That you were already twice married before you took Fräulein Fruzsinka to wife."

"I twice married!" exclaimed Ráby. "What do you mean?"

"That they are still alive," answered Petray with a perfectly serious face. "They both are here," he added, "and I beg that they may be confronted with Mr. Ráby."

"Well, I should like to see them."

And thereupon through a side door they admitted two women into the court. One was a pretty young Rascian in her picturesque national costume, the other was a coquettishly clad peasant from the Alföld, of imposingly tall stature. They were each cited by name, though Ráby had never heard either before.

"So these are my wives, are they?" he cried, half amused, half angry.

"They are indeed," answered Petray unabashed, "and pray do not attempt to deny it, for they are both ready to prove it."

"Why, when have either of you ever seen me before?" demanded Ráby sternly of the two women.

The little Rascian was obviously ashamed of herself, for though the paint on her cheeks effectually hid her blushes, she buried her face in her handkerchief to suppress her confusion. But her companion was not so easily daunted. Her arms akimbo, she placed herself in front of Ráby and began to abuse him roundly.

"So you mean to say you don't remember me, do you, my fine sir?" And she forthwith began a string of voluble reminiscences which Ráby in vain strove to stem, beside himself with indignation, but he could not get in a word edgeways.

At last the judge intervened. Till then he had contented himself with pulling his moustache the better to control his ill-suppressed amusement.

"That will do, woman, we have had enough of your tongue. We must have documentary evidence. Have the parties marriage-certificates to produce?"

The little Rascian drew out the desired document from her pocket, whilst the rival claimant in great haste dived into a huge bag she carried, and produced the certificate wrapped up in a coloured handkerchief.

They were to all appearances genuine enough. One was drawn up by the registrar at Szent-Pál, the other dated from the commune of Belovacz on the military frontier. Both documents were countersigned by the parish priests, and bore the official seal of the ecclesiastical authorities.

"But I have never in my life even been in the neighbourhood of these places," cried Ráby in desperation, fairly trembling with rage. "These registered formulas are falsified; I charge the man who produces them with forgery."

The little Rascian girl here began to wring her hands and weep, but her Hungarian rival gave her tongue its rein, and she poured forth such a flood of abuse on Ráby that his every fibre thrilled with indignation.

With much trouble the heydukes restored order, and the judge called on the court to be quiet.

"Silence, his honour is speaking; the judgment will now be given, so let the litigants retire from the court," was the order.

It was hardly five minutes before the contending parties were recalled and the verdict given.

"The case as heard by us is very complex. It lies between two parties who prefer counter-accusations against each other. The one says his opponent has robbed him of his wife, whilst the accused becomes plaintiff in his turn, and incriminates his accuser as a bigamist, and therefore incapacitated for demanding the restoration of his runaway spouse. Therefore, we beg to refer the case to the united courts of the provinces of Pesth, Pilis, and Solt, that they may adjust the relations between the contending parties satisfactorily. Meantime the case is dismissed." And herewith followed in legal phrase the reasons why the said courts should be pressed to institute an inquiry into the whole suit between Ráby and Petray, and its complications, and the parties were adjured to leave the court.

Ráby was sorry enough he had ever come, for what had it all availed him?

Scarcely had the door of the court closed behind him than he heard the end of it all, the horrible mocking laughter which burst forth from the whole room, directly he had left it—a sound which followed him out into the corridor.

He was completely staggered. The shame, the exasperation, the deception of it all, and this persistent persecution—how powerless he was against them! His very senses seemed deserting him. So distracted was he in his bewilderment, that when he reached the end of the passage, instead of going straight out, he took the flight of steps which led down to the cells. Through the prison doors came the sound of merriment. Even the criminals were mocking him. And that was likely enough, seeing that the two women who had impersonated his wives, had been requisitioned from the ranks of the prisoners.

For three days did Ráby remain in hiding at his inn, not daring to show his face. He fancied all Pesth and Buda were making merry over his fall.

Only on the evening of the third day did he venture to set out for home. And even then he muffled himself up in his mantle so that he might pass unrecognised.

But as soon as he reached the open country, the fresh air exhilarated his drooping spirits and he saw things in a different light. It was certainly very impolitic to betray his vexation, for in this case he was sure to get the worst of it. It would be far wiser to disguise his real feelings.

The first person he sought out was his uncle.

"Remember, my boy, it's just what I told you. Didn't I say that if you would insist on marrying Fruzsinka you would have wife enough. And, sure enough, here you have three! And by the time you have done, it may be a great many more."

"How do you mean, uncle?"

"Why, as soon as the news spreads that the marriage certificates of these women were forged, other 'wives' will be turning up from all parts, and a nice dance they will lead you."

Ráby, in spite of his real misery, could not forbear a grim smile.

"Where did you say the two marriage articles came from, eh?"

"One was from Szent-Pál, the other from Belovacz."

"So that's it, is it? Well, Szent-Pál was utterly destroyed by the insurrection of Hora-Kloska three years ago, and Belovacz is a haunt of freebooters. In neither place is there priest or sexton, church or register, as I happen to know, so seek all your life long, you'll never find proof of the forgery."

"Now I see why the witnesses came from so far afield; it was manifestly a part of the plot."

"By the way," said his uncle, "you'll want some one to look after your house, for in your absence your maid Böske has been locked up."

"Whatever do you mean?" demanded Ráby indignantly. "My servant locked up! why what is the meaning of it?"

"H'm, it was by order of the municipality."

"And pray what for?"

"That, no one can say. I only knew through the neighbours coming round to tell me that I ought to send my servant over, for your cows were standing at the gate, and that there was no one to let them in, seeing that poor Böske had been marched off between two officers to the police-station."

"The deuce she has!" cried Ráby, and he seized his sword. "But I won't stand that!"

And without another word he dashed out of the house and down the street at full tilt, in the direction of the police-station, which was close to the post office. He thrust open the door, without announcing himself, and shouted so furiously to the unlucky porter that the latter nearly died of fright.

"Where is the jailer? In heaven's name, tell me," thundered Ráby.

"He is drinking in there," said the man, pointing to a door.

Ráby dashed into the room and found the jailer, seized him by the lappet of his jacket, shook him, and yelled:

"You brute, you scoundrel, what have you done with my servant, I want to know?"

"Your worship, the judge had her locked up in 'the Hole.'"

"Let her out, then, at once, you hound! If you don't, I will slay you on the spot, and willingly pay up the forty gulden fine I shall be mulcted of for killing a peasant. Where is the cell, where are the keys? I tell you, you are to give them to me directly."

The frightened official said humbly that he would soon get the keys, but Ráby held him by the scruff of the neck, and dragged him to the door of "the Hole," made him open it, and called out, "Come out directly, Böske!"

Directly she appeared he seized the girl by the hand, and led her out of her captivity. And he never let go her hand all the way home, in spite of her wish to withdraw it.

"You are a good, honest girl, Böske, who have only been persecuted on my account; there, there, don't cry, they shall pay for this, sure enough!"

And he flourished his sword so threateningly, that all who met them were quite scared and hastened to clear out of their path.

The gentry had robbed him of his wife, and now the burghers had stolen away his servant; it was truly "adding insult to injury!"

"And now just come in," said Ráby, "and tell me all about it."

"Oh, but I've no time to," exclaimed Böske, "besides, it's a long story. First of all I must run and look after my cows. I've not seen them for two days. They weren't milked either, and perhaps they are starving."

"Oh, it's all right, the postmaster's maid tended them."

"Ay, what does Susanne know about it, I should like to know? The dun cow, she won't give a drop of milk if anyone else milks her, and the dappled one, if she knows that a stranger is there instead of me, will kick over both pail and milking-stool. And no one can feed them as I can. Just listen, gracious master, how they begin to low when they hear my voice."

And away ran Böske into the cowhouse. Not for anything would she have told her own story till the cows were looked after. They recognised her also directly, and the dun cow licked her red arm affectionately, when she went to tether her, and Böske made them a nice turnip "mash," in a wooden bowl, and fed her favourites. Then she washed the pail clean, and when she had put everything in order, she sat down to her milking, and here Ráby found her.

"Now you can tell me, while you are at work, all that has happened," he said kindly.

"If the gracious master does not mind listening to me in the cowhouse. It was like this. When I was setting the yeast to rise the day before yesterday, for baking, in the kitchen, in came two police-officers, saying I must go with them to the police-court. I told them I had not stolen anything. Thereupon, one said, I was not to make a noise, and he threatened to lay his cane about my shoulders, and if I didn't go of my own free will, he'd make me. I told him my master was away. He said that would be all right, and that we could shut the door and leave the key under a beam outside, where I could find it again. So what could I do? I had to leave the yeast in the trough where it got all sour and mouldy, and go off to the police-station. When I got there, I saw lots of men sitting round a table, and they all looked at me and asked me questions, and told me I'd got to be sworn. I thought they meant being married, so said I didn't mind if there was anyone there I liked well enough to marry. Then one of them said it wasn't a question of marrying, but that I must swear to what I knew about the master."

"A regular inquisition," muttered Ráby.

"'I'll swear fast enough,' said I, 'that I know nought of him but what is good.'

"'Then,' says the notary, 'what about the peasants that he sets on to rebel against their landlords?'

"'Nothing of the kind,' says I; 'the man who says that ought to be hanged.'

"With that, he asks if my master did not throw Dacsó Marczi and the surveyor into the river. So I told them it was a wicked lie."

"That was quite true, Böske!"

"Then they asked me if you were not a sorcerer, and did not call up evil spirits at night-time."

"And, pray, what did you say to that?"

"Why I just laughed outright, and told them I had never even heard my master say 'the devil take them,' much less call up evil spirits. But they said the Devil himself would carry me off if I didn't tell the truth. And when they asked me to swear that the gracious master was a sorcerer, I just swore by the Crucifix it was not true. But they were so angry that they just packed me off to prison, then and there, and there I was left without food or drink till the gracious master himself came and fetched me out."

Poor Böske finished her story with a burst of weeping, for up till now she had not had the time for crying. But now she had got her tale over, and the milking done, she cried her heart out into the corners of her apron.

"That was quite enough for once," muttered Ráby to himself. But he deceived himself if he fancied it was enough, for there was yet more to come.

When they had recovered the key from its hiding-place under the beam, Böske went first to open the house, but she started back in horror, and dropped the pail of milk she was carrying, as she exclaimed,

"Gracious master, just look, thieves have been in! We have been robbed!"

Sure enough it was so; the whole house had been completely rifled of valuables. So thoroughly had the work been done that only the empty chairs and tables remained.

Böske broke into a wail of despair.

"Hush, be quiet," ordered Ráby sternly, putting his hand over her mouth.

"But they've broken into my trunk," she cried; "they have stolen my new petticoat, and best kerchief, and my shoes with the rosettes."

"Never mind," said her master consolingly, "to-morrow I'll take you to Buda, and buy you some fresh ones. These are trifles. The thieves probably came after my papers, but those I luckily had with me."

At this Böske was appeased, also she remarked it was a comfort the lady-mistress had taken the embroidered quilt with her, so the thieves were done out of that at any rate.

"But where is the house-dog?"

They found the poor beast, by the well, stiff and dead.

"The brutes!" cried Böske, horrified; "they have drowned him, they have not even left us the dog alive."

Ráby drove the weeping girl into the house and spoke earnestly to her:

"Now, Böske, listen to me. You must never tell anyone what has happened, and that the house has been robbed, for if you do, they may put you in prison again, and you may not get out for years."

With which piece of parting advice Ráby repaired to his uncle's. Here he collected his papers, and stowed them away in the pocket of his coat, he likewise donned his fur mantle, told his uncle shortly what had occurred, and then started to go back home.

It was already nightfall when he took his way down the street to his own home.

As he passed Peter Paprika's house he heard a curious whizzing noise near him, and at the same moment was conscious of having been struck a blow on the side, which so staggered him, it nearly made him lose his balance. He looked round; there was not a soul in sight in the street. He could not imagine from whence the mysterious report had come. But after he had got home, he found a little round perforation on the left side of his coat, which was plainly a bullet hole.

When he drew his papers out of his breast-pocket, out fell a leaden bullet which had evidently bored through so far and been turned aside by the packet of documents.

The whizzing sound our hero had heard had been the report of an air-gun, and had he not placed the papers in his breast-pocket, it would have been all over with him.

CHAPTER XXI.

The jest was surely now at an end, said Ráby to himself; it was no use trifling with these people but best to go straight to the point with them.

So the next day he set out for Vienna, nor did he conceal the purport of his journey. For he had to induce the Emperor to remove the Szent-Endre authorities and order a new municipal body to be set up in their place. As a land-owner, he had full right to demand this to be done.

Meanwhile, he left Böske to keep house, only stipulating she should have someone to be with her in his absence.

In Vienna all fell out as he had wished, and after forwarding his plans there, he returned home.

As he reached the gate of the town he wondered what new developments would greet his return; he had a foreboding something strange was preparing, nor was he mistaken.

For when he came to his own house, there outside sat Böske in tears, surrounded by various bits of furniture, which had evidently been thrown out into the street.

"Why, what in the world have you got there?" asked Ráby, amazed, of the weeping maid-servant.

"What have I got?" cried Böske, "why, honoured master, don't you know your own furniture when you see it? These are all our things, and they have turned them out here, and me with them."

"What?" yelled Ráby, as he leapt from the coach.

But no answer was needed, for just then the door opened, and out came the notary.

He leaned with the utmost sang-froid against the door, while he filled with tobacco his clay pipe, from which he proceeded to puff eddies of smoke right into Ráby's face. He was quite drunk, and behind him stood a couple of boon companions.

"Pray what has happened here?" inquired the astonished master of the house.

"Only that I am taking possession of my own property," was the insolent answer.

"Your property, why it's mine, considering I paid the price for it in due form," retorted the puzzled Ráby.

"But I repent of having sold it, and I've taken possession again," rejoined the notary, as he re-lit his pipe. "And now since you, my fine gentleman, have nothing further to look for in this town, and are no longer the master here, you may just pack off and go!"

"But I paid you ready-money," remonstrated Ráby, his voice fairly shaking with rage and shame.

"You'd better bring it before the tribunal," sneered the notary, and he laughed so immoderately that the pipe dropped out of his mouth.

Ráby heard the laughter echoed in the yard without by a dozen other voices.

He strove no longer. He told Böske he would send a coach to fetch her and the furniture away, and till then, she must wait there. Then he hurried off to his uncle's and told his story.

"This is beyond a joke," said the old man. "We will not stand this sort of thing from these insolent wretches."

"But to whom can I complain?" asked Ráby. "To the judge, Petray, who is my personal enemy; to the county court where I am accused of bigamy and scoffed at?"

"To none of the lot! There is an edict which provides that whoso appropriates unlawfully the property of another, can himself be turned out by the lawful owner."

"But where can we procure the methods of force necessary to drive these people out?" demanded Ráby. "The whole township is in their pay. The municipality gives no formal help, and the military would not move in the matter. If I myself incite the people to act, I shall be accused of instigating to violence."

"Leave all that to me, my boy; we old folks know more than you young ones give us credit for. No need to go either to the tribunal or to the barracks. We'll just get the good people of Bicske and Velencze to help us. The gentry in these towns fight like dragons. But in all their history there is not a single case of either having ever taken their disputes before the county courts or the provincial tribunals. For, being of noble descent, there is a tradition among them that all quarrels which arise between them shall be settled by the military officer who happens, for the time being, to be in command of the defendant's town. They are satisfied with this judgment, and never do either judge or lawyer have a fee out of their pockets."

"That sounds quite patriarchal," remarked Ráby.

"Now why can't we acquire just such a right among our people here?" pursued his uncle. "In a fortnight's time there will be a fair at Stuhlweissenburg. During this time I will go round and discuss the matter with the heads of the departments. You yourself can remain here in the meantime and look after my work in the post office. In Velencze they are just electing Stephen Keö, Knight of Kadarcs, as the judge. You ought to propound your plan to him. He has a fine fighting record behind him, for he went through Rákóczi's campaigns with the great leader himself, and still wears the shabby wolfskin coat in which he used to parade in the old fighting days. He is very proud of his military record, as well as of his ancestors, who came from Asia with the horsemen of Arpád himself. Remember this point; it will be an excellent passport to his good graces, and don't forget to give him his full title, and always to address him as Knight of Kadarcs. As soon as I'm ready with the legal points we'll go to Stuhlweissenburg and set our scheme afoot. Meanwhile, have no fear, we'll soon drive those brutes out of your house, my boy, and send them packing!"

Ráby agreed to all of it. He was so exasperated that he positively yearned for a fight of some kind, whatever it might be.

So it was arranged he should stop and look after the post office, while his uncle went to collect materials for his campaign.

CHAPTER XXII.

It was Stuhlweissenburg fair. In the chaffering, chattering crowd of market folk, cattle-drivers and swine-herds jostled country land-owners accompanied by their lackeys, and shepherds in gay cloaks, while gipsy horse-dealers, with their ragged coats bright with silver buttons, trotted out their prancing nags to attract possible buyers. Here and there flitted strangely clad figures—a Wallachian boyar with his sheepskin cap, or a Servian with his scarlet fez, and turbanned Turks, the remnant of the expelled Mussulman population, who had come to sell their last sheep, and then follow the rest of their folk.

The encampments begin with rows of shoemakers and furriers, then come variegated groups of merchants from outlying provinces. Foreign wares there are none, for the "dumping" of useless foreign commodities is forbidden by an imperial edict. What are exposed here are all genuine native products, whether it be in fabrics, pottery, or copper-ware, while there is a great rush for the booths where pewter plates and dishes are for sale.

Everything is paid for in ready money, so that if a well-to-do purchaser buys a herd of sheep and has not the price forthcoming, he leaves his silver knife and fork (which he carries about with him) as a pledge, and the seller knows well enough they will be redeemed in due course.

Towards mid-day, the "market-kitchen" becomes thronged. Here too the famous gipsy stew needs no advertising, for its savoury odour betrays its whereabouts, and it only wants good wine to wash it down to make it complete. But this same good wine is dear, and only for the gentry. The Velencze people have already annexed a table near the bar, and sit round it and listen to their favourite song:

"See I will drink with you,So I can clink with youA glass of good wine:But if you do not choose,To pledge, I'll not refuseAlone to empty mine."

But now come the Bicske contingent, each one of whom brandishes a huge weighted stick, or copper axe, while their neighbours have already deposited their weapons on the table.

These late-comers observe that the others have already annexed the best table, and proceed accordingly.

"You gentlemen from Velencze have come early," growls Bognár Laczi, the leader of the Bicske party.

"Yes, and by this you must have caught plenty of mud-fish." (This is intended as a graceful allusion to the Lake of Velencze.) "And what's more, have swallowed them by this time," sneered a pugnacious looking, thick-set fellow, who also belonged to the Bicske gang.

As is well known, the worthy dwellers by the Velencze lake do not relish this kind of reflection on their sport, and they resented it accordingly.

But the fight does not yet begin, for who is fool enough to fight over the fish he eats? Besides, eating is the first and most important business, so they sink differences in order to make a square meal.

"Now, friends," says Bognár Laczi to the Velencze contingent, "what say you to some music? We have brought our own piper and a cornet-player with us, so I propose that we take it in turns; first your gipsies shall play, and then our musicians."

"All right," agreed the others, and thereupon the noble representative from Bicske had his favourite tune played on the bagpipes.

"I've a house and a sweet little wife of my own,And bread and bacon and crops that I've grown."

And everything progressed smoothly, for while the music was going on, no one could talk, and if one guest called to someone else at the other table, he did not forget to address him as "noble friend." But at the second round of wine the company began to sing with the music, and it was not easy to stop their efforts. Finally, the two parties insisted on singing different songs at the same time, the result being an uproar, wherein cymbal, fiddle, bagpipe, and cornet strove for precedence in a very rivalry of tumultuous discord.

The Velencze leader could not stand such an annoyance, and he promptly hurled an empty bottle at the wall just above the head of the Bicske chief, so that the fragments fell on the latter's head. He then seized his axe, struck the beam with it, and cried out defiantly, "Let's see who is the better man?"

The valorous Bicske men and their ten Velencze companions, were equally ready to join in the fray thus begun. So they seized their axes and clubs, and began to brandish these in a highly menacing fashion. For there is no fighter like your Magyar when his blood is up.

At this perilous juncture appeared the representatives of peace and arbitration, in the person of Sir Stephen Keö, the "Knight of Kadarcs," and his companion, Mr. Postmaster Leányfalvy, who led between them Mathias Ráby, and presented him to the company.

The old campaigner, with his shabby sheepskin over his shoulders, and a short pipe between his teeth, pressed into the ranks of the combatants as calmly as if the Geneva Red Cross had sheltered his breast. Not a bit intimidated by the uproar, he brandished his pike, and cried out in a shrill voice:

"So you are at it again, are you! Be quiet, you fellows; and so early too, for you can't have drunk much yet. But listen to me, friends. This gallant gentleman whom you see here is Mr. Mathias Ráby of Rába and Mura, the son of the late Stephen Ráby, that noble patriot, who so often stood up for Magyar rights. During his absence from home some bullies in Szent-Endre have ejected this noble gentleman from his own house, and occupied it. Now he calls upon us, the patriots of Velencze and Bicske, to come to his aid, and will pay us a salary of two gulden per head, to drive out the illegal occupiers from his lawful domicile. Therefore I suggest that you adjourn your mutual quarrel till the next Stuhlweissenburg fair (and chalk it up so that you do not forget it); but meantime, come with us, and help to right the wrong done him."

Whereupon the twenty men present cheered loudly and signified their readiness to go.

"We have four carriages here," said Sir Stephen. "Four must stay with the horses, so that there will be sixteen all told for the expedition."

And so it was arranged.

But Bognár Laczi urged immediate action. "Let's be off, all of us, only let us send on a scout who shall warn the Szent-Endre people that we are coming in full force. They shall not say that we take them unawares, but should get their fighting gear in readiness."

It took some time for Ráby, the postmaster, and the knight to agree to this arrangement, for they deemed such a proceeding would be pure folly. Szent-Endre might be too strong for them, if it had time to collect all its forces. But at last they gave in, and sent on their scout ahead, delaying their actual start till nightfall.

By morning they had reached the "Pomázer" Inn safe and sound, so they halted and baited the horses. The passengers sprang from the carriages, and stretched their drowsy limbs. Then they roused the hostess and ordered some coffee, and everyone knows what "Hungarian coffee" means; it consists of red wine, ginger, and pepper, and is drunk boiling hot. But this beverage kept them going all day, so invigorating was it.

While the horses fed, the messenger they had dispatched to reconnoitre, came back with the news that all Szent-Endre was agog, the municipality having brought together a rabble armed with sticks, pitchforks, and flails, who had collected in front of Ráby's house, while the townsmen in the courtyard were armed and ready for the attack.

"Heigh ho," shouted the assailants. "What joy! We shall have someone now with whom we can fight! So let's drive on so that we can be soon in fighting array."

"Stop a bit, my noble friends," said Sir Stephen Keö. "First of all, let us exercise a little strategy. For this will be the decisive struggle, and remember I am in command! Before all, we must know the fortress we are about to conquer. Now the house has two doors, the one opening on to the Buda street, the other behind into the garden. Therefore we must divide into two parties. The one must begin the frontal attack from the street, the other will go round into the vineyard and take their chance under shelter of the garden. The Velencze men will lead the one attack, and those of Bicske the other."

The old fire-eater was not only an accomplished strategist, but likewise a great student of character. He knew his people, and that if he placed the two factions side by side, they would quarrel at least over precedence if over nothing else, that neither would give in, and that all chance of success would consequently be ruined.

"Now who will lead the attack from the street?" asked their commander-in-chief.

It was settled by drawing lots; the garden position falling to the Bicske party.

"So we are to go behind, are we?" questioned Bognár Laczi sulkily.

"Noble friend," pleaded the old knight, "for those who tackle a seven-headed dragon, there is no 'behind,' for on every side there is a head. You will attack the enemy's rear-front."

He was obliged, however, to make this concession to the Bicske assailants, that they should travel first in two coaches to reach the garden by a roundabout way, and yet be there at the same time as the Velencze contingent.

These delicate points of precedence being settled, they drove off in fine style, two of the vehicles turning towards the vineyard, and the other three to Szent-Endre.

They could hear as they drew nearer that the whole place was in an uproar. In the Buda Street the citizens had organized an impromptu army. There they were in little national groups, the Magyars with clubs, the Serbs armed with flails, the Rascians provided with pitchforks. It looked as if it would be a hundred to one.

The space in front of Ráby's house was occupied by a mixed mob of hangers-on of all kinds, who were carrying sticks, and lances, and old flint muskets.

In front of this phalanx stood the lieutenant in full gala dress, with the big drum slung round his neck, ready to give the storming signal, and inciting the mob with warlike exhortations.

But it was in reality no joke, and the antagonists, seeing the attacking party, retreated into the house and endeavoured to close the door behind them. Only when they felt themselves safe did they begin their defensive operations.

The crowd without did not take an active part in the fray, but only looked on.

The Velencze contingent tried first of all to break in the door, but it was barricaded too fast from within. So a regular attack had to be essayed.

The old Knight of Kadarcs directed operations from the coach where he still sat.

"Just take the stakes out of the well-posts, and you can jam in the door with them."

Four of the party managed to wrench out the stakes, and jammed them against the great door like a Roman battering-ram, whilst three others worked at the smaller door with their stout clubs. But those inside defended themselves bravely enough, it must be owned. In the court stood logs of wood piled up, and these they hurled at the besiegers, who naturally returned the projectiles back from whence they came.

Within could be heard the directions of the defenders to those inside to fire on the assailants if these effected an entrance.

But all the attacks of the Velencze men had been perfectly futile, had not the Bicske auxiliaries come up just in the nick of time to the rescue.

They, in fact, decided the issue of the battle. All at once they uttered a tremendous yell which scared the enemy back into their entrenchments. Hereupon, a frightful tumult ensued, the crowd without shouting and seeking to find an outlet over the walls of the neighbouring houses, or in the out-houses and stables. Then the Velencze party made a tremendous dash for the barred door, and succeeded in effecting an entrance. What followed is indeed difficult to describe.

"Take care to hit them on the head," shouted the old commander-in-chief from his perch in the coach, while the mob laughed loud and long, as one after another member of the town council crawled out on all fours over the neighbouring roofs into safety, whilst first one and then another of the Szent-Endre worthies were thrown out like cats on to the ground below. The last to be turned out was the notary, his clothes torn, his temples bleeding, and his teeth knocked out, yet there was not a soul who seemed to sympathise with him.

The mayor had bethought him of a refuge in the chimney, but they lighted straw below, and he was forced to push his way out. But the chimney being too narrow, he only succeeded in getting his head and arms out, and there he stuck, gesticulating wildly like a jack-in-the-box, till the siege being over, they could take off the chimney-pot and so free the prisoner.

When the coast was clear they opened the doors and re-installed Mathias Ráby in his own house again.

"Now, noble sir, what did you think of the operations?" asked the Knight of Kadarcs, as he cleaned out his pipe for a smoke.

"A nice piece of work; it's a pity that sort of fighting has gone out of fashion!"

But the worthy burghers had learned a twofold lesson. First, that when a plebeian fights it out with a noble, it is the plebeian who gets the worst of it; and secondly, that the people themselves, if they see their superiors thrashed, not only turn their backs on them, but regard it as a good joke.

But after drinking to his health, the rescuers took leave of their host, now settled again in his own home.

"We shall be at your service whenever you want us," was their parting salutation.

CHAPTER XXIII.

When Ráby was left alone he began to see that what had been done was really a foolish proceeding.

To attack a peaceful town with armed force, beat thirty or forty of its citizens, to say nothing of its magistracy, black and blue—this was beyond a joke in any civilised city.

Besides, those who had their heads broken in the fray, would not be silent about their grievances. For that matter, Böske had already seen several vehicles full of people with bandaged heads, proceeding in the direction of Buda.

Mathias Ráby therefore determined to go himself to Pesth without waiting to be sent for, and then to testify to what had occurred.

Of course he could not think of leaving Böske behind alone in the empty house, where there was nothing now left to take care of. The cows had long since been turned into butcher's meat for the benefit of the invaders, who had likewise drunk up every drop of wine in the cellar.

And it was lucky Ráby took Böske with him, as we shall see later.

Again he alighted at his old inn, and, donning his official dress, he caused himself to be taken in a sedan-chair to the palace of the governor.

When he entered the ante-chamber the first people he saw were the Szent-Endre officials waiting likewise to see his Excellency, just as they had come from the fight. One had his arm in a sling, another showed a black eye, and a third a bandaged hand.

But even these grievances were for the moment, it seemed, thrust aside directly Ráby entered, for on seeing him they all began to talk and gesticulate noisily. He could not follow what they said, for most of them spoke Rascian, then the language of the Hungarian middle classes, whereof he only knew a few words, but from their tone and gestures, he gathered that the conversation concerned him, and that they were preparing to make things hot for him.

So he did not feel exactly comfortable as he turned his back on them and withdrew to the window.

All at once the noise ceased suddenly as the usher announced "His Excellency is coming," while the audience began at once to cringe and whine, and put on a woful air all round.

The door of the ante-chamber was thrown open, and his Excellency came in.

He nodded grimly at the waiting crowd, for whose woes his face betrayed no particular sympathy, but when he saw Ráby he went up to him, slapped him on the shoulder, and his face relaxed into a smile.

This was indeed a rare event, for it took a lot to make his Excellency smile! Moreover, he greeted his guest with a dignified cordiality.

"Well met, my friend! I'm glad you've come. You are on the right road. Walk in here, and don't let anyone disturb us," he added, turning to the usher, "as long as his Imperial Majesty's representative is with me. But you," and he turned to the expectant crowd of suppliants, "you can just go to where you came from; you have only got what you deserved."

But those left behind in the ante-room looked at one another, and did not exactly know what to make of it, till his Excellency's secretary told them that the hurts they had received were fully recognised by the law, and that they would have redress later if they now went home quietly.

His Excellency, meanwhile, plunged into the matter straight away.

"Now see here, my worthy sir, you can only obtain satisfaction in Hungary from the Magyar laws themselves. The thing is to know how to profit by them, for we have excellent statutes; there is no need to supplement them. I should like to know if the collective tribunals of Austria itself would settle your affair so thoroughly and effectually, nay and cheaply, as the captain of the Velencze company has done. But you have been to the Emperor again with your denunciations, and even now, I daresay, have your pockets full of imperial instructions. Don't take them out if your case is brought before me, for I warn you, I shall not open them. I wonder if his Majesty knows, by the way, that I never read the instructions he sends me."

"But I now bring other orders from his Majesty," said Ráby, who did not think it worth while to say all he knew. "His Majesty has thought a great deal about his Hungarian subjects, and has great projects for bettering this city."

"What may such projects be, pray?"

"First of all, he is giving permission to the Jewish community in Pesth to build a synagogue."

"A synagogue for the Jews!" cried his Excellency, springing up in horror from his seat. "Impossible! Pesth will not be bettered by that, it will be completely ruined. Why in a hundred years' time, if that is allowed, the Jews will be having all the rights of citizens. Heaven forbid they should be permitted a place in the Assembly, for they will want to get in there. Well, that is enough for a beginning; is there anything else?"

"Of course," pursued Ráby, and since his interlocutor was standing at the window, he too went there and looked out at the view over the Danube and Pesth. "Does your Excellency see the great square plain on the edge of the Pesth woods, that is bordered on one side with willows?"

"I see, and what of that?"

"His Majesty has ordered that a large building two stories high, with nine courts, and two thousand windows, shall be erected there. He has, himself, shown me the plans of the edifice which is to be built at his own expense."

"Good heavens! What's that for? is his Majesty going to shut up there all those who do not respect his edicts?"

"No, it is for a hospital for the city of Pesth."

"A hospital, indeed! As if the ordinary lazaretto was not enough."

"It will also serve as a foundling asylum."

"What, for the children who are deserted by their mothers? Why, there are none such in Pesth. The citizens won't tolerate such worthless women in their midst. Such folks must do penance as the Church directs, or else be driven from the city."

"It may be so now, but in course of time, when Pesth is raised to the rank of great world-cities, the magistracy will have something else to do than to control the private lives of its citizens."

"Now, how in the world can Pesth become a great city, I should like to know? Will the Emperor come and live here himself?"

"Perhaps not now, but he means to make it a great place for trade."

"Pesth a place for trade? Why! what are you thinking about? You will never see any trade done in Pesth but by rag-merchants and swine-herds."

Ráby smiled.

"The Emperor means to raise Pesth to the level of a great commercial centre by certain big schemes he has in view. He proposes, for instance, to have a canal cut which shall connect Pesth with Trieste, and so bring it into direct connection with the coast."

"Connect Pesth with Trieste! Why my good young friend" (the speaker had dropped his previous formalities in his astonishment), "don't take me for a fool, I pray! Remember it is not the first of April. What is the Emperor thinking of? What about the Carpathians, pray?"

"The mountains will be tunnelled, and the canal is to run under them."

"Now just listen to me, my good sir! If you do not respect my official capacity, otherwise the Imperial Hungarian Presidency of the County Assembly, which I represent, you should at least have regard to my grey hairs, and find some other fool to impose on with your scheme. Why, this would take millions of money."

"The actual estimate amounts to sixty millions."

"Sixty millions! What are you dreaming of? Why, the Emperor has not got as much as that out of the whole Hungarian revenue in twenty years."

"The financial provision for this undertaking lies ready to hand. A syndicate has been formed which will answer for the needful funds, and directly Pesth is brought into connection with the sea its commercial possibilities can be developed. Imagine a water-way from Pesth to Trieste, one of the great emporiums of the world's trade in the centre of Hungary!"

But his Excellency could not imagine it.

"Tut, tut," he cried, and his eyes flashed angrily. "What do you mean by taking such a chimera seriously? A canal from the centre of Hungary to the coast, what does it mean but foreign traders sucking the life and strength out of this country to glut their markets with our wealth. We won't have anything of the kind! The ruling classes of this country will have something to say to that. We will not let the people of this nation be plunged into misery thus. Why, foreign traders would just exploit our mineral wealth to their hearts' content, and leave the poor folk of this country starving. No, no, my friend, don't you think we will ever have anything of the kind."

Ráby would not give in; he was by this time quite at home on these questions. He could, moreover, give excellent reasons why every land that has a seaport is prosperous, for trade does not impoverish people, it enriches them. To which his Excellency retorted that of course trade was a good thing for nations who knew how to get the best of their neighbours, but for a simple unsophisticated folk, like the Hungarians, it meant ruin.

In the midst of this heated controversy, the two did not perceive that the district commissioner had entered without being announced, and was listening with much amusement to the debate.

The district commissioner could not abide wrangling, so he promptly turned the conversation on to neutral topics.

"Eh, what is all this about? We, at any rate, have nothing to do with the nation's economics. Tell us rather what is going on in Vienna. For remarkably funny events have happened surely since we met." And the speaker laughed slily, as if struck by some comical reminiscence.

Ráby knew well enough what caused his companion's mirth. He was thinking, doubtless, of Fruzsinka and the two other "wives." And the thought pierced him with a sudden stab of pain.

The good-natured official suppressed his ill-timed laughter, however, as he diverted the subject.

"Now tell us something about the capital, my dear fellow? Have you been to the National Theatre and seen the latest comedy there?"

"I had no leisure," said Ráby drily, "to go to the theatre, and see what the comedies were like. You will have more time for that probably than I shall."

Which retort surprised the worthy district commissioner not a little.

Then Mathias Ráby turned to the governor with a deeply respectful bow, only waved a careless "adieu" to the district commissioner, and withdrew.

"He is put out with you about something or other," remarked the governor to his companion.

"Yes, he snapped, didn't he, like a puppy when you tread on his tail."

But just then, in came the secretary with despatches that had just arrived by the last post.

"One for you as well, worshipful sir," said the secretary to the district commissioner. "Shall I send it into your office, or will you have it here, seeing it is marked 'personal.'"

"All right. Give it me here, please," was the careless answer.

And the light-hearted official broke the seal and began to read the missive, stretched at ease in his chair.

But he did not remain so, for hardly had he perused its contents than he got up, and his face grew suddenly pale under its cosmetic.

"Be kind enough to read that," he stammered, embarrassed, "the Emperor writes an autograph letter to summon me to Vienna, and I am dismissed from my post as district commissioner."

"And in my despatch your successor is already nominated."

"I do not understand it."

"But I do. Now, my friend, you will have time to judge for yourself what the comedy at the National Theatre is like."

The ex-official pressed his hand to his brow.

But as his Excellency took a pinch of snuff he said drily: "It is not a puppy who snaps, but a big dog who can bite when he wants to. And he has flown at you, my friend, that's clear."

CHAPTER XXIV.

It was horribly hot and depressing at the "White Wolf" at Pesth, where Ráby had elected to stay. The atmosphere was mephitic and close, and in the dusty inn parlour the flies swarmed uncomfortably, while outside it was horribly dusty, as it is even to-day.

No wonder Ráby was glad to get out of it, and elected to take a stroll in the direction of the wood outside the city, his head full of many conflicting thoughts.

Certainly, his plans for bettering the people were prospering. The Emperor had recalled the easy-going district commissioner in consequence of Ráby's representations, and had appointed to the post an able and strenuous, yet cold and reserved man, a wealthy landlord, who undertook the office on account of the honour it conferred on its holder. Perhaps what best qualified him for the post was, that he was not on intimate terms with anyone in the neighbourhood.

His first care was, in view of Mathias Ráby's complaints, to suspend the magistrate of Szent-Endre and his satellites, and to order a fresh election of such representatives in that town, which meant a complete clearing out of the old gang. Then the deposed notary would be either compelled to show the new officials the bricked-up passage to the treasure chamber, or, if he refused, the "pope" would reveal the secret of the other entrance; this promise Ráby had succeeded in extorting from the new authorities.

Once the treasure-chest was unearthed, the oppressed townspeople, whose money had been wrung from them to fill that coffer, could be compensated for their wrongs. What rejoicing would there not be when the poor starving husbandman could receive back the four or five hundred gulden unjustly extorted from him, and one could tell him that though it had been reft from him unjustly, now his wrongs were redressed. What a splendid mission for him who undertook it!

Ráby's soul revelled in the very thought of it: no sordid considerations of selfish interest poisoned his joy, for he had renounced all personal reward and only taken the work upon himself on the condition that he had no share in the treasure when it was discovered. Legally, indeed, he was entitled to such a share, but how much greater claim had he to be heard if he was empty-handed in this affair!

And if he rejoiced at the fulfilment of his aims, he, it must also be admitted, felt a distinct satisfaction in the thought of revenge. The great coffer held not only the secret treasure, but also the private accounts which would make it clear which of the powerful officials were concerned in the affair. The whole shameful story must then be brought to light, and all, who up till now had pursued him with their malice and mocked him to his face, must then stand as prisoners at the bar, however high they had held their heads.

Obsessed by these and the like reflections, our hero came to the edge of the wood and there found stretched out before him the great waste plot of land bordered with willows, which some hours before he had pointed out from the window of the palace to his Excellency. The surveyors were already working on it, taking measurements, and staking out the ground where the first foundations for the new building should be laid.

All at once Ráby's reverie was disturbed by someone addressing him. He had not observed how the man who spoke to him had come up, but then he had of course as much right as Ráby to walk there. The stranger appeared to be a worthy Pesth citizen; he wore the Magyar dress and had the consequential air of a man who cannot learn anything from other people, however wise they be. His short curling moustachios lent his face a genuine Magyar expression, but of Hungarian he apparently understood not a word, but expressed himself in bad German. Ráby answered the "Guntag" of the stranger politely.

"Does the gentleman happen to know what the surveyors are planning here?" asked the new-comer.

Ráby was naturally ready to satisfy worthy curiosity.

"That," he answered, "is a great hospital the Emperor is erecting. A building we much need," he added.

And they talked of various other things, in the course of which it came out that the new-comer was a pork-dealer in Pesth, whereupon Ráby opined that he had the honour of speaking to a member of the famous "Guild of pork merchants." But this new friend talked of many things beside his own trade.

They had now come to the winding path which led along the side of the wood, but the stranger's fund of conversation continued to be apparently inexhaustible. He mentioned, among other things, that he preferred this walk because the road was not yet made. Since it had been the fashion to have the roads in the city paved, he said, he no longer cared to walk in the streets. The whole paving scheme had been a hobby of the present burgomaster, who, as everyone knew, had been a German shoemaker, and had only introduced paving-stones so as to give the German shoemakers preference over the Hungarian bootmakers, for since they had had pavements to walk on, people naturally wore fewer boots, for you only need shoes for the paving stones.

It was not long before the two reached the little inn, which stood there even then for the refreshment of travellers.

"What do you say to turning in for a glass of beer?" asked his companion, "you get a capital brand here."

Ráby answered that he did not drink beer, whereupon the pork-dealer pressed him to touch glasses with him, and promptly drew out his purse as a proof of his readiness to pay the reckoning. But Ráby insisted that he only drank water.

"Well, if that is the case," returned his fellow-wayfarer, "you cannot do better than have a glass; the water here is of unusual excellence. Just wait here, and I will go in and get some beer for myself, and send you out a glass of water. It comes from the famous Elias spring; there is no such water in the world."

Ráby gladly assented; tired and thirsty as he was with his walk, he longed for just such a refreshing draught.

So into the inn the good man hurried, but he soon reappeared, followed by a neat little waitress bearing a wooden tray with a large pewter mug of water on it. The girl looked at him while he drank, with her innocent blue eyes, so that Ráby hardly noticed, as he returned her scrutiny, that the water left a curiously bitter after-taste in his mouth. When he set the mug down, he observed that there was a white sediment at the bottom of it.

Rather scared in spite of himself, he asked the girl if there was anything in the water.

"I don't know," she answered, "if so, the gentleman who has just gone, put it in."

"Has he gone?"

"Yes, he went out by the back door. He did not even wait to take the change which I brought him."

The man was no pork-dealer, but a hired assassin. Ráby had been poisoned, that was clear. The trees already had begun to dance before his eyes, the blue sky became blood-red, and his feet refused to carry him, while his head was so heavy, it felt as if it would burst. He had not even the strength to stagger as far as a sedan-chair, but bade the inn people carry him back to the "White Wolf," which they promptly did in terror.

Had not poor Böske been there, Mathias Ráby's history would have come to an untimely end with that glass of water.

The servant-girl was the only one who had the presence of mind to give the patient some warm milk, and then tickled his throat with a feather, so as to induce violent vomiting, while she applied hot fomentations.

But in spite of her care it was needful to send for a doctor. Yet it was not so easy to find one, for physicians in those days were few and far between, and there were, as a matter of fact, but two in the whole city, the municipal doctor and the town leech, and neither would come when sent for. The municipal practitioner maintained that the law did not allow of him seeing patients out of their own houses. The town physician again found his excuse in the plea that he could not interfere in cases which had already been referred to his municipal colleague.

So there was no one to look after Ráby, since neither doctors would come to him, even though his life was in danger. Thus for fully four-and-twenty hours the poisoned man had no other assistance than that rendered by a poor servant-maid. For only on the evening of the following day, when it was getting dark, did a surgeon from Pilis appear, who, it had fortunately occurred to Ráby, was likely to answer the summons.

He set about curing his patient immediately, but he bound Ráby on his honour not to say a word as to who was treating him, otherwise it would be ruinous to his professional career in the town. It was only through the urgent prayers and tears, he said, of a good woman, that he had come to do what he could for the sick man.

As a matter of fact, the kind-hearted surgeon had to leave the city in consequence of having succoured Ráby in this way. But it was ten weeks before the patient fully recovered.

CHAPTER XXV.

During those ten weeks, Ráby had abundant leisure to reflect on the riddle these events presented. Who had thus attempted to poison him? Was it the offended councillors who had thus intrigued against him, some jealous courtier who had a grudge against him, or his own fugitive wife?

But all that time, except the surgeon and Böske, not a living soul knocked at his door to see him.

His enemies were, of course, countless, but it was just as certain that he had devoted friends. Where was his uncle, and Abraham Rotheisel, and the Servian "pope"; where too the grateful crowd of poor people that he had befriended?

Over and over again too did he inquire if this or that one had yet called, but Böske always answered that visitors had come only when the gracious master was asleep, and she had not dared waken him, or that the doctor had ordered that no one was to disturb the patient.

"And why don't you let people come in and see me?" asked Ráby querulously of his nurse. He was so cross that at last she lost patience, and told him plainly that during the whole course of his illness, not a soul had been near.

But Ráby would not believe it; it was impossible, and he asserted she was lying and trying to deceive him.

Which remark so upset poor Böske, that she burst into tears, and, in her own justification, admitted that people shunned him on purpose, that they were afraid of him, and spoke all imaginable evil of him. Nay, was it not true that everyone was saying he deserved to lose his head for being a traitor to his own country?

The simple maid-servant had only spoken the truth. Her master was, as she had hinted, virtually an outlaw, and his name was by all, from their Excellencies to the shoemaker's apprentices, only mentioned with hatred and scorn. But Ráby, incensed, was so indignant at Böske's well-meant candour, that he gave her notice then and there, and paying her a year's wages, refused to have her any longer in his service.

Thus it was that Ráby dismissed his faithful domestic who had simply told him what men said of him, and now he was absolutely alone in the world.

As soon as he had fully recovered, he set out for Vienna, but this time, in a wine-freighted barge which was to be towed by horses to the capital, for he was too weak to stand the tiring journey by road. They took eight days to reach their destination, and the fresh air did much to restore his shattered health. By the time he reached Vienna, Ráby looked quite himself again, save that he was much thinner than of old.

He related all that had befallen him to the Emperor, who advised him not to bring the crime home to the culprit, as if it came before the courts, he considered Ráby's cause would be ruined. Thereupon, he furnished him with directions of all kinds, and gave him carte-blanche to take his own line in all disturbances that might arise.

When Ráby came back to Buda, he wore armour under his coat, for this time his mission would be no jesting matter, that was evident.

In pursuance of the Imperial instructions, when he arrived at Buda, he handed the new district commissioner the Emperor's orders, and it was duly signified to the prefect of Szent-Endre, that the court of inquiry would meet on a given day, but in the prefecture.

At the same time, the Szent-Endre magistracy and their underlings were to be dismissed, and new officials were to be elected in their place. That choice of fresh functionaries might be made in due order, a big military force was held in readiness in case of disturbances arising.

When the order to quit came to the officials, the prefect hurried to find the notary, who was so angry that he forthwith broke his best porcelain pipe, and flung his cap down on the table in a rage.

"It's all up with us," admitted the prefect to his crony. "Now they will go ahead, and the enemy will spoil us utterly. The new district commissioner doesn't know his place, he did not once say, 'Your humble servant,' when I went to see him. All I could get out of him was that he was 'going to act conformably to instructions.'"

"That's well enough, if we knew what the 'instructions' were. But it's the soldiers I don't like, with Lievenkopp at their head too."

"But, surely, he is an old acquaintance."

"Yes, that's just the mischief of it. He knows a great deal too well the ins and outs of my affairs."

"I know he has had loans at one time or another from your worship."

"But unluckily he's always paid me back. Hardly a fortnight ago, he paid me up to the last ducat. I never dreamed an officer would remember his debts so accurately. I wish he had forgotten them! The world is going to the dogs, that's plain. And then just think what the commissioner has said. That he, in consequence of the denunciation of this good-for-nothing fellow, will insist on a strict search, not only in the Town Hall, but also in your house and mine. They will go from top to bottom in the prefecture."

"They can ransack my place as much as they will; they won't succeed in ferreting anything out. They will never find the great coffer; I can answer for it."

"With you perhaps they won't succeed; you hide your savings so well. But they are bound to scent out my chests."

"Why, how can they know anything of them?"

"How can they know? Don't be a fool! Just remember, Fruzsinka, doesn't she know?"

"Do you think she told Ráby?"

"Not Ráby, but Lievenkopp. I heard her with my own ears as she was wandering about one day in the maze with the captain, whom she wanted to marry her. That is why she told him all about the coffer and what it contained, so Lievenkopp knows all. But they can pounce upon the old contracts which are in my possession and want to know how I procured the money which, when I came here, I took for certain pledges left with me. And if they convict me?"

"We can easily prevent that; hide your chest so none may find it."

"That I know without a fool telling me. But whom can we trust? All these men here are knaves, anyone of them to whom I trust my treasure will betray me directly he knows that a third of the money legally belongs to whomsoever informs against the owner. If I bring the money here, someone will see it, and know where I have hidden it. The whole world is full of spies. We are the only two honest men in it, friend Kracskó."

"Don't you trouble, I'll hide your little savings effectually for you. Good! Well, go home, and come back soon with an empty box under your cloak, so that everyone can see you are carrying something. Thus no suspicions will be aroused when you go away again."

Mathias Kracskó did as he was bidden; he went off, and returned shortly with an empty municipal cash-box under his cloak.

Mr. Zabváry had his own box ready, sealed not only at the lock, but at the four corners.

"Here it is. Hide it away by all means, and directly the commission is off our track you can restore it to me again. And give me your written promise to give it me back as soon as I ask for it. For it's a sad world, and we are the only two honest men left in it."

So the notary signed the document, tucked the chest of savings under his cloak, and hid it carefully away.

Mathias Ráby was taking his way to Szent-Endre to attend the inquiry into the municipal scandals. On the road he met his uncle, who appeared to be looking for someone.

"Halloa, uncle! what are you waiting for?"

"I'm waiting for you, nephew, to have a talk with you. Remember, it's some time since we met!"

"Surely, uncle, that is not my fault," exclaimed Ráby, "considering that you never once crossed my threshold during my illness."

"No, indeed; small chance of doing so, seeing that every time I came, I found a heyduke before your door, who told me that only the doctor was allowed to see you."

"A heyduke!" cried Ráby in amazement, "why who could have placed him there?"

"That was just what I asked him, and he told me the municipality had done so."

"But what does the municipality mean by planting a heyduke before my door? And why did not Böske tell me?"

"Because the good soul had only one idea in her head—as sweet simplicity ordinarily has. She wormed out of the fellow why he stood there, and he told her he was ordered to look after a maniac inside, whom, if he tried to go out, he was to seize and bind. Had Böske told you a man was waiting for you then, nervous and feeble as you were, you would have sprung out of bed and had a hand-to-hand fight with him, and he would have bound you, weak invalid as you were, and carried you away to the mad-house, whence you were not likely to get out again. So Böske was silent."

"And I was so angry with her. But now we are good friends again, aren't we?"

"To be sure we are. But what shall we do with the others?"

"With my enemies?"

"No, with your friends! You can always be even with your foes, but your friends are another matter. The heads of the magistracy have not been idle during the ten weeks you were ill. To-day you appear with the imperial orders to elect a new municipality in Szent-Endre. Yet you will see that the folks here will choose exactly the same lot again."

"That surely is impossible!"

"Unluckily, it's not at all so. The mob whom you befriended, have been clearly bought over by the magistracy, who have not spared their wine for the last three weeks to convince the townsfolk that the present municipality are the best set of men going. They have befooled the peasants into believing they won't have to pay tithes next year, and blackened you in their eyes, so that the whole town is enraged against you. They say you have come to 'rectify' the taxes, and instead of the six thousand gulden it has paid up till now, Szent-Endre will have to yield thirty thousand, and that is why you trouble about their money matters."

"But all this is surely midsummer madness!"

"My dear fellow, the mob believes everything it is told, if it is only dinned into its ears often enough. You will see for yourself how popular feeling has changed towards you since you were last in Szent-Endre. Take my advice, and don't allow yourself to be seen in the town before the military arrive. But I know you will go your own way in spite of it!"

The old gentleman was right. Anyone else would have profited by such a warning, but it made Ráby only more keen for the fray.

"I must be on the spot," he answered; "and that soon, for I must have some talk with the people before the others appear, so good day, uncle!"

"Well, adieu, but come again soon!"

So Ráby hastened on to Szent-Endre to the big market-square, where the forthcoming election was to take place. On the way, he noted many suggestive signs, showing which way the wind was blowing. The shopkeepers who lounged at their thresholds withdrew indoors directly they caught sight of Ráby. Some acquaintances whom he met retreated to the other side of the street as if they had not seen him.

In the square, a large crowd had already assembled. In the front ranks Ráby recognised many old friends who often had interceded with him for the grievances of the common folk. Formerly, such men had hastened to kiss his hand; to-day they did not even raise their hats, and when he spoke to them they only ignored his greeting. One man to whom Ráby stretched his hand, actually shook his fist at him, and answered the question he put in Hungarian, in Rascian. Evidently no one here wished to understand Magyar. In vain did Ráby try to address them, the crowd only interrupted him with loud shouts, accompanied by threatening gestures.

His uncle was right, the mob had wholly changed, and by now believed that Ráby had bought over the town for the Emperor. They yelled noisy acclamations as his enemy, Kracskó, came across the market-square, hailing him as their benefactor and the defender of their rights. So Ráby thought the best thing was to go home and postpone his speech till the commission should formally cite him to appear before them. In the court he could have his say, and there he would have witnesses to support him.

So he went back to his deserted house to think over the situation.

Whilst he paced through the empty rooms, he suddenly caught sight of something sparkling on the floor. It was a metal button which had fallen between a crevice in the boards. He picked it up, and it awoke memories of Fruzsinka, for it was to one of her gowns that it had belonged. He remembered so well the one; she had worn it that day when she had thrown her arms round his neck and besought him not to sacrifice his own and her happiness to an ungrateful people. Had he listened to her, perhaps she would have remained a good and true wife to him, and peace and happiness would have blessed his married life. Now it was all over and done with, and there without the mob was howling for his destruction.

He threw the button out of the window, hastening to do away with such souvenirs.

Presently from the market-square burst forth that indescribable murmur which rises from a distant crowd. The minutes seemed hours as he waited.

At last a trampling of hoofs was heard; it was a lieutenant with an escort of half a dozen dragoons come to conduct Ráby to the court.

"The magistrate, the notary, the councillors, are all re-elected," was the news they came to announce.

Ráby was much annoyed that they should send an armed escort for him.

"I can find the way by myself, and am not afraid of anyone," he said, and with that he took his documents under his arm, and set off to walk to the Town Hall.

His self-possession impressed the crowd who silently made way for him. Besides, they stood in a wholesome awe of the dragoons who were drawn up in the market-place.

Ráby entered the court-room where the commission was sitting. It was intolerably warm, and he could have fairly swooned as he entered the hot oppressive atmosphere, yet his strength of mind conquered his physical weakness and steeled his failing nerves.

He began by making a formal and solemn protest against the way in which the election had been conducted, but it was not listened to.

Then the district commissioner read out Ráby's protest and asked the complainant to formulate his grievance.

Ráby laid his documents in order at the other end of the table, where they had prepared a place for him, and began to state his case at length; he quoted his documentary evidence, and promised to call witnesses for the prosecution.

It goes without saying that his statements did not pass unchallenged by those most interested.

After the case for the prosecution had been thus stated, the examination of its witnesses followed, but these were not so satisfactory as they might have been.

None could tell much about the great treasure chest, except that they had heard such an one existed, but they had never seen it, and only knew of it by hearsay.

Finally, no other evidence for the prosecution being forthcoming than the incriminating bills and the collected taxation-accounts, it was left for the municipality to justify themselves.

For the defence of the officials collectively, the notary was called upon to speak.

In the whole of his discourse, however, there was not a single word of justification of the officials concerned, or any refutation of the impeachment; it consisted solely of a violent torrent of invective against Ráby, who, according to his accuser, was a sorcerer who had dealings with the devil, a bluebeard who kept seven wives, a revolutionary who incited to revolt, to say nothing of being a highwayman who robbed harmless travellers. In short, there was nothing bad enough for Ráby, whom, finally, he denounced as a vampire who was robbing the poor folk of their trade and fattening on their labours—this last an indictment which fell rather flat, in view of poor Ráby's attenuated appearance, for he looked little more than a skeleton.

And so it went on, the heap of vile calumnies growing as he proceeded, yet their victim listened with a smiling face, for Ráby was really rejoicing in the absurdity of this collection of impossible impeachments.

But there is nothing that annoys an uneducated angry man more than ridicule from his opponents. And the more he raged, the more did it visibly excite Ráby's mirth.

Suddenly the features of the notary became distorted and his face turned livid, while his discoloured lips foamed and his eyes nearly started from their sockets, as the man he was vilifying continued to smile at his traducer unperturbed. At last the notary dealt his master stroke.

"And what think you of this, worshipful sirs, I tell you that he has actually boasted to the prefect that he has not only played bowls with the Emperor, but that he has constantly put on his Majesty's gold-embroidered coat and walked about in it. What say you to that?"

At this, the crowning accusation, Ráby could restrain his mirth no longer, and he burst out into a peal of hearty laughter which reverberated through the hall.

But at that sound, the speaker suddenly was silent, as if a shot had struck him, his mouth remained open, but his head sank back, and his eyes rolled till only the whites showed themselves; for an instant a spasm convulsed him, then he fell back—dead!

The laugh had killed him, as surely as if a bullet had been lodged in his heart.

They seized him and dragged him out into the fresh air, believing it was only a swoon, but in vain did they endeavour to restore life: it was all over with him.

When they were convinced that the notary was indeed dead, their despair knew no bounds.

But most of all was Mr. Zabváry quite desperate; wringing his hands, he wailed: "Kracskó, Kracskó, do not die till you have told me where my treasure is hidden. Wake up, I say, and tell me where you have put my little money-chest."

"But our big one," moaned the magistrate, "where's that? Haven't I always said that if only one man knew, and the devil carried him off, what should we do? Fetch a doctor, a surgeon, some of you. He must live till he tells us where the great treasure-chest is."

But no earthly aid could avail them for the man they called on lay there dead, and he had hidden the treasure so effectually that no one would ever find it.

The despairing survivors ran fuming with wrath back into the court-room. "Murder, murder," cried Zabváry as he rushed on Ráby. "I am a beggar, I have been robbed! Hang the murderer who has killed the notary."

"Not quite so fast," exclaimed Captain Lievenkopp, placing himself before Ráby. "There are others here as well you might hang."

"That's the man," shouted Zabváry, shaking his clenched fist at Ráby. "String him up at once!"

Whereupon the district commissioner rose and insisted on a hearing.

"It is quite true," he said, "that the notary died in consequence of Mr. Ráby having laughed at him during his speech, but our law does not reckon laughter as an instrument of manslaughter. I advise you not to lift a hand against this gentleman, for whoever does so, will be taught by the military to respect lawful authority. Now be off home with you!"

This appeal to armed force effectually quelled the malcontents, who sulkily beat a retreat.

The district commissioner turned to Ráby when they were alone. "We must prorogue the inquiry till all this has blown over. But if you, Mr. Ráby, will take my advice, you will leave this town as soon as possible, and will place yourself under Captain Lievenkopp's protection till you get away."

CHAPTER XXVI.

After the foregoing experiments, it was time for Ráby to seek for exterior means to attain his purpose, and he determined to extort an avowal from the Rascian "pope," who alone now knew the hiding-place of the great coffer, and if this was revealed, the whole intrigue could be unmasqued. The heaped-up treasure and large number of bonds, which represented a large amount of money, constituted irrefragable proof against the guilty.

It was to this end that Ráby sent for the "pope" to come and meet him at Pesth.

This time our hero did not alight at a frequented hostelry, but put up at an inn where the country people were wont to go, and chartering a room there, only went out at night.

But none the less had his enemies ferreted him out, without his having the slightest suspicion that two or three spies were on his track wherever he went.

One morning, Ráby was able to write to the Emperor and tell him that the "pope" was ready to present himself in Vienna, and divulge all, as soon as he received direct instructions from his Majesty. He read the missive to the "pope" before sealing it up, so that the good man might approve of it throughout, and carried it himself to post, so that it should pass through no strange hands. Then he invited the ecclesiastic to dine with him, taking care to provide that worthy's favourite national dishes, a savoury Paprika stew and the Servian "Csaja."

As they sat there doing justice to them, who should come in but Judge Petray.

It was surely some unlucky chance which led Petray to Ráby's table.

They exchanged greetings with a certain amount of embarrassment, and Petray's contemptuous tone in opening up the conversation (which Ráby had willingly avoided), was not lost on the other.

"Well met, friend! I beg pardon for disturbing you, but you are the very man I wanted to see," said Petray, as he sat down beside them. "Yes," he went on, "about that letter which you have written to the Emperor."

"What do you mean?" cried Ráby, beside himself with astonishment.

"Why, you know well enough that the municipal council has forbidden complaints to be formulated to the Emperor regarding any matter affecting its internal regulations."

"But who can possibly know what my correspondence contains, I should like to know?"

"Well we happen to know, because we intercepted the letter at the post-office, you see."

"What, you have dared to intercept my correspondence!" cried Ráby enraged.

"Yes, and what's more, we have opened the letter and read it, and have submitted it to a committee of inquiry."

"But this is an unheard-of insult!" exclaimed Ráby, rising from his seat in uncontrollable anger.

"Oh, you are getting angry, are you? I guessed you would be, when you heard it; that's why I begged your pardon when I came in. But it doesn't alter the fact that I am sent to arrest you in the name of the municipality, on a charge of treason against the authorities, and am ordered to commit you to prison forthwith."

Petray said all this in such a jesting tone, that the "pope" who had kept his seat at table, imagined he was simply joking. He poured out a glass of wine and offered it to the judge, saying as he did so:

"Here have done with your jests, and drink this, your worship; no one believes what you are saying! Come, let us toast one another!"

The "pope" was a vigorous, dignified looking man in the prime of life, with a round rosy face. He beamed again with benevolence as he pledged the judge.

Yet Petray did not take the proffered glass, but stiffened himself and stood in a judicial attitude, with his hand on the hilt of his sword, while he said in a stern tone:

"Here there is no matter for jesting, I am sent by the Pesth County Assembly to arrest Mr. Mathias Ráby as a criminal, wherever I may find him."

And with that he stepped to the door and pushed it open. Without, stood half a dozen heydukes armed with swords and carbines and the town provost.

At the sight of them, the "pope" turned suddenly pale; his rubicund face became a ghastly grey, his hairs seem to bristle in terror. There was a rattling sound in his throat, and then he fell back senseless on the floor in an apoplectic fit. In vain they strove to revive him. He was dead! Fright, or rather the apoplexy had killed him. And as he was the only living soul who had known the secret of the buried treasure, his death forbade the entrance ever being discovered.

Yet Ráby had not seen what had happened, for as soon as ever Petray had opened the door, the provost had immediately arrested him with the threat that if he did not yield, he would be put into irons.

Ráby simply answered that he would not oppose armed force, and that he put his trust in a Providence that would bring truth and justice to light. And with that they marched him off, and led him down out into the street.

Before the gate stood three coaches. They made him take the front seat in the first, and placed two guards opposite him with their swords pointed against his breast. The others followed in the remaining vehicles. So they drove through the streets of Pesth till they reached the Assembly House, where Petray ordered Ráby's conductors to "obey orders."

So they proceeded to "obey orders." First they loosened his silver-hilted sword from his side, took his purse and gold watch from his pocket, drew the signet ring from off his finger, and searched him from head to foot. In the breast-pocket they found the passport of the Emperor, commanding that Mr. Mathias Ráby should pass unmolested wherever he went. The provost read it through with a mocking laugh. Then he brought out fetters, rivetted them on his prisoner's hands and feet, opened a narrow iron-barred door, and without further ceremony, pushed him into "cell number three."

From that moment they called Mathias Ráby with justice, "Rab Ráby,"[1] for does not "Rab" mean in Hungarian, a prisoner?

[1] I cannot but help feeling that the sudden death of the "pope" in this last chapter will strike the reader as a somewhat bold license, even for the novelist, seeing how closely it follows on that of the notary. I am aware that as romance it could not be justified, but seeing that this is a true story which I am telling, I cannot do otherwise than follow the facts however extraordinary they may appear, seeing they are set forth in the hero's own autobiography.—(AUTHOR'S NOTE.)

CHAPTER XXVII.

Nine feet long and six wide was the underground cellar wherein they had plunged our hero.

In this space, a select company was already assembled, eighteen individuals all told. And Mathias Ráby now made the nineteenth in the already overcrowded cell, and how he was to find a place there was a knotty problem. It was lucky that the window over the door was not filled with glass, but with an iron grating, which let in some air.

As a matter-of-fact, this cell was the best in the whole Assembly House, as could be testified to by old Tsajkos, the eldest of the prisoners, who was now quartered here. He was an old acquaintance of our hero, by the way, and Ráby had often provided the old man with tobacco, a luxury which the prisoners were not allowed to smoke, but might chew, if they could get it.

Nor was Tsajkos long in recognising the new-comer. He limped up to him, rattling the heavy chains he wore on his legs, and clapped Ráby on the back in greeting, while the other occupants of the cell looked on in wide-eyed amazement.

"So you have come to it at last, have you, my young friend? Now who would have thought the likes of you would ever have tumbled into this company? Why, I've always known you to be a well-brought-up fellow, who never eat an apple that was not peeled. What can they have against you, I should like to know? 'Not guilty' may do well enough up above there, but you know as well as I, it does not do down here. Folks don't come to a place like this for nothing, we all know that! Now tell us what it is."

Disgust and repulsion almost choked Ráby's powers of speech. He covered his face with his hands.

"Come now, none of that sort of thing! We want no blubbering here. Don't disgrace the company. If you want to cry, be off to the women's prison; we know you've got two wives already there!"

At this, the whole crew yelled with hoarse laughter.

"Aha!" exclaimed a voice from the furthest corner. "So that's the celebrated husband, is it? Well, I can tell you what he's here for; the women themselves told me, and they had it from the heydukes; he is a spy."

At these words, the whole band were roused to sudden uproar. "A spy! a traitor!" they yelled in chorus. "He'll strangle us at night. Let's squeeze the life out of him now."

"Be quiet, all of you," cried old Tsajkos, as he thrust the crowd back. "You don't know what you're talking about. Stop your barking and listen to me. He may be a spy, but he only betrays the gentry, and he'll never turn on us poor folk. If a great lord robs or steals, he's down upon him, but never on us."

"That's another matter," shouted the rest. "Then we'll be friends with him."

And Ráby had thereupon to submit to the rough greetings of his new comrades in misfortune.

"They are not a bad sort," remarked Tsajkos, and he proceeded to point out each individual member of the crew to Ráby, specifying which was a horse-stealer, and which a highwayman, identifying as well the thieves and incendiaries among them. Most of them, however, it turned out, were murderers.

To Ráby the whole thing seemed more and more like a ghastly dream. Yet his five senses warranted its reality: the low vault of the cell which surrounded him, the fierce criminal faces of the prisoners, the clinking of the fetters, the dirty grimy hands that grasped his own, the damp, mouldy odour of the dungeon, the taste of the brackish water from the prison well that the old man handed him to revive him—all these things warned him that this was no dream, but a grim reality from which he must find a speedy means of escaping.

He looked round, but his companion misconstrued the glance.

"You are wondering how you will manage to get forty winks here, eh, comrade? Yes, it's a difficult matter, I warrant you; all the places are taken, and each one has a right to his own. Unless Pápis will let you have his corner for the night, I really don't see how you are going to manage it."

"Why not, pray?" exclaimed a voice from another corner. "Of course I will, if I get well paid for it!"

Pápis was a gipsy felon, already pretty advanced in years, his complexion wrinkled and tanned like parchment, yet his hair was quite black, and his teeth shone like ivory.

"Bravo, Pápis!" cried the old man, while the lithe gipsy crawled between the others and grinned at Ráby.

"Don't have any fear, Pápis," said Tsajkos, "the gentleman will pay you, sure enough; he has no end of money. How much do you want for your place?"

The gipsy did not hesitate. "A ducat a day," he retorted promptly.

Ráby began to enter into the humours of the situation. He reflected a minute on the proposal.

"That is not much, after all," he said politely.

"Ah, you are the right sort, you are," cried old Tsajkos. "I only hope you'll be long with us. You shall just see what a good place we'll make for you against the wall with no one on the other side, and my knees can be your pillow. We can't do feather beds down here, or even run to straw, but one sleeps soundest on the bricks after all."

"But where will Pápis sleep himself?"

For all his own misery, Ráby could not repress the question.

The whole crew burst out laughing. As soon as they had stilled their mirth, the prisoners looked at each other embarrassed, and then at their leader to explain.

The old man smiled slily.

"Where will Pápis sleep? Why, in the bucket, to be sure, up above there," he answered.

Ráby looked up, and saw from the roof two chains hanging, through the links of which two poles were thrust, and on these hung the great bucket in which every evening the prisoners had to carry the water needed in the kitchen of the Assembly House above.

They showed him how Pápis got up. One of the prisoners seized the little gipsy by the legs and hauled him up to the roof, after which, Pápis took the cover off the bucket, crawled inside, and disappeared from sight.

Ráby was still more astonished.

"But how can the man sleep in that pail?" he asked, puzzled.

Everyone laughed, but quickly suppressed it, and all looked again rather sheepish.

Tsajkos patted Ráby's cheek patronisingly with his greasy hand, and cried,

"Bless my stars! what a simple greenhorn it is; Pápis will sleep sounder to-night, thanks to you, on a comfortable bed."

"How may that be?"

"I'll whisper it in your ear. He will leave this place this evening on your account."

"On my account, how can that be?" cried Ráby astounded.

"Ay, sure enough, and come back early to-morrow morning again."

"Why, how is it possible?"

"That's not our affair. All that matters is he will come back. He does this whenever some poor devil has a message to send to anyone outside. To-day Pápis will do it for you. Do you want to send a letter to anyone? Have it ready, and he'll see they get it. And what is more, you can trust him with gold; he'll bring back what you give him, even were it a hundred ducats, all safe and sound. The Emperor himself has no more trusty courier."

Ráby's head began to whirl. How if he should take this means of informing Joseph of his present situation?

"Yes, but how can I write a letter?" he exclaimed anxiously; "they have not left me a single morsel of paper, or even a pencil-end."

"Ay, you shall have any amount, only turn your head away, and don't look where I get it from; we don't want new-comers to learn these things all at once."

The prisoners were already bent on widening their dungeon by breaking through the roof with implements which Pápis had procured for them. They had removed first one stone and then another from the roof, and each night and morning the stones were laid back in their places, in order to arouse no suspicion, the clefts being hidden with bits of bread, and the breach carefully strewn with mortar dust. The warder would thus not notice it. In the cavity from which two of the stones had been removed, they kept the more dangerous implements required for the work, and likewise the writing materials.

A table was also improvised for Ráby. At a sign from the old man, one of the prisoners, a broad-backed fellow, placed himself on all fours in front of him, so that Ráby could make a desk of his shoulders.

"To whom is this letter addressed," inquired Tsajkos.

"To Abraham Rotheisel, in the Jewry," returned Ráby.

"It will be all right. Take it, Pápis!"

The little gipsy stretched his arm from under the lid of the bucket, and seized the letter.

How he was ever going to get out with it was a mystery which Ráby did not pretend to fathom, but the gipsy clambered down again from his hiding-place. It was growing dark.

The prisoners prepared a sleeping-place for Ráby in a corner, spreading a bit of old sheepskin on the floor, so that he might not find it too hard.

When the guard was changed at six o'clock, and the great outer gate was closed, a rattling of keys was heard without, and the gaoler came into the dungeon to visit the prisoners and bring them their food. He came first to Ráby, tested the fetters on his hands and feet to see if they were fast and then handed him a piece of black bread.

But the new-comer did not feel hungry and threw it away.

While the gaoler tried the fetters, two prisoners hauled the bucket down, and the gipsy slipped into it under the lid.

Then the two men took the poles on their shoulders, and accompanied by an armed warder, their chains clanking as they went, marched to the well, Ráby wondering the while how Pápis was feeling during this expedition.

He had leisure for reflection, for he did not get a wink of sleep the whole night; how indeed could he close his eyes in this horrible place?

He had full scope for his imagination, for he knew every nook and corner of the building, so familiar to him since his boyhood's days, from the great council hall to the dainty little parlour, where the spinning-wheel had hummed its well-remembered song. Only up till now had the subterranean part remained unexplored ground to him; now he had had the chance of seeing it for himself. How long was he to remain here? That was the question. It was certain the Emperor would take steps to free him, once he had his letter. But it would take at least four days, two there and two back, and a day more for Rotheisel to convey the missive to the Kaiser. Full five days therefore he would have to spend in that frightful hole. But what would have been his thoughts could he have foreseen how long his captivity was to endure? He would surely have dashed his head against the wall in despair.

At last day began to break, and the rattling of keys and the gaoler's footsteps were again audible outside. One night had gone!

Then the orders for the day were given as to which of the prisoners were to sweep the court, and which to carry water.

Two of them thereupon lifted the bucket again on their shoulders, and off they went, their fettered footsteps echoing along the corridor. Those left had now more room, so they stretched themselves and tried to sleep once again, for it would be some time before the others returned to the cell.

It would soon be the hour for the gaoler to come again on his rounds, and Ráby began to dread lest he should note one of the party were missing. But none were wanting. When the roll was called, the little gipsy rose from a corner where he had apparently been huddled up, and showed an abnormally distended grin on his brown face.

Directly the gaoler's back was turned, the gipsy wriggled up to him and produced from one side of his mouth a many folded note; from the other a roll of fifty ducats. No wonder he had grinned so broadly. He lay both in Ráby's hands.

Ráby could fairly have embraced the mannikin, repulsive as he was. The note, however, contained nothing more than these words: "To-day, steps will be taken," and by the side of it, the cipher which represented fifty ducats. Moreover, not one of the latter was missing.

How in the world had the fellow managed it all? But this demands another chapter.

CHAPTER XXVIII.

That a prisoner should break bounds in the evening, return again the next morning, and be present each time the roll is called, with fetters properly rivetted on hands and feet seems, humanly speaking, an impossible feat to achieve.

But Pápis was quite ready to tell how he had managed it. While the gaoler had been occupied with testing the fetters of each prisoner, he had crawled noiselessly into the bucket which stood close at hand. In the half-dark cell no one could have noted his disappearance.

When the examination was over, two prisoners lifted the bucket and carried it to the well, which was one worked by means of a pulley, the chains which let the bucket up and down clanked, and the axle creaked so loudly that under cover of the noise, and unseen in the tub, Pápis could strip off his fetters, for there were no rings too narrow for the pliant gipsy to draw his hands and feet through. Then the carriers removed the lid of the receptacle and began to fill it from that of the well-bucket, taking care the while that the heydukes could not see there was anything else inside. They had of course to pour the water over the gipsy, and as it came up to his chin when the bucket was full, he held his missives tightly between his jaws.

The two prisoners then carried it into the assembly house, where it was emptied into a water-tub. If a maidservant happened to be lounging in the kitchen by any chance, the two men would deliberately frighten her away by their foul talk. The water-tub stood close to the mouth of an oven; whilst the two others transferred the water from the bucket into the tub, the gipsy slipped away as nimbly as a squirrel into the oven, clambered up the chimney, and waited there till the coast was clear.

As soon as he heard the pass-word shouted from the guard in the courtyard below, he knew that it must be ten o'clock. So he clambered up out of the top of the chimney on to the roof of the Assembly House, as far as the gable-end. In the yard of the building stood an ancient pear-tree, which the governor would not cut down, as it bore an excellent crop of pears every year, although it was obviously dangerous in the neighbourhood of prisoners. Pápis swung himself dexterously from the roof on to this tree, whose branches jutted out over the two fathoms of wall which shut in the court towards the street, that had now to be scaled.

But the returning was a more difficult matter than the setting out in this case, for Pápis had not only to break out of prison, but the next morning to break in again, which is a different matter.

And this was how he managed it. The pear-tree had a great hollow in its trunk, and in this a rope-ladder was hidden; this, the gipsy wound round an overhanging bough, laid himself flat on the edge of the wall, and waited till the guard, who patrolled the space below, had turned his back. Then he let down the ladder, and slid along it into the street below.

But this would doubtless have been seen by the sentry the next time he passed by, so to obviate this peril, the cunning Pápis fastened a string to the other end of the ladder. As soon as he reached terra firma, he threw the ladder back. The dun-coloured string which fell down over the wall no one was likely to notice in the dark.

By the time the sentry had returned, the gipsy was in the neighbouring street. From there it was easy to reach the Jewry direct, and find the way to Abraham Rotheisel's.

He returned by the way he had come up the ladder over the wall, over the pear-tree on to the roof, through the chimney into the kitchen of the Assembly House, and into the bucket again, and so back into the dungeon. When the gaoler came for his morning rounds, Pápis lay fettered hand and foot in his accustomed place.

CHAPTER XXIX.

Abraham Rotheisel hastened to Vienna as fast as the lumbering diligence could carry him. He lost no time in presenting himself before the Emperor.

Before long, the courier was on his way back, furnished with a document which the Emperor had signed and sealed himself, after he had heard of the dismal situation in which Ráby found himself.

This important missive soon found its way to the governor.

"Eh, what is this?" demanded his Excellency, as he recognised the superscription and private seal of the Kaiser. He was just in the act of dictating to his secretary, so put the imperial missive into a basket, which was filled with documents of all sorts, and went on with his dictation, pacing up and down the room the while.

He was just trying to finish, when the district commissioner entered without any announcing.

"Has your Excellency received a courier from his Majesty?" he asked abruptly.

"I have."

"What does he say?"

"How should I know?"

"Where is the letter?"

"Where all the others are." And he lifted the cover from the basket and pointed to the collection within of yet unopened correspondence.

The district commissioner raised his hands with a little deprecating gesture, as he whispered anxiously: "But your Excellency, these are in the Emperor's handwriting; they should not lie here; they are urgent, surely?"

His Excellency looked at the speaker as a fencer measures his antagonist.

"Urgent, are they?"

The district commissioner looked puzzled.

"Your Excellency," he began, "this affair is not done with. His Majesty has sent a second letter to me by special courier, and I have read it. He orders me in it to come to you immediately, and express the gravest disapproval that Mathias Ráby, notwithstanding the imperial safe conduct, has been made a prisoner and placed in the dungeon of the Assembly House, among the scum of convicted criminals. I am to take care that he is released, and that he is allowed to defend himself as a free man without hindrance."

"That procedure won't be according to our laws."

"Perhaps not, but in view of the accusation brought against Ráby, his Majesty orders that he be detained in a place of confinement more befitting his rank and calling."

"That shall be done," said his Excellency, and therewith he rang the bell.

The lackey answered it, and he gave him the order:

"Go at once to the Assembly House at Pesth, and tell the lieutenant he is to wait on me immediately."

Then he turned to his interrupted dictation as a sign his guest could go.

An hour after this, Mr. Laskóy was announced. He had come to represent the Council, as the latter was engaged over the vintage.

His Excellency looked ready to eat his visitor.

"What is all this foolery in the dungeon of the Assembly House, pray? Is this the way you keep order? Mathias Ráby has only been imprisoned four days, yet already the Emperor has had a letter from him, telling him all about the thieves' den where he is shut up. Could you not manage things better, and fetter him so that he could not write a letter, even if he had pencil and paper?"

Mr. Laskóy stammered and stuttered and lamely excused himself, and finally got enraged, and vowed to himself he would soon find a way out of this business.

He tramped back to the Assembly House, and after a short confab with the gaoler, new arrangements were soon made regarding Ráby.

Among the underground vaults was a cell where wood was kept, but this was hastily turned out. The little vault had an iron door, with a tiny air-hole in the middle, so small it could hardly be seen, and the door could be locked fast. A more fitting place for Ráby could not be found.

Our hero had already passed four days in the company of criminals, and was counting the minutes and hours till the Emperor's orders should arrive which were to free him from this frightful hole. And now the time as it seemed had come.

He was eating his supper of rice soaked in water—the usual prison fare—when they came to fetch him. But they only rivetted shorter fetters on his hands and feet alike, led him down into a deeper vault, and thrust him into a cold, dark, mouldy cellar, wherein not a single ray of sunlight, nor the sound of a human voice could penetrate.

Yes, this was a worse place than that he had longed to escape from. Above there, they might be evil men, but at least they had had human faces. Their words had been hateful indeed, but they had been human voices that uttered them.

When they clanged the door behind him, and the cold, dark, deathlike silence closed around him, Ráby lost consciousness.

In the afternoon the district commissioner again called on his Excellency, who was engaged in his favourite game of billiards.

"Dare I venture?" began his visitor.

"It is all right. Ráby is transferred into another cell. Now just watch, my friend, what a good shot I shall make."

"Yes, but perhaps they've put him in a worse one still?"

But his Excellency was looking after his ball, for he knew what he was about at billiards, and scored heavily.

The next day the district commissioner went to the Assembly House to investigate the sort of cell Ráby had been removed to. But when he could not find it, and moreover, could, by no means whatever obtain from the officials where the prisoner might be housed, he went again to the governor to demand an explanation.

This led to recriminations between the two functionaries as to the respective limits of their jurisdictions, and they parted on very cool terms.

"I don't envy his next visitor," whispered the secretary to one of his colleagues, "whoever it is, he won't get a warm welcome."

And sure enough, one was just then announced.

The governor was busy writing to the Kaiser, and he resented this intrusion.

"Excellency, it is a petitioner," ventured the secretary timidly.

"Send him to the devil, then!"

"But it is a young lady, Excellency."

"I don't want any young ladies here. What the deuce does she want with me, I should like to know?"

But the secretary whispered a name that caused the angry governor to spring up hastily, and ask:

"What is she doing here? Has anyone come with her?"

"Excellency, she is alone."

"Alone? Let her come in, then."

It is easy to guess who the stranger lady was. She wore her ordinary morning-gown, just as she had slipped out from her household duties, without anyone knowing, but in her blue eyes lay woe unutterable.

And it was only with those same eyes that she spoke; not a word did she utter; not a gesture did she make. She sank at the feet of that hard man, and seized his hands in both of hers, and hid her face and wept at his feet.

"Come, come, this won't do, little one! I can't have tears! Now, child, tell me" (he was her godfather), "what brings you here alone? How if anyone met you in the street? What is it? What is the matter? Can you not say a word? Shall I have to talk instead? Shall I guess what it is you want? You come here on behalf of that scoundrel, Ráby, eh? Nay, there's no dungeon deep enough for him, the rogue, the graceless knave, the good-for-nothing that he is——"

But Mariska—for it was she—suddenly pressed both hands over the speaker's mouth to stop his denunciations.

"Ha, ha, ha!" laughed his Excellency maliciously. "So you've come in case I am treating him too harshly, have you? Never mind, he shall carry fifty pounds weight of chains on his feet before we've done with him."

But at these words the poor girl pressed her hands to her heaving breast in dumb entreaty, and her breath came in short gasps.

"Come now, don't cry, it's all right," whispered the stern old man, as softened by her grief, he kindly drew her to him. "Foolish child, were you really so fond of him? There, there, rest easy, we will deal gently with him. Eh? if you go on like this, I shall want to throttle the fellow outright. Silly child, can't you forget him? Ah, Ráby, you may thank your stars you've got such an advocate, otherwise the Emperor himself hadn't been able to help you."

His visitor uttered a little smothered cry of joy:

"My dear, good, kind godfather!" she murmured, as she covered the horny hand with grateful kisses.

"Why, how pleased she is! Silly child that you are!"

He rang the bell, and a secretary appeared.

"Sit down and write thus:

"'To the Lieutenant of the Prison.

"'By this present, I instruct your worship that you cause the noble prisoner, Mathias Ráby, to be released from the cell where he at present is confined, freed from irons, and be forthwith put in a place of honourable custody befitting his rank, till his trial takes place.'

"You will take the letter immediately to Pesth, and you will remain there till you have seen with your own eyes that the prisoner is transferred to proper custody, and further, will say, that I, myself, shall follow in half an hour's time to see whether my orders have been executed."

The secretary hastened away to fulfil his commission.

Mariska was beside herself with joy.

"So my foolish god-daughter is satisfied at last, is she? Go back to your pastry-making, for I want some cakes badly. Yet no more tears, please! But come back with me," he added, "and I'll take you home. When your father hears you've been to me to plead for Ráby, he'll be mighty angry. So you had better let me take you back and smooth it over for you at home. But I tell you, you must promise to put the fellow out of your thoughts! No, no, I'm not going to say anything against him; for pity's sake let's have no more weeping. Rest easy, no harm shall happen to him. He'll soon be set at liberty, and go back to Vienna, and then he'll cease to trouble us."

The girl's only answer was a deep sigh.

His Excellency led his god-daughter downstairs, and placed her in the coach which was waiting for them. And little Mariska returned home in state.

Janosics, the castellan, met his Excellency at the gate of the Assembly House, and bareheaded, bowed low before him.

"What about the prisoner, Ráby?" asked the governor shortly.

"He is already conveyed to number three on the first floor, your Excellency," was the respectful answer.

His Excellency nodded, took his companion by the hand, and led her indoors.

Tárhalmy knew nothing, and was astonished beyond measure at seeing the governor with his daughter.

"I'm bringing your little deserter back," said her god-father, jestingly. "Don't be angry with her! Judge the case for yourself; she came upon me unawares with her cause, and who could withstand such pleading, eh?"

The head-notary now understood. Father and daughter looked for a minute at each other, then the girl threw her arms round his neck.

He kissed her forehead, and whispered:

"You were the only one who could do it!"

It was a consoling word for her. Yes, if everyone else in the world had the right to persecute and vex the prisoner, she, at least, had the equal right to protect and console him.

She said nothing, but ran away into the kitchen.

Their guest could hear that outside a hen was being killed, and guessed what was going forward. He stopped on chatting with Tárhalmy, so that Mariska should have time to fulfil her kindly task. When she re-entered the room, after half an hour's absence, her face was red, as if she had been standing over the fire—or was it some deeper cause? Her god-father patted her cheek, and promised to come again, as he took his leave.

But he would not permit his host to accompany him, for he wanted to go and see the culprit for himself, so he made his way to cell number three.

It was a pleasant spacious room, with two beds in it, as well as other furniture. There was no one else in it but Ráby.

He was seated at the table, and eating a freshly cooked fowl, which he seemed to be relishing mightily.

But when the governor entered, the prisoner rose, and was evidently anxious to show a brave front.

"Your humble servant," murmured his guest, as he looked round the room. "Well, is your worship content with your new quarters, pray?"

"As far as any man who is innocent of the crime whereof he is accused can be content with his prison," answered Ráby.

"Ah well, that will be proved at the trial. But at least as long as the affair lasts you are well lodged here, I hope. Also you have something to eat, I see, and some clean linen."

"I fancy my former serving-maid must have brought it for me from home. She was a very devoted servant."

"Oh, you think it's she, do you? Well, there are other devoted people in the world who remember Mr. Ráby's needs, I fancy, as well. Books too, I see, and well-chosen ones. Well, there's a difference between this and your earlier lodging at any rate."

Ráby felt the blood mount to his head, but he would not betray his resentment.

"My arrest was a wholly unjust one," he said bitterly. "If no regard is shown to the Hungarian nobleman, at least, the imperial mandate should be respected."

"So you think that the turn for the better your affairs have taken is owing to the Emperor's intervention, do you?"

"I am convinced that his Majesty would not allow his devoted servant to perish," answered Ráby.

"You are right in what you say of our illustrious sovereign; he is, indeed, gracious. You soon found means, it seems, of advising the Kaiser of your situation. I admire your promptness! The Emperor did not lose time either; yesterday, early, I had his despatch in my hands."

Ráby's cheeks grew red with indignation.

"And why, then, in spite of this, was I yesterday afternoon cast into a far worse dungeon than the one I was taken from—a cold, dark hole, where I fainted."

"Yes, I know all about it. But I suppose you know what happened to the Emperor's letter?"

And his Excellency brought out of his pocket, the imperial missive, with its great seal still unbroken, and held it out to the prisoner.

"You have not even opened it!"

"No, nor are any of them opened when they arrive. And I tell you plainly, that all you write to the Emperor from here avails nothing. If you have anything to quote from the Hungarian laws in your defence, do it, and justify yourself. But every effort to act independently of those same laws is worse than useless. It means only lost time and trouble, and only rivets your fetters more closely. But at any rate your captivity is bearable."

Ráby shook his head, and as the door closed on his guest, he buried his face in his hands.

CHAPTER XXX.

One morning there was an unwonted stir in "Number 3" cell. Some women came in to scour the room and fleck away the cobwebs. Moreover, they placed a fine silken coverlet over the second bed, and the warder came and fixed a nail in the wall. A new prisoner was expected, they said.

Ráby was naturally curious to see what his room mate would be like; nor had he long to wait.

About eleven of the clock, arrived the expected captive; they could hear him talking as he came along the corridor, and noted how the gaoler kissed his hand respectfully, as he opened the door ceremoniously for him.

It seemed to Ráby as if he had seen his face somewhere before, but he could not remember where. The new-comer had his hair carefully powdered and dressed in the fashionable cue, and he wore his rather fierce-looking moustachios stiffened in the Turkish fashion. His dress was, however, distinctly Hungarian, for his green coat, variegated hose, and gold-laced boots were all in the prevailing Magyar mode.

The heydukes who accompanied him all seemed at his service. One drew out his pipe from a large leathern case, a second handed him his snuff-box, a third his pocket-handkerchief, whilst yet another spread a bearskin by the side of his bed, and set out bottles and boxes of cosmetics in a row. The stranger appeared quite oblivious of the presence of another person in the room, and comported himself as if the whole Assembly House had belonged to him.

The worthy Janosics evidently thought it time to repeat his instructions to the captive, so that he might recognise his limitations.

"May it please your worship, the prisoners are forbidden to smoke," he said obsequiously.

But his worship, ignoring the observation, remarked with a lordly air: "If the tobacco runs out, just cut me fresh, will you, Janosics? But don't leave it to the heydukes, they don't understand it as well as you do. Good tobacco, mind, and don't let them bring inferior. My cook must have my orders," he went on, but the castellan interrupted him respectfully:

"May it please your worship, the prisoners' meals consist of pudding three times a week, and meat three times, with vegetable broth on Fridays."

"My cook, I say, must have my orders," went on the other, not heeding, "and must make me fish-soup on Fridays, and I must have my wine sent in at once."

"May it please your worship, the prisoners are not allowed to drink wine."

But his protest availed little, for the new-comer proceeded airily:

"And please, Janosics, see that the wine is well re-corked once it has been opened. And take care there is some fresh water in the wine-cooler, as well as plenty of it for washing."

Then he looked round him. "Tell my cook to provide two covers; I don't like eating by myself, and don't want other people to look on while I dine."

"The gentleman here is on invalid diet, and has light meals served from upstairs," said the gaoler.

Ráby turned his back on the new-comer; he did not want him to think he troubled his head about him.

"Never mind that, let the dinner be served for two, I tell you, and there will be all the more over for those who want it."

"May it please your worship, the prisoners must go to bed at eight o'clock every night, and make no noise, for the deputy-lieutenant lives just overhead."

"All right. But, Janosics, you must not let the prisoners go clanking up and down the corridor with their chains; the noise gets on my nerves, I can't stand it! Now you can go, and if I want anything, I'll just knock on the door, so the guard had better be on the alert. But let them take care to wipe their boots before coming in."

The gaoler and heydukes blundered out of the room, and the new arrival turned to look at his companion. He appeared a jovial sort of person, and to be very genially disposed.

"So it is Mr. Mathias Ráby after all," murmured the stranger with a smile.

Ráby looked sharply at him. "You have the advantage of me," he said.

The new-comer laughed slily. "Ah, I recognise you well enough, but perhaps you don't remember me, though we have met before?"

Ráby had to admit that he had no such recollection.

"Ah, that's because I was—well, differently dressed, perhaps, yet it is so, I can assure you, and what's more, I spoke four words to you, although you have so short a memory for them."

And the speaker sat down and began filling his pipe and lighting up for a smoke.

Ráby in vain sought for a solution to the mystery. After the smoker had taken a couple of pulls at the pipe, he went back to where our hero sat, and planted himself on the window-ledge letting his legs dangle, while his spurs rattled.

"Is it possible they didn't tell you who the prisoner was that was to share your cell?" he asked.

"I did not even ask," admitted Ráby, "who it might be."

"Then I will tell you—his name is Karcsatáji Miska."

"Gyöngyöm Miska?"

"Don't make a mistake!" pursued the highwayman, "and think I let myself be taken: I am here solely through my own fault. It's a strange story, I'll tell you more about it later, I can't talk on an empty stomach!" And thereupon, he took out a big flask of brandy from a case, and produced some glasses and white bread, and called upon his companion to join him. But Ráby stood coldly aloof. He could not forget that before him stood the man who had so cruelly wronged him, the man who had been the chosen lover of Fruzsinka! All the manly pride of his nature revolted at the thought. Yet he could not help a feeling of satisfaction that the man for once had been judged on his deserts, and what those were, Ráby knew only too well. But that his rival should be thus sharing his prison and partaking the same fate—this was indeed a strange turn for events to take.

When dinner-time came the highwayman knocked on the wall for the heydukes, who promptly responded to the signal, and hastened to serve quite a luxurious meal, but Ráby excused himself on the score of his dining at a later hour. His host did not press him, but so vigorously tackled the good fare, that soon the dishes were cleared completely.

Ráby, the while, had leisure to meditate on the course events had taken. It gave an exquisite edge to his misery to be penned up in the same room with a man he hated. Yet such a man, since he was still keeping up apparently his relations with the world outside, could help him vastly, and would be a better prop to rely on than the gipsy-carrier: he had simply to give letters to the heydukes, and they would deliver them as bidden. Yet his better self revolted at the notion of being helped by Karcsatáji, for, in his inmost soul, he had nothing but the bitterest contempt for this highway robber, who had been the lover of Fruzsinka. No, he would receive no favours, were it liberty itself, from such a hand!

CHAPTER XXXI.

As soon as Karcsatáji had finished his meal, he turned to Ráby.

"Are you inclined for a chat, Mr. Ráby?" he said, as he lighted his pipe. "Because if you are, this will be our chance to discuss the world in general, and our own corner of it in particular."

"I am all attention," answered Ráby coldly.

"You will be still more so when you hear my story, I fancy. We two are companions in adversity (only you have got over the worst of it), since we are both the victims of a worthless woman, curse her!"

"I will not curse her," said Ráby quietly.

"No? Then you are a man out of a thousand, but I am only of very ordinary clay, I fear. And I am not the only one she has fooled. If I mistake not, Petray is also in the same boat. But the fellow can talk as well as I can ride—which is saying a good deal. And it is that precious tongue of his which bewitches the women. Yet I have more to complain of than you, I consider. She took refuge under the wing of Petray, and meantime the fatal letter she had written to me was intercepted, in consequence of which Lievenkopp and you both challenged me to a duel near the old Zsámbék Church. The end of it was that Petray, as soon as he heard how matters stood, let the lady know some home-truths, so that for sometime they lived as man and wife, though leading a cat and dog life. At last my lady became sick of this honey-mooning, and one fine day she left Petray and came to me."

Ráby buried his face in his hands and groaned. How could he endure this talk?

"You need not bear me a grudge," said the other. "Know, by that time I had given up robbery, and would have buried my ancient feud with the law. I was seriously thinking about setting my house in order, and I told my old companions to come no more to see me, and promised, if they were in need, I would send out supplies to them in the forest. I was not going to be 'Gyöngyöm Miska' any longer, for I had made up my mind to reform my way of life. Then it was that your runaway wife fled to my protection. You were well rid of her, yet how many times I have cursed you in thought. I knew it was a deadly sin to take another man's wife. Small wonder that Fruzsinka brought me nothing but ill-luck. I gave her to understand from the first, that I was changing my life, and I set about building a church in our village, moreover I repented of my sins, fasted, and did penance and abjured my old evil ways. But easy as it is to befool women-kind, it is difficult to deceive them, if we want to get rid of them. Their suspicions are so easily aroused. If I were Emperor, I would trust the police-espionage to women. She began with intercepting my correspondence. Good heavens! what an experience I had, and I thought she would tear me to pieces. So angry was she that she left me, and I naturally concluded she was going to be reconciled to you."

Ráby ground his teeth.

"I know now that she was not. She began to work me further mischief. Do you know, that to her I owed the denunciations which were shortly afterwards, from some mysterious source, made to the ecclesiastical authorities against me, of blasphemy and sacrilege, and though the charges were true enough, I am sorry to say, I did not reckon in expiating my past sins so sharply. For it was on these very charges that I was arrested by order of high ecclesiastical dignitaries and condemned to two years imprisonment; and many a thaler has it cost me already to avoid being put into irons."

At these words he blew into his big pipe-bowl so energetically, that the sparks flew up and illuminated his face in the darkness with a strangely sinister light.

"And now, friend Ráby, who has the greater ground of complaint, you or I?"

He did not wait for an answer to his question, but began to curse away furiously for some minutes with a virulence terrible to hear. When he had finished his round of imprecations (and it was no limited one), he threw himself on his bed and fell asleep.

As for Ráby, he pondered long and deeply all he had heard about his faithless wife, and once more she seemed to be spinning beside him, yet there was a grim satisfaction that others had suffered beside himself. Was he not avenged on the highwayman at last, seeing that the biter was bitten!

CHAPTER XXXII.

The Emperor sent urgent orders to the governor to set Mathias Ráby free immediately, so that the inquiry into the Szent-Endre frauds, established on his accusation, could be brought to an end.

The letter was laid by with the rest, as usual, unread. The governor however hastened to answer that the orders would be executed in due course—when the depositions of the municipality had been taken—an explanation which satisfied the Emperor, who little knew what the "due course" extended to.

It really meant that the culprit Ráby was brought out of his prison, not to be freed, but rather to be fettered hand and foot. That is usual when a prisoner is to be tried, and this was his first examination.

In the presence of the whole court, and of the district commissioner, they subjected him to an insidious cross-examination for fully four hours, till he was ready to drop from sheer exhaustion. Only half of the accusations brought against him would have sufficed for his condemnation.

Finally, he was conducted back to prison. He staggered into the room he had left, but the gaoler called him back.

"Oho, there, Mr. prisoner, that's not your cell. Those who wear irons don't lodge there!"

And he led him into a neighbouring cell whose door was furnished with three massive locks, whilst the window was protected with iron bars and a grating. The only furniture was a plank bed; of table or chairs, there were none. The prisoner's books had not been sent in either.

Although it was dinner-time, and he had eaten nothing, no dainty meal awaited him, such as those he had been accustomed to, nor even was he allowed the ordinary prison fare allotted to well-born culprits. A heyduke brought in a great earthen pitcher with a crust of black bread.

"Here you are, my fine sir," laughed the heyduke mockingly, but, as he bent to set it down on the stone floor, he whispered, "The bottom comes off!"

Then he left him, carefully locking the door behind him.

Now was Ráby's wish fulfilled, he was rid of unpleasant company and was alone. But solitude had been more welcome if they had allowed him his books. As it was, he only had his own thoughts for company, and these were not cheerful companions.

Ráby's soul was full of rage against the whole world, but most of all was he angry with his own weak body that was so sensitive to hunger and cold, that trembled at the thought of death, and felt the pressure of its chains so keenly. Why could not he carry his body as defiantly as he bore his soul within him?

But he knew that he needed some support, therefore he began to eat mechanically the black bread, but had it been the daintiest fare possible, it had tasted all the same to him. Only when he raised the pitcher to his lips, did he remember the words of the heyduke about the "bottom coming off." He began to examine the pitcher, and presently, by dint of close scrutiny, he found that it had a false bottom which screwed on, and found a cavity in which was concealed a bottle of ink, pen and paper. With them were some slices of cold meat, as well as a note containing these words: "Fear nothing; the Emperor knows all. Your friends will not forsake you. Write once more to the Emperor."

Now he no longer feared solitude. The phantoms and fears which had tormented him hitherto, vanished with the sight of pen and ink. A written thought is a substantial friend. So he committed to paper all that had befallen him, hid the writing again in the bottom of the pitcher, and re-screwed it on. The meat, too, revived him, and the consciousness that he was not left to his fate, and that he could still communicate with the outer world, was strangely comforting. Who his unknown friend might be, he could not conceive. It must be some one more powerful than the weak girl whose part in this business his own heart had already suggested to him.

The next morning, in came the gaoler with the same heyduke, who carried away the pitcher, and at mid-day brought him his rations as before.

Ráby could hardly wait till he had gone, to unscrew his pitcher. Sure enough, he found some writing materials therein, and the money for covering the fee of a special courier for his letter. His friends must be wealthy people.

He quickly hid all again, however, for steps were approaching his cell.

The door opened, and three men came in, who proved to be Laskóy, Petray, and the lieutenant of Szent-Endre. The latter handed to Ráby the bill of his indictment.

The prisoner immediately handed it back to him.

"It is not you who are the accusers in this matter, but rather I," he said haughtily. "It is for me to impeach you, not the reverse. I refuse to accept it."

"Take care," cried Laskóy. "Weigh well the consequences of this rejection. If you do not receive the indictment, we will soon tackle you as a contumacious criminal."

"I dare you to do it," returned Ráby.

"The man is a fool; he shall take it," cried Laskóy, beside himself with rage.

Ráby folded his arms proudly, so that they should not force it on him.

"Mr. lieutenant, witness that he will not take it and draw up a warrant of attainder for contumacity."

The lieutenant proceeded to carry out these instructions.

"And while you are about it, certify that I threw the document out of the room," said Ráby, suiting the action to the word.

This was an unheard-of audacity. The three men withdrew uttering violent threats.

After a time, in came the castellan with a very long face.

"Now I would not give a cracked nut for your chances," he cried. "They are going to pronounce judgment immediately. The executioner has been told to hold himself in readiness for to-morrow. We have martial law on our side, and the Emperor himself cannot gainsay it."

These words caused Ráby to think over what he had done. It was, of course, only too likely that their legal right could be strained before the Emperor had any chance of interfering; in this case, he would have lost his head before the latter could prevent it. The thought tormented him the whole night through. The strong soul in vain reminded the weak body which held it that dying was not to be feared, but philosophy availed nothing before the thought of imminent death.

The next morning found the prisoner restless and wakeful. It was hardly day ere he heard a number of footsteps approaching his dungeon. The iron door was thrown open, and a whole crowd burst into his cell, the magistrate and the lieutenant among them, whilst following them, came a man he took to be the public executioner of Pesth.

A sudden faintness overcame him; all seemed to swim before his eyes, and he heard nothing of what they said. The man who looked like the executioner began to undress and roll up his shirt-sleeves. Ráby imagined they were going to execute him in prison. The forbidding-looking wretch then called for assistance, and bid them bring him his tools.

Ráby heaved a deep sigh and folded his arms across his breast, whereat the whole company burst out laughing. The tools which the man had asked for were a hammer, a trowel, and a tub of mortar. He was, in fact, no executioner, but an ordinary mason, who was going to block up the window in Ráby's cell which overlooked the street, and bore an air-hole in the ceiling. They were going to shut out the prisoner from the outside world altogether. Henceforth his cell would receive no light but what fell from the tiny opening over the door which gave into the court, and was darkened with a narrow iron grating.

Moreover, from this day forward, Ráby was subjected to daily cross-examination, and every means was tried to entangle him and make him contradict himself.

The twenty indictments first formulated against him rapidly lengthened to treble that number. And so it went on for a month, nor did they ever succeed in incriminating him. But it was a painful process for the accused.

One day the gaoler brought a bird into Ráby's cell, a magpie, who by his chattering mightily cheered the captive. The feathered guest sat on his hand, and pecked his finger in a playful way as if it had been an old friend. And Ráby stroked the soft plumage tenderly, and he guessed it was Mariska who had sent it to cheer his loneliness which had become well-nigh unbearable, and he welcomed it as a comrade. Whilst he listened to it, as it sat on his hand, he would almost forget the irons that fettered them, and would, on his return from the court each day, whistle to his little friend on re-entering his cell.

But one day there was no answer to his greeting; all was silent. Ráby sought for his pet in every corner of the cell, and at last found the bird strangled, tied to the iron grating, killed by his enemies because of the pleasure it had given him.

Had Ráby seen one of his own kith and kin dead before him, he could not have grieved more than he did for this feathered friend. Nor did he get any sympathy from the gaoler, who only laughed when he heard of it. But Ráby implored him not to tell Mariska of the fate of her pet.

That official, however, promptly reported the whole affair to Mariska, and took care to carry her the dead bird. Bitterly she wept over her favourite, but remembering her father might see she had been crying, she soon dried her eyes.

But Ráby must not be alone; that was the main thing. So she did not long delay in sending another feathered pet, a titmouse this time, in a cage, which she intrusted to the gaoler to carry to the prisoner, but on no account to let him know who sent it. As if Ráby would not guess!

The warder placed the cage on the prisoner's bed, murmured some excuse for bringing it, and left him. He did not see Ráby fall upon his knees before the cage in a transport of almost hysterical joy. And the little bird soon became as dear to him as the magpie had been.

But one evening, when he came in from the wearisome cross-examination that seemed as if it would never end, lo, and behold, there lay the titmouse dead in his cage. Someone had fed him with poisoned flies.

Ráby implored the gaoler not to bring him any more birds. Henceforth he determined not to have these feathered friends sacrificed to him.

All the same, he soon found another pet in the shape of a little mouse, which, like himself, lived in captivity. At first it only timidly put its head out of its hole, and glided shyly and warily along the side of the wall; gradually, however, it perceived that the cell's occupant had strewn bread-crumbs on the floor, and furtively yet nimbly it picked them up. And by degrees it came nearer to the prisoner, and presently ventured to run up his knees and dared to eat the crumbs that the stranger hand held, and finally, in that same hand, sat on its hind legs, looking at Ráby with the most whimsical expression imaginable on its diminutive face.

Poor Ráby! The mouse might well look at him; perhaps it wondered who this haggard, unkempt man was, with the tangled growth of unshaven beard and lank hair drooping over the hollow eyes, framing a pale, lean face, disfigured by suffering.

This was the beginning of their strange friendship. The mouse would sport round him the whole day, or gambol about on his shoulder, and at night, would, as he lay on his plank bed, watch him from the ceiling, with bright, friendly eyes. Did Ráby call to it, it would answer him with a little responsive squeak, and try to gnaw the links of the chain that bound the prisoner, with its tiny teeth. But did anyone enter, the mouse would hurry back into its hole.

But alas, there came a time when he had to lose even this humble companion. One evening he missed him, and only found the poor little beast dead in a corner—someone, apparently, having placed rat-poison in its hole. What the prisoner's feelings were, words do not express; his whole heart welled over with bitterness at this fresh proof of the malice of his enemies. They were, indeed, evil hearts that could find their pleasure in thus tormenting their victim.

CHAPTER XXXIII.

When the points in Ráby's indictment had mounted up to eighty, he thought it time to make his protest to the presiding judge:

"I am shattered in mind and body alike; I desire to withdraw the accusation I have made, seeing it in no wise profits the oppressed people in whose interests I lodged it, but rather tends to their further hurt."

"That avails nothing," was the answer. "The accusation has been presented to the Emperor, and the complainant must justify it. Is the treasure to which the impeachment relates, found, a third of it falls to the informer; is the information thus lodged proved to be false, the informer forfeits his head forthwith. So out with your proofs!"

"Proofs? How can I furnish them I should like to know, fettered as I am, from a dungeon?" cried Ráby in desperation. "Are not all my documents in the hands of my enemies? Have not the archives of Szent-Endre been destroyed, and my private papers abstracted, so that I am denied all means of procuring the proofs I need?"

"How do you know that?" asked the judge, dumbfoundered.

"I know it only too well. Nay, I know too, it happened at the instigation of the authorities."

"This is the gravest evidence we have yet had of your guilt," cried the judge; "this shows you have held intercourse with the outside world, although forbidden by the law to do so."

"It only proves I am right," retorted the prisoner.

"Pray who are your accomplices who helped you in your correspondence?" demanded his accuser angrily.

"No one and everyone body. The bare walls, the air itself, the iron door, my fetters, my guards—all are my accomplices if you like to call them so."

"Well, we will just make your chains a little faster so you can't move about quite so easily, my friend, that's all."

"That avails you nothing," exclaimed Ráby. "Their clanking sounds even now in the ears of one who is your imperial lord and master, and will shortly be here in his city of Pesth to sit in judgment upon you. Let the guilty tremble before him, I have no need to do so."

These bold words enraged the judge beyond measure. How did Ráby know that the Emperor was about to come to Pesth for the military manœuvres, and there review the troops in person. Did he know as well that the Szent-Endre people were only biding their time to send a deputation to the Kaiser to ask for Ráby's release, and to demand an inquiry into the conduct of the Pesth authorities in imprisoning him. It never occurred to them that an ordinary water-pitcher with a false bottom held the letters which Ráby wrote and received, and that each heyduke who carried it, was an involuntary courier.

In vain did they interrogate the heyduke who brought it, and ordered him to be beaten; for each stroke the man received, he was sent by some unknown hand a gold piece, so he was not inclined to complain.

When the Emperor did arrive in Pesth, the following August, he learned with surprise that his emissary was still detained in prison. He straightway sent for the head magistrate, expressed his displeasure, and ordered Ráby's immediate release on pain of all the authorities of the city being dismissed from office. This was an order which had to be obeyed.

So forthwith in the Emperor's presence, the mandate was sent that Mathias Ráby be immediately released from custody. The command was peremptory and admitted of no evasion.

But the next night someone thrust under the door of Ráby's cell, a note containing these words:

"Be ready this night! Your true friends are coming to fetch you away. They will overpower the gaoler, take away the keys from him, and set you free."

"But it is evident," reflected Ráby, "this is not from my friends; we don't conduct our correspondence like this. They have heard the Emperor has ordered my release, and now they want to convict me of trying to escape by force." And he gave the letter to the gaoler.

But, alas, it only made an excuse for a fresh inquisition, and they based on it the pretence of "a plot against the public safety." Moreover, it was held to justify a still more rigorous treatment of the prisoner, who on this fresh charge of conspiring with bandits, was declared to have merited imprisonment anew. And the inquiry which followed lasted late into the autumn, whilst the Emperor was too much occupied in his fresh war with the Turks to be aware of this new turn of affairs.

And Ráby's fetters were meantime rivetted more closely than ever, so that he could not write any more, and his wretched prison fare grew worse and worse. The winter too had come, and the prisoner was well-nigh frozen in his cell, for the dungeon was not warmed, and he had only his summer clothing which was now in tatters. On his complaining of the cold to the judges, they gave orders that Ráby's cell should be heated three times a day.

The end of it was that they placed a stove in the cell which was so violently overheated that it burst, and Ráby had to press his face to the wall in desperation to cool his scorched brow. Yet he could have escaped had he chosen, for the door of his cell was often left open, as if to abet his flight. But Ráby, when he did leave prison, meant to leave it proudly and fearlessly, as an innocent man who is rightfully acquitted before his country's tribunal, not as a fugitive.

One day the gaoler came in to say that permission had been given for the prisoner to be shaved, and for his irons to be removed—a grace for which Ráby hardly knew how to be thankful enough. It was a deadly pale, if clean-shaven face that the barber's mirror reflected, but small wonder, seeing that Ráby had not seen the sunlight for a year and a half. This luxury was followed by an amelioration of his prison fare, and fresh bedding, for both of which benefits, especially the last, he was duly grateful, for it meant a good night's rest.

However, that very night, Ráby was awakened from his first sleep by a tremendous rattling at his cell door, and the next minute it was burst open, and the light of the full moon flooded his dungeon. The prisoner thought he must be dreaming, but the same instant the cell was suddenly filled by a band of masked men in Turkish attire, with huge turbans on their heads, and armed with an array of weapons, including swords and muskets.

Ráby was wondering in what language to address his strange visitors, when one of them accosted him in Serb, and then Hungarian.

"Fear nothing, Mr. Ráby. We are true friends from Szent-Endre, and have bribed the guard and occupied the Assembly House. We have come to set you free from this wretched dungeon by the Emperor's orders."

"But I do not wish to purchase my freedom by force," answered the captive, "and if the Emperor wished to deliver me, it would surely not be by masqueraders sent by night, but by his accredited emissaries in the full light of day."

"Here's the order signed by the Emperor," and the head of the band of maskers handed Ráby a document which contained detailed and definite instructions anent the Szent-Endre affair, set forth in Serb, which was the Emperor's favourite language.

Ráby protested against the idea of flight, but they overpowered his resistance, and made a show of armed force. "Silence, or you are a dead man," was their only answer to his protestations, and the prisoner, weak and enfeebled as he was by his privations, and dazed by the sudden surprise which had thus overtaken him, fell at last in a dead faint and lost all consciousness.

When he came to himself, he was dressed as a woman, in the coloured bodice and embroidered apron of the Serb peasant girl, and his hair tied with gay ribbons; it was for this, no doubt, that he had been shaven.

Ráby's entreaties availed nothing. In vain he implored them to desist, and reminded them the military would be sent to overtake them, and then all would be over! His representations achieved nothing with his rescuers, and finally a rough, but powerful-looking fellow of the party seized Ráby and carried him off on his back out of the cell, followed by the whole crew shouting and howling. The inhabitants of the Assembly House must have been stone deaf, had they not been aroused by the tumult. The band dashed in the moonlight through the court and gateway, past the guard-room where four-and-twenty were wont to sleep, without being questioned by a single soul as to their escapade.

It was towards the Kecskemét gate that they hurried, as the likeliest one to be open, so as to get off thus with least delay, and thence away to the river-bank.

At that time, communication with the other side of the Danube was kept up by a so-called "flying-bridge," that was a work of art in its archaic way, consisting of a flat raft-like contrivance, whereto was attached a thick cable, which half a dozen small boats served to keep out of the water. Behind the last boat, at the so-called "Nun's Ferry," below Hare Island, the cable was fast anchored. Linked to this cable, the raft was towed by a single oar to and fro. At night the ferry was not generally used and the ferry-men were not there, but this time they were at their posts ready for the expected passengers. The masked Turks took their places on it without delay, and off they drifted.

Poor Ráby was trembling in every limb, principally from the bitter cold of the December night, which, after his long confinement from the outer air, struck his senses with the sharpness of a knife. Moreover, he was not quite sure that these strange rescuers would not throw him overboard into the river, to find there an unknown and unhonoured grave.

However, they did nothing of the kind, but the party reached the other side safely. There horses, ready saddled, awaited them, and a coach and four. Three of the sham Turks sprang into the vehicle, and dragged Ráby with them. The rest mounted the horses, and they took the way along the Old Buda road.

One of the escort had the kindness to throw his cloak over the freezing prisoner, the coach leading the way, the riders following. But gradually the horsemen dropped off till, when they reached Vörösvár, not one was to be seen.

By this time the released prisoner had succumbed to the unaccustomed strain on his already exhausted and overwrought nerves, and had lost all consciousness of what was going on around him, so that he had to be lifted out of the carriage in a swoon when they stopped at an inn.

When he awoke from his stupor late the next morning, he was in a comfortable bed. Only two of his late companions were to be seen, and they no longer wore Turkish dress, but the garb of the well-to-do Serb peasant, and, indeed, turned out to be respectable peasant-proprietors of Szent-Endre.

Yet neither their names nor faces were known to Ráby.

For the rest, his two guardians showed themselves full of consideration for their patient. They procured him warm clothing, caused light invalid food to be prepared for him, and begged him not to be too anxious to try his strength with the journey. When Ráby had sufficiently rested, the coachman received orders to drive slowly, so that it might not exhaust the traveller, and they set out again, not without many misgivings from the fugitive as to whether they could not be overtaken and their flight intercepted.

One of his companions, who told him his name was Kurovics, besought him to make his mind easy on this score. He pointed out how they would get the start of the authorities before these could mobilise their forces. Then no one knew of the disguise in which Ráby had escaped; from the description which the Pesth court would issue for his recovery, no one would recognise him, so he had no cause for fear.

They only made two stages a day, so that the journey to Pozsony (which was their goal,) lasted eight days, through resting at the inns on the road. His companions gave themselves out as pig-dealers, and said Ráby was their cousin. The third day they fell in with a party of armed heydukes who were searching for their charge. They stopped the cavalcade, and told them of their quest. At each wayside inn Ráby could read the notice which posted him up as a criminal and outlaw, for whose identification a reward of two hundred ducats was offered. To his relief, the description of him corresponded to the appearance he had presented in prison, with an overgrown beard, tangled hair, and pale face, wearing a faded silk coat.

Little did his pursuers imagine that in the shy Serb maiden, with her cheeks painted red, who understood nothing but her native tongue, that the fugitive they sought stood before them. More than once it even happened that Ráby and his pursuers slept under the same roof.

Meantime, he became more and more attached to his two friends, whose worth he began to realise increasingly.

CHAPTER XXXIV.

The fugitives had only one more station to accomplish before they reached the Austrian frontier, where the Hungarian jurisdiction ceased. Was there trouble at the frontier over Ráby's identification, at least it meant that he would be taken to Vienna to prove it, and not back to Pesth.

They heard from travellers they met on the way that the Emperor was back in the capital, owing to the army being in winter quarters, and hostilities against the Turks being suspended for the time being. Ráby, thereupon grew more anxious than ever as to his possible reception by the Kaiser, whose concurrence he still doubted in his forcible rescue, though, by this, the Emperor had doubtless seen that his formal orders availed nothing, and he probably thought it impolitic to use military force to free his representative.

It was revolving such thoughts in his mind, that Ráby and his guides came to the wayside inn where they were to pass their last night on Magyar territory. It was a poor little "csárda," as such hostelries are called in Hungary, between Pozsony and Hainburg, wherein only now and again travellers passed the night, driven thereto by stress of weather. The accommodation left much to be desired, and its reputation was none of the best. It was whispered, indeed, that travellers had been murdered and waylaid there, and even now the host was serving his term in the Pozsony prison, where he was a frequent inmate. In his absence, his wife looked after the inn.

There was no proper sleeping-rooms, so the guests had to rest on the straw thrown down for them in the public dining-room, where they forgot their differences of rank as best they could, while the only light was a single tallow candle suspended from the ceiling in a hanging tin-candlestick.

Laying about on the benches, or on the long table, were a crowd of guests that included peasants and shepherds, pedlars and smugglers, while the air was rank with odours of strong cheese, onions, and tobacco-smoke. The hostess ministered herself to the wants of the guests, and handed round the wine.

It was among this company that Ráby and his companions took their places; as there was no other woman present among the travellers, the hostess expressed some fear that the pretended Serb maiden would find it somewhat uncomfortable.

The two men thanked her, but said they would look after their sister, and ordered a stewed fowl and some wine, for which the party paid in advance. The water was too bad for anyone to depend on, so Ráby had to drink wine, which, unaccustomed as he was to it, soon made him feel drowsy.

In a few minutes he was fast asleep, with his head pillowed on his folded arms on the table.

His slumbers, however, were soon to be disturbed, for there was a loud noise heard outside as of the trampling of horses and the clash of weapons. The hostess said it must be a party of heydukes, and sure enough it was.

Now Ráby had ceased to be fearful of discovery by these pursuers, as from the description of him so industriously circulated, they could not recognise him in his present disguise. Moreover, he had been carefully shaven every day since his flight, and his face newly painted, the better to sustain his rôle.

But this time he had cause for anxiety, for the first voice he heard without was a hatefully familiar one—that of the castellan, Janosics. How did he come to be here, for they were now in the jurisdiction of Pozsony not of Pesth. He heard the castellan giving orders for one man to come in with him, and the other to remain with the horses.

Ráby stole a glance at the door which was half open. A cold shudder seized him as he caught sight of Janosics wearing the Pesth uniform, and carrying a carbine in his hand and a sword at his belt.

Ráby pressed his head down lower, so his face might not be seen. The big sleeves of his bodice helped him to hide his features the more easily.

"Up all of you fellows, and let me have a look at you!" shouted the castellan. Those present immediately obeyed, and submitted to the inspection.

"The man I want is not here," grumbled Janosics, as he rapidly ran over the assembled faces, but when he came to Kurovics, he laughed aloud.

"Aha, Master Kurovics, so you are here, are you? What brings you out this bitter winter weather, pray?"

"Oh, we must look after our business you know," answered the other, without the least embarrassment.

"Where's your passport?"

"What do I want with one? I don't cross the frontier."

"Well," shouted the other, "what may you be doing here?"

"Hush! not so loud," retorted Kurovics, with a glance at Ráby. "I've got my little cousin to look after."

"Oh, that's the game, is it? Soho, I see; and a nice little baggage it is, I'll be bound. Oh I don't want to wake her if she's tired."

And the castellan sat down between Ráby and Kurovics, and asked the latter for a bit of his tobacco. Then he smoked, but always keeping an eye on Ráby.

"Pretty, eh?" he asked, and he made as though he would raise the coloured kerchief that half hid the sleeper's face.

"Let her rest, Mr. castellan, I beg. She's wearied out with the journey."

"Well, well, let her be then, but you, hostess, bring us some wine, and take some to the heyduke outside."

"And what may you be doing in this neighbourhood, if I may be so bold?" inquired Kurovics.

"Oh, an important police-mission. A dangerous felon, the notorious Mathias Ráby broke out of Pesth prison last week, and the descriptions circulated of him are not correct, as I could have told them had they asked me. The fellow is not bearded as described, but he was shaved the day before he got out, and had a face as smooth as any girl's."

Ráby felt as if the beatings of his heart would burst his bodice, as the newcomer went on:

"When I heard of it, I went to the authorities and told them the mistake they had made, and offered to make it good by riding after the runaway myself to see if I could identify him. And there are two hundred ducats for the man who brings him back alive."

"A nice round sum! I only wish I could find him," answered Kurovics.

"I mean to take him myself," said Janosics coolly. "But hark ye, Kurovics, is it possible that you yourself are leading my prisoner away in a girl's garb? Just let me have another look at her."

Ráby would have swooned, only that the castellan was now smoking so closely under his nose that he was nearly choked by it. He was on the point of springing up and surrendering in sheer desperation; it was with the greatest difficulty he mastered his feelings, above all his inclination to cough, for raising his head would betray him directly. And the suspicion too arose in him that perhaps, after all, his guides were accomplices in a comedy which had for its dénouement the arrest of the fugitive just as he was making sure of safety.

"Now I must see her face," said Janosics, and Ráby felt his enemy's clammy hand laid on his brow.

"Won't you look at me, little one? I can speak Serb quite well," sneered his persecutor. And the castellan forcibly raised Ráby's head, and looked him in the face with a grin of malicious triumph.

But just then the heyduke, who had been waiting outside, dashed into the room in hot haste, crying excitedly, "Villám Pista is here!" With that the scene was changed, and Janosics had to make way for a mightier rival. The very name of the renowned robber-chief spread consternation, and the carabineers, on hearing it, promptly threw their weapons away, the better to run for their lives, while the whole company scattered pell-mell, some out of the window, and others up the chimney, in their hot haste to get off. There was no one finally left in the room but Ráby and his two companions, and the hostess.

Outside, they heard some shots fired, followed by a feeble groan that seemed to come from Janosics. Then the door flew open, and Villám Pista himself entered, accompanied by two comrades, his rifle in his hand still smoking from the recent shot. He was a fine-looking young fellow, with no trace of beard on his smooth, handsome face. His bearing and air showed that he was accustomed to be master of the situation wherever he was. His dress fitted him admirably, a richly embroidered cloak fell across his shoulders, on his head was perched a jauntily feathered cap, and a short pipe was in his mouth.

"They are a cursed lot," he cried, as he threw the weapon on to the table. "But I've paid them out; they won't ride quite so merrily back as they did in coming, I'll be bound. I'm sorry, however, the shot did not finish them."

Then he looked round the room. "Bless me, what a miserable light! Is that what you call lighting up?" And he whistled to the hostess, who hurried up with a dozen candles, and promptly placed them on the table in as many sticks.

Ráby's companions had placed themselves before him, so that their mantles rather screened him from the highwayman. But the latter spied him out at once owing to his dress, and seizing Ráby by the hand, he dragged him out into the middle of the room. For a moment, they looked each other steadily in the face, and Ráby recognised in the robber-leader, his wife, Fruzsinka!

And thus it was that they met. But the supposed highwayman still did not betray the situation. He drew Ráby closer to him, and whispered hastily in his ear, "Pretend you are frightened, and make your escape by the door."

Ráby obeyed, and with a bound across the room, in a trice was outside. Fruzsinka followed him, and grasped his hand in hers.

"We have no time for talking. A whole gang of heydukes from Pesth is on your track. Come away immediately; here are the horses of your persecutors; up and ride for your life till you have left the frontier behind you. Do not trust even your companions who will follow you, but do not wait for them."

And so saying, she helped Ráby to mount, only he was so exhausted he found it difficult to keep his seat, and was crying like a child.

"Weep not thus, wretched man," she cried impatiently. "Shame on you for your weakness! Why do you look at me like that? We have nothing more to do with each other, you and I. But fly, and look not back, and beware of ever setting foot in this accursed country again, for whose sake you have made both me and yourself so miserable."

While she spoke, she cast her cloak about him to protect him from the bitter cold of the winter's night.

Ráby would have spoken one last word, but she cut him short by switching his horse's flanks with her riding whip, whereat the animal bounded away over the ground, where the snow already lay a foot deep. And the last sound Ráby heard from the "csárda" was the cracking of Villám Pista's whip.

CHAPTER XXXV.

It really looked as if Ráby's flight had been a predetermined affair, so that allowing him to get off in woman's clothes, the authorities might recapture him to lead him back to Pesth in triumph, more degraded than ever in the public eyes, only that the appearance of Villám Pista somewhat disturbed this hypothesis.

Villám Pista, otherwise Fruzsinka, in fact, had learned from spies that Ráby had escaped from prison, having pitched her camp in the neighbouring forest—a fitting abode for the half-crazed woman who now lived at enmity with all the world, though she boasted that what she robbed the rich of she divided among the poor—a sentiment which caused the ten thousand ducats to be taken off Gyöngyöm Miska's head and set on hers. But when she heard of the pursuit of Ráby, her heart smote her with pity for the man she had so cruelly wronged, who was now a persecuted fugitive.

With her companions she had lain concealed in the forest near the inn, till the arrival of the Pesth heydukes warned her that the time for reprisals had come—with what results we have seen.

But she only learned in what disguise Ráby had fled, when she saw him. In an instant her plan was formed. The Pesth pursuers were all around; if Ráby escaped them, he would be taken at the Austrian frontier, where, seeing the Hungarian trappings of his horse, they would relegate him to the Pesth authorities to deal with. And meditating on this thought, she re-entered the inn. "She has escaped me," she cried, "and has dashed off on one of the heyduke's horses."

"You don't mean to say my cousin has run away!" cried Kurovics anxiously. And he made as though to follow the fugitive Serb maiden.

"Not so fast, my friend," exclaimed the robber-chief, "besides you have not told me your name." And she questioned the two closely as to their antecedents—questions which they did their best to evade.

"Well, by way of passing the time, suppose I teach you how to dance! We'll just see what you can do?"

And with that, the pretended brigand took out an axe from under his coat and dexterously threw it at Kurovics, so that he jumped up nervously as it fell with its edge close to him.

But the noise of shots fired without, arrested these diversions. Villám Pista did not stop even to pick up the axe, but snatching the rifle from the table bounded out to face this new alarm.

Outside there stood her horse, which quickly mounting, she shouted to her followers who were awaiting her orders, and galloped away into the night. The fresh party of heydukes, with this new enemy to run down, forgot all about Ráby (for on his head only two hundred ducats were set, while it was a matter of ten thousand with Villám Pista). And that chieftain was thinking that this delay would give Ráby time to cross the river, while the frontier guards' attention would be distracted by the shots fired. Two of the pursuers at last succeeded in running down Villám Pista, and in cutting him off from his comrades.

They were closing upon him in a thicket, and no outlet remained.

"Is it the ten thousand ducats you are seeking?" laughed their enemy contemptuously, as she took two pistols out of the holster, and seized the while her horse's bridle in her mouth. And just as the assailants approached closer, the robber fired, aiming not at the riders, but at their steeds. Both beasts fell, the one with his rider under him, the other on his knees, so that the heyduke was thrown over the horse's head.

Villám Pista clapped his hands and laughed aloud. "Now you can overtake my husband," cried the false highwayman, and for the moment the old Fruzsinka asserted herself.

Then she vanished into the thicket, the gathering fog hiding all trace of her, even as might disappear some wild valkyr of the old legends.

CHAPTER XXXVI.

Ráby succeeded in crossing the frontier, the thick mist which veiled the moonlight favouring his escape. The shame of the situation nearly killed him. To be freed by a woman masquerading as a robber-chieftain—and that woman his wife! His wretched spouse had done him many wrongs, yet this one, although intended to benefit him, smote him as with a lash, and the memory of her last words stung him to the quick.

But he had by this reached the adjacent river, whose waters were not sufficiently frozen over to bear the weight of both himself and his horse. So he had to dismount and leave the animal behind, and then cross the ice on foot as best he could.

This was undoubtedly better than arriving at the Austrian frontier on horseback, for a woman riding alone at that time of night would certainly arouse the suspicions of the Austrian officials, and they would probably escort him back to whence he came. So he dragged himself to the first wayside inn he could find, and explained his presence there with a story of his brothers having fallen into a snow-drift. The kind-hearted people believed him, and when it was light, set out to find his kinsmen. But whom, strangely enough, should they come across but Ráby's two friends, who, after the fight with the heydukes, had set out to follow him, not without many mishaps in the snow which bore out Ráby's tale.

It was a right merry meeting, and the three could eat and sleep in safety now that they were free from their pursuers. They thought it best to say nothing of the heydukes, in case they might be cited as witnesses. There still lay a two days' journey before them across bad roads ere they could reach Vienna. His friends' readiness to accompany him convinced Ráby that they were in the service of the Emperor, and not mercenaries of the Pesth authorities. In view of chance separating them again, Kurovics made over to Ráby thirty gulden so that he might not be without money.

On Austrian territory, Kurovics became quite communicative, and let out that he was no Szent-Endre burgher, but a well-to-do landed proprietor, whose father had been ennobled by Maria Theresa, and that he was in the Emperor's confidence.

"And won't I just give you a reception if you ever come back to our country," he cried, "not with passports, but with police and dragoons at your back. I promise you I'll kill my finest sheep and roast it whole in your honour, and open a bottle of the best wine my cellar contains to drink your health in."

"How do I know if I shall ever return?" queried Ráby sadly.

But at last they reached Vienna, and put up at the "Dun Stag" by the Red Tower Gate. Kurovics was evidently well known in the capital, and Ráby's doubts about him were henceforth set at rest for good and all.

Our hero had willingly taken a few days' repose after all the fatigues of his onerous journey, but Kurovics would not hear of it. "Get to work directly," he urged, "the Emperor is anxiously awaiting your explanations. Write down your indictment, and do not wait to change your clothes, but just come as you are into the palace, and we will come with you as far as the Hofburg. For you know here in Vienna, everyone who comes into the city has to report himself immediately, and state his business here. It is possible that the Vienna police have already received instructions from Pesth, in this case they will perhaps lock you up before you can get a hearing with his Majesty, so be beforehand and get the start of your enemies."

And Ráby thought it as well to take this advice, so he proceeded to put on paper his report as simply and briefly as possible. He was, moreover, convinced that Kurovics was a genuine friend of the people, for he gave him many proofs of gross abuse of authority on the part of the Pesth officials.

Hardly was the ink on the paper dried, than they chartered a coach and drove off to the Hofburg, in order to be in time for the daily audience which the Emperor was accustomed to hold for those who sought a hearing. The audience chamber led straight into the Emperor's own private cabinet, and was daily, from the hours of ten in the morning till one o'clock, filled by a crowd of all sorts and conditions of people, who came furnished with written petitions, or preferring requests, unannounced and in every-day dress, to seek a personal audience of the Emperor, which was always granted to them in turn.

Joseph spoke all the languages of the polyglot races he governed, and was equally versed in all the various patois, though he usually conversed in German with the petitioners of higher rank.

It was a mixed crowd which now stood awaiting the imperial pleasure—prelates, soldiers, Jews, mourning-clad widows, finely dressed ladies, and peasants in their varied national costumes, jostled one another in the antechamber in which Ráby and his friends found themselves. There was no precedence of rank observed, for the Emperor would speak to whomsoever he willed first, though none were overlooked.

All at once a hush fell on the chattering crowd, and only a subdued whisper was heard here and there, as the moment for the Emperor's appearance had arrived. Ráby was not a little shocked to note how his imperial master had altered: camp life had apparently not suited him. His cheeks were hollowed as with sickness, and his features bore the unmistakable marks of the ravages of both bodily and mental suffering; only the clear blue eyes he remembered so well of old, were unchanged.

Amid the crowd of suppliants, the Emperor seemed not to observe Ráby and his companions. At last Ráby ventured to press into his hand his report.

"What is this?" asked the Kaiser in German, as he pocketed the document without looking at its contents.

All those who had spoken with the Emperor had to withdraw directly the audience was over, and Ráby and his friends were at last the only ones left. The Emperor seeing that they still waited, demanded of Kurovics what it was they sought?

Kurovics thereupon with a low bow, gave him to understand they were only accompanying the lady.

"I have received her petition already," said Joseph, "what does the girl want?"

"Does not your Majesty remember me?" asked Ráby in a low voice.

The Emperor scanned him sharply with no sign of recognition.

"I have never seen you before," he exclaimed coldly. "What is your name?"

"Sire, I am Mathias Ráby!"

His Majesty clasped his hands with a vivid gesture of surprise.

"Ráby! is it possible? Have you lost your reason then that you dress thus? Whence do you come in this masquerading attire?"

"From the dungeons of the Pesth Assembly House, Sire."

The Emperor seized him by the hand, and drew him without a word into his cabinet.

Two secretaries there were very busy sorting documents. The Emperor led the Serb peasant girl up to them.

"Now, gentlemen, say, do you recognise this lady?"

The secretaries were perplexed, and denied all knowledge of the new-comer.

"Come, come, gentlemen," said the Emperor jestingly, "tell the truth, for I'll wager that you have often met before, to say nothing of the lively correspondence you have carried on of late."

The secretaries called heaven and earth to witness they had never seen the stranger in their lives before, and had not the slightest idea who she might be.

"This lady is no other than Mr. Mathias Ráby."

At these words, in defiance of all court etiquette, both burst out laughing, and in their merriment the Emperor himself joined heartily.

Only Ráby looked grave, and did not share their amusement. Even now through the paint on his cheeks, the angry colour flamed—a fact which did not escape the Emperor.

"But however did you manage to put on this disguise?" he asked.

"Simply because I heard your Majesty had ordered I should do so," answered Ráby.

"I? Why whatever put such a thing into your head, I should like to know?"

"Here are the instructions I received," and Ráby handed him his friends' paper.

The Kaiser shook his head as he went through it. "Of course I understand Serb," he said; "but I never wrote this. Where did you get it from?"

"From the leader of the twenty-four men dressed as Turks, who, in your Majesty's name, dragged me by night from out of the dungeon of the Assembly House in Pesth. Two of them came hither with me. Your Majesty saw them in the other room."

"Bring them in here," ordered the Emperor.

One of the two secretaries went then and there to fetch them in, but returned immediately with the news that the two men had already left the Hofburg.

"The police must be notified," said Joseph.

But all their trouble was in vain. The two unknowns on leaving the palace had made direct for the river-bank, where a boat manned by four oarsmen had awaited them, and carried them away in the fog which overhung the river.

Here was an enigma to clear up! Why the men had conducted him to the palace; why they had waited for his meeting with the Emperor and then deserted him entirely; whether they had been indeed friends or foes in disguise, Ráby could not imagine. It remained an unsolved mystery.

CHAPTER XXXVII.

That year saw the appearance of a strange and new phenomenon in Vienna, namely the first Hungarian newspaper. Then for the first time did the Magyar feel he had a purpose in life, and see that by providing the world with a certain quantity of news (whether true or otherwise it mattered not to him), he could get for that same news a certain amount of money.

Such was the début of the Magyar Hiradó; it was edited in Vienna, and then circulated in Hungary forthwith. Little it mattered to its readers what were the news it contained; as long as there was something to read was the main concern of its eager public.

And so it was that a copy of the Magyar Hiradó found its way to the Assembly House in Pesth, for the head-notary, Tárhalmy, had been extravagant enough to invest in one. His neighbours borrowed it freely, and many were the messages that Mariska received to ask her to procure for the senders the loan of the coveted news-sheet. And even the girl herself was not without curiosity to see what this famous journal contained, though she was too ignorant of Hungarian to be able to understand its contents. She fondly imagined that everything that happened in the world would be written down there as news, and she often tried to spell out the strange Magyar sentences.

One day, however, after more futile efforts than usual, she summoned up courage to ask her father the question she had at heart!

"Father, is poor Mathias Ráby released?"

Tárhalmy looked at her sadly, he guessed well enough the reason of her study of the Magyar Hiradó.

"This time he is free, child," he answered; "but if he runs into danger again, he won't get off so easily."

"Is he really a bad man, father?"

"He is the best man alive, and both just and honourable."

Mariska shook her head with a puzzled air, yet she would find out still more now that the ice was broken.

"And the men who prosecute him—are they just also?"

Tárhalmy did not shirk the answer: "No, they are unjust men," he said shortly.

Mariska grew bolder still, "How is it that a man who is really good can be ruined by those who are evil?"

"Because it is the way of the world, my child," returned her father.

"Are you vexed with Mathias Ráby?" she inquired in a low voice.

"No, I love him as if he were my own son," was the answer.

"And yet you cannot defend him against those who intend him ill?"

"I cannot."

"And why not?"

"Because I myself am on their side."

The girl gazed at him in astonishment.

"My father taking the part of the unjust against the just, how can that be?"

"It is a big question which cannot be judged by ordinary standards. Besides, how should a child like you understand?"

Yet Tárhalmy marvelled at the girl's questions; they reached their mark. But he felt he owed her an explanation.

"I will try and make it clear," he said. "Our Emperor is a very well-meaning man who has the welfare of this country at heart. He honestly wants to benefit the people he rules over. But one thing he does not understand, and that is the love of the Magyar for his native land and his Hungarian institutions. If our mother is sick, do we cease to love her? And so it is with Hungary, we, her children, know her weakness and her wants, but we do not cease to love her the less. The Emperor does not understand us; he wishes to civilise us before we are ready for it, to mould us to his own ideals of a nation. He does not want, as other rulers have done, to crush us, but he would have us develop by new and unfamiliar methods. Against force we could oppose force, yet he does not attempt to coerce us, but seeks only to impose on us the weight of his authority. Thus it is that he sends orders which no one obeys, and there are none of his officials who dare carry them out. The whole body of Hungarian opinion in this land is dead against his reforms, and will continue to oppose them tooth and nail."

Now all this did not trouble Mariska; she understood so little of it. Moreover, what her father said must be true. Yet she could not see what the Emperor's dealings with Hungary had to do with Ráby's imprisonment.

"It is a bit difficult for my little girl to grasp, isn't it?" went on Tárhalmy kindly. "Unfortunately the Emperor does not understand how to deal with our constitution. For instance, the members of our governing body are chosen every three years, so that if any among them are proven to be unworthy of the office, they can be rejected at the end of their term. But the Emperor stretches his prerogative, and rules that these offices are to be held for life. And as long as he persists in tampering with our constitution and interferes with the existing order in the state, so long will Hungarians put every hindrance in the way of his emissaries. Nay, they would rather condone the misdeeds of corrupt officials than reach the hand of fellowship to an idealist like Ráby, who is inspired by a noble belief in the righteousness of his mission, and sincerely imagines he is going to free the people of this land from long-standing ills. That is why they make him suffer for his boldness, and will make him suffer yet more, if an evil chance brings him hither once again. He will find the anger of the entire nation aroused against him. Moreover, now that the whole nation is incensed with the Emperor for carrying on the war against the Turks with his Russian allies, and is refusing him both subsidies and recruits, it is less likely than ever to view those who carry out his reforms with favour. And meantime, we honest well-meaning folk who only desire to live at peace with God and our neighbour as Christians should do, have to stand shoulder to shoulder with rogues and vagabonds to protect our country's interests."

The head-notary turned sadly away and left the room, and Mariska sunk into a silent reverie. Her father returning, suddenly put his head in at the door.

"Are you quite sure, little one, that you understand all I have been saying?" he asked somewhat anxiously.

"Father dear, I am going to write it all down straight away," returned the girl, "and may I send it to Ráby?" she added shyly.

"You may if you like," whispered Tárhalmy, strangely touched at her request.

And Mariska set about making herself a new pen in order to do justice to the projected document.

CHAPTER XXXVIII.

Mathias Ráby kept as far as possible out of Vienna society after his arrival in the capital. He never appeared at Court, and rented a modest apartment in Paternoster Street without giving his address to anyone. It was not only that he wanted to be undisturbed so as to fulfil a difficult and important work, but that he felt that a turning-point in his life had come, which implied a momentous decision on his part.

His common-sense told him that so far the tragedy which he had lived through was only a huge jest for the Vienna public, who enjoy nothing so well as a joke. That the bold Magyars had played off this trick on the Emperor himself made the whole jest all the grimmer. For them it mattered not one jot who the victim was, as long as they had their laugh.

So Ráby avoided his nearest friends, and even reading the papers irritated him. With so many big affairs going on in the world, what did people care about the Szent-Endre happenings, or the machinations of the Pesth government authorities, at a time when in the East, Russia was shaking the Ottoman power to its foundations, and the rising of the German Netherlands was threatening Austria with the loss of her finest province, whilst like an ever darkening storm-cloud, the French Revolution was already lowering on the political horizon. With such contingencies, Szent-Endre affairs might well go to the wall.

Ráby worked so unremittingly at his task, that by the beginning of January, he could hand over his report to the Emperor.

It was a straggling and long-winded, but exhaustive, document. To make the tangled threads hold together and get a grip of the facts was no light business, but at last the bill of indictment was drawn up.

Nor were the Pesth authorities, meantime, slow in preferring their counter impeachment against Ráby, and a black one it was—instigator of rebellion, breaker of the peace, calumniator of the council—he was all these, and much more according to this weighty indictment which brought forward as many arguments to prove the case against him, as Ráby had adduced against his adversaries.

It was between them the Emperor had now to judge, and that impartially, as justice demanded, and not swayed by his own feelings.

Ráby handed his report to his imperial master, and gave him a brief sketch of the contents, and the proofs of his charges, the Emperor listening intently the while. Joseph held in his hand the counter-indictment.

Then he said: "I will consider the whole report carefully. Till I am ready to see you again, take this document and read it at your leisure. I have glanced through it, and by letting you read it, I shall show to you that my trust in you is still unshaken. If you can bring it back to me, faithfully deny all the charges it contains, and prove that they are false, I will tell off two of my most trusted police-agents to look after your personal safety, protect you against the wiles of your enemies, and procure for you all the witnesses and documents you need to establish your innocence. But if you find one serious indictment against you which can be substantiated, then say no more about it; I promise you I will not ask any questions, for what has hitherto happened may have been through my own fault in dealing with this people. At the St. Petersburg Embassy there will soon be a legation-secretary wanted; it would be just the berth for you! I'll give you to the end of the month to think it over. At our next meeting it depends on you to say whether you go to Pesth or Petersburg."

And with these words the Emperor dismissed Ráby.

And what better offer could he have had? A new life in a new country where all the old unhappy past could be for ever blotted out and forgotten, with no remaining links to bind him to his old days. Nothing more tempting could the Emperor have suggested.

He took the fatal indictment with him, and returned home to study its contents—and a bitter reading it made. By turns he laughed at the horrible tragicomedy, and then ground his teeth in rage at the stupidity and malice of it all; the whole thing was put together with such a grotesque lack of reason. The heaped-up charges would have sufficed to condemn the accused over and over again, and Ráby hardly recognised himself in this double-dyed traitor, who had been guilty of almost every crime. There would be no judge living who, had such charges been proven, would not have passed on him without mercy the capital sentence. And to think that this avalanche of lies had been heaped up by those for whom he was labouring to free from oppression, those for whom he had suffered so much, and was still suffering, who were now vilifying him as a traitor.

At that moment he was very nearly throwing over the cause of the people for good and all, and fleeing to a country where he should never hear the name of his native land again.

And then a terrible struggle began in Ráby's soul. On one side all his vanity and self-respect rose in arms to urge him to flight. Was he to labour without reward for this miserable people, and make its most distinguished leaders his enemies? Was his name to be dragged in the mire through the length and breadth of the land to gratify their malice? Could he not turn his back on it all, and find in a foreign capital that field for his gifts where they would have a worthy scope for their display, and be cherished and rewarded? Fame and wealth on the one hand, misery and disgrace on the other, and at best, the doubtful credit of the informer—that was the choice!

Long did the two strive for mastery, and darker and more hateful grew the picture of what he might expect if he returned to his self-imposed work. Was it not better to root out from his soul all thoughts of his fatherland?

And in the midst of it all there arrived Mariska's letter, which was the only one of all his missives he opened and read just then.

Twice, thrice, he read it, with its too well-understood appeal: "Do not come back again!" And her words decided him.

And indeed if Ráby had not, after reading it, sprung up and cried, "Now I will go back!" he had not been worthy of having his history written in this record.

What if he owed it not to his people or his prince to go back, at least he owed it to Mariska, and he would remember his debt. To her, at least, he would prove that he was a man who did not turn his back on danger, but went boldly forth to brave it when duty and his country called, and to justify himself at that country's tribunal.

And what love did not the letter breathe for him for whom she wrote it—no gross earthly passion, but rather the pure love of a devoted sister for a brother, of a tender mother who seeks to ward danger from the head of a dearly loved son—that was love as Mariska felt it.

And Ráby thought sorrowfully how many anxious hours that letter must have cost her poor little head, ere she could clothe her thoughts in words and achieve the difficult task of reporting faithfully her father's ideas—ideas which must of necessity have been hard for her girlish mind to grasp in their fulness, much more to put on paper.

And like a horrible nightmare arose the thought of that other woman who had betrayed her husband, and as if to make herself still more unworthy in his eyes, had flaunted her shamelessness by masquerading in man's attire.

And the temptation suddenly arose to procure the deed of separation which the free and easy Protestant marriage laws made only too possible, and forswear the solemn tie that bound him to Fruzsinka. But he put it from him as one more temptation to be resisted, not less powerful because it came from within instead of from without.

Poor Mariska, how the aim of her well-meant letter had failed! It was to have just the contrary effect she had intended.

After reading it again, Ráby hesitated no longer, but took the documents under his arm, hastened to the palace, sought the Emperor's presence, and said simply, "All that stands written here is false from beginning to end! I beg your Majesty to send me back to Pesth."

"Good," said the Emperor, "and if they dare to lay a hand on you, I will come myself and set you free."

CHAPTER XXXIX.

The Emperor sent Ráby two agents of the secret police, who were told off to accompany him wherever he went; both had full powers to claim admission everywhere, to arrest anyone they desired without respect to rank, and to draw the requisite funds they might need from the public banks.

One of them, named Plötzlich, was a famous detective, and never so happy as when he was tracking some notorious criminal to his lair, or dexterously unravelling some-deep-laid plot. His personal courage was everywhere recognised, and he had won high distinction in the performance of his duties in Vienna, where he was generally respected and feared; in fact, Ráby could hardly have had a better man to protect him.

However, even Mr. Plötzlich had his limitations, as Ráby found out by the time they were fairly on the road in the diligence. The police-commissioner had never been out of Vienna, and a country journey was a new experience.

At the sight of the sparrows (which had been exterminated in the towns) he cried, "How very small the pigeons are here!" Then, seeing some country peasants hunting marmots out of their holes, he asked what kind of an animal they were, whereupon the farmer he addressed told him it was an Hungarian mouse. From which it will be seen that the accomplished detective's knowledge of zoology was limited, to say the least of it.

When they put up for the night at an inn on the road, Ráby noted with some surprise that Plötzlich drew his sword and laid it in the bed beside him. Ráby assured him that no danger was to be apprehended, as all the doors were barred against possible attacks from robbers.

"Ah! that may be," returned the other, "but," pointing to a mouse hole, "suppose an Hungarian mouse should get in!"

Meantime the long formal document which officially announced Ráby's readiness to appear before his judges to refute the charges against him, had been drawn up and sent to Pesth, and the head of the police there, as well as the district commissioner were properly notified of the same.

It was growing dusk when Ráby and his two conductors arrived in Buda. And this was just as well, so that they should not be recognised. So ere the street lamps were lit they hastened to the police-station, where it had been arranged they should stay. Over the door hung the great Austrian eagle, and below a soldier guarded the great shield bearing the imperial coat of arms, which showed that here no Hungarian had jurisdiction.

But the chief of the police complained loudly when he heard who his guest was, and made a very wry face at Ráby's name.

"H'm," he said doubtfully, "I have received orders from the governor of the city to deliver over to him the prisoner Ráby if he should come into my power."

"But we bring you the imperial mandate," exclaimed the others, "that you give a shelter here to the noble gentleman, Mr. Mathias Ráby, who is one of his Majesty's chamberlains."

"Well, my friend," answered the Buda official, "remember that his Majesty is far away, while his Excellency is near."

"Surely the Emperor is a greater man than the governor of Pesth," cried Mr. Plötzlich indignantly.

"Well, you will see for yourselves," retorted the Buda chief, "you don't know the Pesth authorities as well as I do."

"Yes, but remember we have instructions from the Kaiser," they answered.

"You had better go and interview him yourselves."

And off they went, leaving Ráby under the shelter of the Austrian authorities.

Arrived at the governor's palace, they were received by his Excellency, who, after seeing their credentials, asked abruptly what they desired.

"We are commissioned by his Majesty to accompany hither Mr. Ráby, who is to appear for the purpose of confronting his accusers at the Pesth Assembly House shortly."

"Do you mean the good-for-nothing fellow who ran away the other day from prison?"

"May it please your Excellency, he is authorised by the Emperor himself."

"And he is likewise my prisoner, don't forget that!"

"Pardon me, he is under our special protection, with an imperial safe-conduct and is here for the fulfilment of a perfectly lawful purpose."

"And I have already ordered that he shall be surrendered to the custody of the Pesth magistracy."

"Then I must emphatically protest in the Kaiser's name. Here is his authorisation."

"Then I recommend you to keep it," returned his Excellency drily. "The Kaiser commands in Vienna, but it is my turn here."

And with that the governor got up and rang the bell.

It was answered by a secretary.

"Go to the Assembly House and tell them to send an escort of police to arrest the runaway prisoner Ráby," was the peremptory order.

The Vienna police-agents both exclaimed loudly at this defiance of their prerogative: "We protest, we protest!" they cried angrily. "This is sheer rebellion."

"Protest if you dare," retorted his Excellency. "I'll have you both placed in irons if you don't make off, and you will have time enough to remember Hungarian justice for the rest of your lives."

And the two commissioners, seeing all protest was futile, thought discretion was the better part of valour, and hastened away as fast as they could, till they reached the shelter of the Austrian eagle. There a council of war was held by the indignant officials and Ráby.

But they had not much time for discussion, for not long after, the provost of the Pesth prison arrived with an armed guard to arrest Ráby.

His Austrian protectors insisted on accompanying their charge, whose forcible removal they strongly resented, though their protests were unavailing.

The Vienna officers naturally thought they would cross from Buda to Pesth by the bridge; what was their dismay, then, to find that the expedition meant to ferry across, and this in spite of the drift-ice which at that season of the year encumbered the Danube and made it dangerous for navigation.

"However shall we get across," they asked, as they gazed in consternation at the river, which did not look inviting, it must be owned.

"Oh, that's soon done," said the provost airily. "You've only to get into the boat here," and he led the way to the ferry-boat which was fastened close at hand.

"Please be good enough to get in," said their conductor.

The prisoner was pushed in first, and the two commissioners dutifully prepared to follow him.

"However are we going to make our way through the ice?" asked Plötzlich anxiously.

"You'll soon see," was the ready answer.

The helmsman cut her adrift, and the rowers pushed from the shore; but scarcely had they put off, before a huge ice-floe drove them back again.

"Ship your oars," roared the ferry-man, and the rowers dexterously trimmed the boat which had well-nigh capsized under the blow, but for their skill.

It was too much for the Vienna officials. "We protest in the Emperor's name!" they yelled, whilst Plötzlich, in mingled fear and anger cried, "I am bound under oath not to allow anyone to cross the river when it is unnavigable through ice, and I won't transgress my own rules, so take us back to the shore!"

And so back they came, and the two Viennese speedily disembarked. "And Mr. Ráby as well," they cried.

"Not he!" laughed the provost triumphantly. "You needn't trouble your heads about him. Whosoever is born to be hanged will not be drowned, of that you may be sure."

And once more they put off on their perilous journey, while the police-agents took out their red pocket-books and made formal memoranda of what had just happened. Meanwhile, with much trouble and long delay, Ráby and his custodians reached the other side, not without narrowly escaping destruction.

The next morning, the river being free from drift ice, the two commissioners took their way to Pesth, and by dint of much threatening and imploring, arrived at the door of the prisoner's dungeon, where they could speak with him.

"Are you there, Mr. Ráby?" they asked anxiously, "and what are you doing?"

"Yes, I'm here sure enough, and clanking my chains for want of any other amusement," was the answer.

"You don't mean to say you are in irons?" cried his questioners.

"Yes, indeed, both my hands and feet are fettered fast."

"Well, have no fear, we will soon free you!"

For this was more than the police commissioners could stand; and they dashed off in hot haste to demand Ráby's release from the authorities, but they found the latter perfectly obdurate to all their entreaties. Finally, they tackled Laskóy, and extorted from that gentleman a promise to remove the prisoner's fetters. They also were invited by him to attend the inquiry next morning, when they might see Ráby for themselves, he said, and escort him away a free man.

So the following morning found the two Viennese again at the Assembly House, but there was not a soul about, save a clerk who could give them but scant information. So they determined to get their news at first-hand, and make for Ráby's cell. On the way they fell in with Janosics, carrying a brazier containing disinfectants, whose fumes filled the corridor.

"When does Mr. Ráby appear before the court?" they inquired eagerly.

"Not to-day," said the gaoler, "the poor man is ill."

"Let us see him and speak with him."

"You cannot, he is much too bad; besides I have to fumigate the whole place on account of his illness."

"But what is his malady then?"

"That I cannot tell you; ask the doctor when he comes out."

And at that moment the cell-door opened and the doctor walked out, carrying a shovel on which some aromatic gum was burning, in one hand, and in the other a pocket-handkerchief soaked with spirits of lavender. He spoke to no one till he had washed his hands in a bowl of vinegar and water that a heyduke held for him, the commissioners looking on somewhat aghast at all these precautions. Ráby's malady must be something very contagious to demand them.

At last Plötzlich summoned up courage to ask what was the matter with the prisoner.

The doctor took a long inhalation of the lavender and then whispered to the official, nervously, "It's the oriental plague."

It was enough for the Viennese. They thought no more of the unfortunate man they were leaving behind them, but without more ado, hastened out of the infected building as fast as their legs could carry them, to take the fatal news back to Vienna. As for Ráby he was as good as dead and buried, as far as the world was concerned, for his death was a foregone conclusion.

CHAPTER XL.

What was really the matter with Ráby the police never learned; but we can tell the reader.

When at about three hours after midnight, they had brought him to the Assembly House, the whole gang of his enemies was awaiting him, including the gaoler.

He was received with a shout of derisive laughter, as he came into the room, thick with tobacco-smoke.

"So the Emperor has given you decorations, has he?" thus they jeered at him. "Well, we'll see what sort of ornaments we can procure for your worship," and such like remarks, were freely fired off at him.

But Ráby bore all the jeers of his tormentors in a dignified silence, and quietly submitted to the searching process, whereby he was stripped of all his valuables, and fetters slipped over his wrists and ankles, the gold lace being cut off from his new coat so that he might not hang himself with it! Then he was led back into the cell he had formerly occupied, and left to himself.

But, he reflected, his captivity could not last long. The two police-officers must be still there, and when all was said, they were the masters. And failing all else, had not the Emperor himself promised to come? Up till then, he would have patience. The visit of his friends on the following day did not give him much hope that their help would avail him.

On the third day, the prison doctor sought him out, and with the help of the gaoler, began to subject him to a long process of disinfecting, which he said, was necessary for every prisoner who came from across the frontier, seeing that in Turkey the oriental plague was raging.

We have seen how the two Viennese officers were smoked out of the city. This left the coast clear for Ráby's examination the following day. His earlier trial had taken place before the district commissioner as a political offender: now he was haled before the ordinary assizes as a common criminal.

The indictment which set forth how Ráby by the help of diabolic arts, had forcibly broken out of custody, and fled to another country, was read. It called for five and twenty years' solitary imprisonment, together with public chastisement; which should allow of his being at appointed intervals set in the public stocks, with a placard showing the nature of his crime hung round his neck.

Ráby, in his defence, demanded that the judges should call one of the twenty men who had forcibly seized him the night of his flight; this was, he said, exacted by the Emperor in his instructions as to the trial.

Laskóy struck the table with his fist. "That is not true," he said, "it is not in his Majesty's instructions."

"I have seen it myself," said Ráby, "the Emperor gave it into my own hands to read."

At these words there was a perfect outburst of wrath and indignation from the whole company, so that Ráby could not speak for the uproar; when the noise had quieted down, he went on:

"The men who freed me are not forthcoming as witnesses. But there are two at least, who must know what happened that night, and this is the heyduke who stood before the door of my cell, and the other who kept the gate. Though I did not see them I know what their names were, for I heard the castellan address them as Sipos and Nagy."

"Let them be brought in," said Laskóy to the castellan with a meaning grimace.

But it was Ráby's turn to be astonished when the witnesses entered. For there before him, stood his two travelling companions, the pretended pig-dealer, Kurovics, and his comrade, who had accompanied him to Vienna! And these, it appeared, were the two heydukes who had been commissioned to play this trick upon their unsuspecting victim. Ráby's brain fairly reeled at the thought of the lying fraud to which he had been forced to lend himself.

But the examination of Sipos was beginning. "It seems you were the guard at the door of the prisoner's cell, the night of his escape?" questioned the judge. "Do you know what happened?"

The witness groaned, and murmured something incoherent.

"Tell us what you know. The truth, out with it!" as the man hesitated.

"Ah, how can I say it!" exclaimed the fellow, while the gaoler shook his fist at him menacingly.

"I'll tell all," he said, "just as it happened. The gaoler ordered four and twenty of us heydukes to disguise ourselves as Turks, then to break open the door of the prisoner's cell, and put on him a peasant girl's dress and escort him to Vienna in this disguise. He gave us money for the journey, and told us the Pesth magistracy had ordered it."

At this outspoken testimony, Ráby could hardly contain himself, he stamped on the floor till his irons rang again. So the whole intrigue was manifest! His enemies themselves had hatched this conspiracy against him, and now they dared to condemn the victim of their own wicked plot!

He attempted to protest, but the whole crew shouted him down. "Hold your peace, traitor!" they cried! "Hold your peace! Not a word will we hear from you!"

And their anger was not less hot against the witness whom they called a liar and false swearer, and then and there ordered him to receive fifty strokes with the lash, and this was Sipos' reward for telling the truth.

"Let the other witness appear," cried Laskóy. "Now, János Nagy, you are an honest man, and will tell us what happened, so out with it!"

Nagy, otherwise the false Kurovics, had the example of his comrade before him, and bethought himself in time of what he might expect if he was too truthful, so he took his line accordingly.

"This is the true history, your worships. When, on the sixth of December last, I was keeping guard before the door of the gate of the prison, and my comrade stood before the prisoner's cell, I heard a loud cracking noise; then the door of Mr. Ráby's dungeon flew open, and he came out in a fiery chariot drawn by six black cats, whilst on the box sat a demon in a red dolman, who gave first my comrade, and then me, such a switch in the face with his long tail, that we could hear and see nothing further—so stunned were we. And then with a noise like thunder, the prisoner disappeared in a flash."

Ráby was astounded—not at the witness, but at his hearers.

"Is it possible, is it credible," he cried, "that you gentlemen, can accept such testimony as this?"

"Be silent, and don't interrupt the witness," yelled Laskóy, "we don't want you to teach us. You know we have laws against witchcraft, and we mean to enforce them. Mr. notary," he cried, turning to Tárhalmy, "please take the depositions of the witness."

And Ráby saw with amazement that Tárhalmy did not hesitate to do as he was bidden. And suddenly there flashed across the prisoner what Mariska had written to him. Here the wise and fools alike seemed to be leagued against him. In vain he protested his innocence in the Emperor's name, and that of the law and common-sense: it availed nothing. Finally they led him out of the room while they debated on his sentence.

It was not long before he was conducted back again to hear it. Of the several indictments against him, several had not been verified, but one at least they indeed had proved, and that was, that by diabolic agency he had escaped from the dungeon. That was enough to condemn him, and "death by the axe" was awarded accordingly.

When Ráby heard it, he could contain his indignation no longer:

"Gentlemen, and you my most worshipful judges," he cried, "hear me before I depart, for there is no tribunal on earth so tyrannical that it will not allow the criminal to justify himself. Why am I condemned? Why have such punishments, ending with the death-penalty itself, been meted out to me? Why have I suffered thus? Simply because I strove to heal the woes of the oppressed; just because the Emperor has sent me hither to inquire into the grievances of the people, whose cry has reached him. The poor were no rebels against the law; they sought only justice, and I desired to help them to attain it. Do you remember what authority is given to you, when you are placed in the seat of law? Is it not a divine commission to defend the right of the individual, as of the people, alike? If you are confident in the success of your cause, I am equally so in that of mine, for my conscience is clear, I have broken neither the laws of God nor of man, and to my convictions I will never be false. I only ask one thing for my people, that they may be freed from the yoke of the oppressor. Is that a crime deserving the death penalty? Well, let my head fall; my blood be on those who shed it!"

Several of the judges could not restrain their tears. Tárhalmy hid his face in his hands; was it that he could not face the prisoner?

Ráby's last words rang with such intense sincerity that not one of those present had dared to interrupt his speech. Laskóy was the only one to speak when the accused had ended his defence, and all he said was, "Take the prisoner away!"

"I appeal then against the judgment of the court," said Ráby as he was being led out.

"That is permitted; meantime, he who is under sentence of death must be heavily ironed till the hour of execution."

"Against that likewise I protest," said Ráby firmly. And they led him out and called for the prison locksmith.

CHAPTER XLI.

Up till now, Ráby had been rigidly fettered, in that his right hand had been fastened to his left foot, while another chain had bound his left hand to his right foot. Now as an addition to this came the whole equipment involved in "heavy irons." Two chains, consisting of six iron rings linked together, weighing in all about a quarter of a hundred weight, were now produced for the prisoner.

These fetters were no longer fastened, as the lighter ones had been, with a padlock, but were to be rivetted on an anvil, so that they could only be sawn asunder when taken off.

For the operation the prisoner was led into the yard of the Assembly House, much to the excitement of the townspeople who gathered to witness so unusual a spectacle, including all the women-folk. They were aghast at seeing a young and richly clad gentleman being loaded with heavy irons. In such a scene the crowd is on the side of the criminal, and they were now.

When they saw Ráby forced to sit down on the paving-stones, and heard him groan with pain as his already fettered ankle received the first stroke of the heavy hammer on the anvil, a cry burst from the bystanders, and they could not restrain their indignation.

"Poor fellow! What has he done to deserve it?" they asked, and the women wept freely. One of them took off her kerchief, and, kneeling down beside him, was fain to bind it round the ankle-bone, so that the iron should not cut it too severely, but the gaoler sternly thrust her away.

"What do condemned criminals want with that sort of thing, you stupid? Away with you and your silly feelings. Would you have his fetters lined with velvet? He'll soon get accustomed to them, I'll warrant you."

And he brutally tore the kerchief off Ráby's ankle.

When at last the work was done, the prisoner had to rise. But this was easier said than done, for with his fettered hands and feet, he was almost powerless to move. Small wonder he fell back in the attempt.

Janosics laughed aloud.

But it is no laughing matter when a man in irons tries to walk.

Meantime, the women became more sympathetic than ever with the prisoner, and openly railed at the heydukes.

"You murderers! It is a sin and a shame to treat him thus! And such a pretty gentleman too! If we were only men we would soon teach you gaolers to mend your manners. Why you are worse than the Turks themselves."

"Drive the women out of the yard," cried Janosics furiously, "and then let us be getting on, for the cage is ready for the bird."

And some of the heydukes promptly drove out the women, while the rest looked after Ráby. In one of them, who helped him to rise, Ráby recognised the man who had brought him the pitcher with the false bottom when he was in prison. The man also evidently pitied him in his stumbling efforts to drag one foot before the other, and showed him how he could best do it by carefully measuring each step forward. But the pain of the irons which had already begun to cut into his flesh, was well-nigh unbearable, and it was with the greatest difficulty he staggered to the cell prepared for him—a small damp dark hole with a little grated orifice for air through which the falling snow was drifting.

No stove warmed the frozen depths of his dungeon, but there was a huge stake in the wall to which was affixed an iron chain: to this the fetters of the prisoner were made fast, so that he could stir no further than the small tether it allowed, and had to lie or crouch day and night in the heap of straw, which was his only bed. An earthen pitcher and a wooden bowl held respectively the drinking water and black bread which were to last him a week, for having provided them, they needed not to trouble further for some days about the inmate of the cell. And there was no pitcher this time with a false bottom!

Now Ráby was to know what it meant to be a captive indeed.

CHAPTER XLII.

Poor Ráby, he was a prisoner in such surroundings that they would have served for the wildest page of romance. No sound came to him from the outer world, as he lay there chained to the blank wall in his living grave—the underground dungeon whose door no key opened. Yet for all this he was not forgotten.

In the deathlike stillness of the night he heard what sounded like a noise of scratching in the roof of his cell, as if someone were trying to bore through the ceiling.

All at once the sound ceased, and from above he heard a well-remembered voice: "Poor Ráby!" it murmured.

At the sound, a thrill of joy shook the prisoner, in spite of his fetters; it spoke to him of life and hope.

"Can you hear me?" asked the voice.

"Perfectly," answered Ráby.

"Trust in God, He will deliver you, He will not let you be lost. If to-morrow you hear a sound of knocking, give heed. Good-bye."

Then there was again stillness. But Ráby slept in his heavy fetters rocked by that hope, as peacefully as a child in its mother's arms.

When he awoke at daybreak, it seemed like a dream, till he was reminded of its reality by a light tapping on the ceiling of his cell.

And then, just over his head, there appeared a long hollow cane thrust down from a small aperture in the roof, and it came lower and lower till it reached his fettered hands.

"Have you got it?" asked the voice. "If so, open it carefully."

Ráby carefully opened the sealed end and found a minute phial of ink, and an equally slender pen made from a crow's feather. Round it was rolled a sheet of paper.

"Write, and I will wait to take it," said the voice, and the prisoner, as might be imagined, was not long in obeying the request of his unseen monitress. Carefully and minutely, in spite of his fettered hand, he traced on the paper a letter to the Emperor, telling him all that had happened, and in the relief of giving this welcome vent to his feelings, he forgot his wretched surroundings. When it was done he rolled up the paper, tucked it in the cane, and pushed it up again through the ceiling.

On the evening of the next day he heard the voice again: "Dear Ráby, take courage. Your letter has gone to Vienna by the Jew Abraham."

Ráby's heart warmed at this news, it would mean at the most only a week more of his present captivity—and for that time he had bread and water enough.

Meantime, before the said week came to an end, his Excellency the governor sent for Mr. Laskóy.

"We are in a nice quandary, my friend, and you will have to get us out of it; hear what has happened," and his Excellency paused as if to emphasise what was to follow. "Three days after Ráby was imprisoned, the Emperor summoned me to Vienna. I went as fast as posts could carry me, to hear, as his first question: 'What have the authorities done with Ráby?'

"I told him that Mathias Ráby had already had a fair hearing before the magistracy, but that owing to a dangerous sickness which had suddenly overtaken him, he was now in the hands of the doctor, pending being confronted with his accusers. The Emperor did not interrupt me, but when I had done, out he comes with a letter written by your prisoner in spite of his irons and fast barred door, setting forth his grievances to his master in very plain terms. And I can assure you he didn't spare either of us."

Laskóy was petrified with amazement. "That means," pursued his Excellency, "that Ráby has found ways and means of writing to the Kaiser from his dungeon. When I had read the letter through, the Emperor said: 'Mark my words, if Mathias Ráby is not released from prison by the day after to-morrow (you will be back in Pesth by then), I shall give orders that his custodians be themselves arrested and put in the Dark Tower for the rest of their lives on bread and water. So you see what you have to reckon with, and the best thing you can do is to set the prisoner free at once.'"

The lieutenant did not want urging, he rode to the prison in hot haste, and demanded to see the head-gaoler. No sooner had Janosics appeared, bearing his huge bunch of keys, than Laskóy sprang at him straight away like a wild cat, seized him by the ears, and banged his head against the door unmercifully, till the keys rattled again in his hands.

"Take that for your pains," he cried, "I'll teach you how to look after your prisoners! What do you mean by letting Ráby write to the Emperor from his dungeon?"

The castellan was dumbfounded with pain and amazement. "All I can say is, your worship," he cried, rubbing his head, "that Ráby must be in league with the Devil."

And though all the authorities of Pesth put their heads together, they could not solve the mystery. The only thing they were clear upon was that Janosics deserved fifty strokes with the lash, a punishment he promptly received.

The following day his Excellency went to the Assembly House, and two letters were put into his hands by Laskóy with a crafty smile. Both were in Ráby's handwriting. The one was dated from Szent-Endre; it contained an expression of the writer's gratitude for his release by the Pesth authorities, and his willingness to abide henceforth by the laws of the land. Further, it announced his determination to withdraw from public life and attend to his private concerns, and the writer begged that the accompanying letter, if it met with the governor's approbation, might be, after reading, forwarded by special messenger to the Emperor.

The second missive contained a formal admission by the writer that he had been led astray by false evidence, that the story of the treasure-chest was a lying invention of the deceased "pope"; further it expressed his regret at having caused the Pesth magistracy so much inconvenience, and his determination not to return to Vienna but to pass the rest of his life in the country, to which end he begged the pension allotted to him might be sent to him at Szent-Endre.

His Excellency immediately dispatched this missive to Vienna, and drove back home. You do not imprison Pesth people so easily in the Dark Tower.

Yes, it was all very cleverly arranged, but perhaps the reader will not be surprised to learn that Ráby still languished in his dungeon a closer captive than ever. At the discovery of Ráby's letter to the Emperor, a contingent of heydukes had visited the prisoner in his cell, searched the dungeon for ink and paper, but in vain, for the thick rime which glazed the ceiling, effectually hid the small hole at the top. The result was that, failing to get any light on the mystery, Ráby was fettered closer than before, the door barred and sealed with the lieutenant's own private seal, and the prisoner was once more left to the solitude of his cell.

And as for the supposed letters, why they were easily accounted for by the fact that an accomplished forger then in prison, who was anxious to please his judges to the best of his ability, which was great, had written them at their bidding.

So Ráby waited till his good angel again provided him, by means of the hole in the ceiling, with ink and paper in the cane, but this time he only wrote the words, "I am still here, your Majesty," and signed it with his blood, for his foot was bleeding profusely through the chain cutting into it. But even this was assuaged by his protectress by means of a linen bandage concealed in the cane, with which Ráby was enabled to bind up his ankle.

Before the week was out, his dungeon-door was opened one morning, and an unusually large allowance of bread, and two pitchers of water were thrust into his cell. Then the man he had seen once before, whom he recognised as a mason, appeared with his assistants, and with their help, took his cell door off its hinges, and proceeded to brick it up. And through Ráby's mind ran old stories he had read of people being walled up alive in the Middle Ages, and a shuddering horror fell upon him, at the fate reserved for him.

CHAPTER XLIII.

The Emperor received both of Ráby's letters—the forged and the genuine one—nearly at the same time, for the latter had been sent by express post. Shortly afterwards, it became known that his Majesty was going to pay a visit to Pesth, ostensibly to review some troops. It was this news that had hastened the walling up of Ráby's cell. The Emperor was not to find him when he came, and when the Kaiser had gone, they meant to restore the dungeon-door to its place. For they did not intend to kill their victim outright by burying him alive.

In order to dry the fresh masonry, they often let the window in the corridor stand open, and so thick was the rime that you could not see the walls for it. Nay, the hair and beard of the captive were white too with it, and from the frozen ceiling, the icicles dropped down upon him as he lay on his straw couch. But the greatest misfortune induced by the cold was that he became so hoarse, he could not answer the voice from above, but could only rattle his chains to show that he still lived.

On the day of the Emperor's arrival, the voice ceased, and he heard men's footsteps above, as if re-arranging the room, in view perhaps of the imperial visit.

In fact the Kaiser had come, and by mid-day had inspected his troops and was sitting down to a frugal mid-day meal in the Assembly House, as was his custom, alone, giving orders the while to the crowd of aides-de-camp, and the various functionaries who came and went. He left untasted the glass of old Tokay, poured out for him by the obsequious Laskóy in a glass of rare Venetian crystal, for to the date of its vintage he was quite indifferent.

"And now," said his Majesty, when he had finished, "tell me what has happened to my commissioner, Mr. Mathias Ráby?"

"Sire, he has gone back some time since to his home in Szent-Endre, and we had a letter of thanks from him just lately."

"I have seen that letter," returned the Emperor drily, "likewise another written from the dungeon of the Assembly House, wherein I learn he is still a prisoner."

"Ah, sire, that is easily explained," answered the lieutenant airily. "The fact is that we had imprisoned at the same time as Ráby, a renowned forger, who has been deceiving even your Majesty by carefully forged letters in your commissioner's handwriting."

"What could he have gained by that?" said the Emperor.

"Probably he knew," returned Laskóy, "that Ráby enjoyed your Majesty's favour, and reckoned that, as you were coming to visit the Pesth prison in person, he would thus recall himself to your Majesty and gain a hearing from you."

"That reminds me," answered the Emperor, "that I have not yet seen the prison, so I will trouble you to lead the way."

And Laskóy proceeded to conduct the imperial guest to the dungeons, even to the most noisome, regardless of the pestilential atmosphere which met the visitor. The Emperor had every door unlocked, and insisted on seeing everything, and it was plain from his sharp scrutiny that he did not trust his guide.

Then he inspected the cells where the "noble" culprits were confined, and among them that formerly tenanted by Ráby. The bed which the prisoner had occupied, was duly pointed out to the Emperor, and then he proceeded to inspect the rest of the cells in order.

Three times did he actually pass the door of Ráby's dungeon (and the prisoner could hear the clink of his spurs overhead), yet did not discover the one he sought. And no suspicion crossed the captive's mind from behind his walled-up door that his would-be deliverer was close at hand.

The deception had been only too well carried out. Not even by coming in person to free him, as the Emperor had promised his emissary, could he succeed in delivering him.

And there was not a single man of them all who would point to Ráby's cell, and say boldly, "There lies the man whom you are seeking."

As for Mariska, she had been sent that very day to her aunt's at Buda, for some of the officers had been quartered at the head notary's, and it was no longer the place for the daughter of the house.

And the Emperor went that day into camp, but Ráby still languished in his dungeon.

CHAPTER XLIV.

Ráby's persecutors were getting tired of their unavailing efforts to break the prisoner's spirit, so they determined on softer measures, and three days after the Emperor had left Pesth, his dungeon was broken open, and Laskóy and Petray arrived to make personal investigations into their victim's state.

Truly it was a pitiable spectacle that met their gaze when at last a breach was made in the masonry and they penetrated into the cell. A wasted and attenuated figure they saw half-buried under the snow that had drifted in on to his straw bed through the grating—snow that was stained red with the blood that had streamed from the captive's wounds.

"Take the irons off!" ordered Petray, "and wrap the prisoner up in warm coverings."

And the order was not unnecessary, for it was some time ere the locksmith could be found, and, meantime the victim was benumbed nearly to death with cold.

Even the locksmith, as he filed off the fetters from Ráby's bleeding wrists and ankles, could not suppress a murmur of pity, for he was only a public servant who did as he was told, and had a kind heart.

When at last Ráby was freed from his chains, he could not stand, and had to be carried by two heydukes to a neighbouring cell, which was one of those he had formerly occupied.

"Let him rest for a little," ordered Petray, "and then I will have a word with him, and meantime, you may bring him some egg-broth with wine."

And the broth revived the wretched prisoner, half-starved and frozen as he was, with new life, and he eagerly swallowed it. He was conscious of a feeling of anger against himself for thus being so ready to accept alleviation for his miserable body, that so little emulated his strong, unconquered soul. One thing alone lightened the memories of his sufferings, and that was the voice that had cheered his loneliness with its encouraging whisper. And lulled by the unaccustomed warmth, he sank into a comforting slumber, and at his awakening, only had his bandaged limbs to remind him of his irons. Yet the remembrance that it was to Petray, of all people, that he owed this amelioration of his misery, stung him as with a lash.

But just then the door opened, and in walked his enemy himself. He came up to Ráby's couch and asked the prisoner how he had slept, and whether he felt better. But the captive answered these hypocritical enquiries by never so much as a word.

"You have to thank me for this change, you know," pursued Petray, "for I have been chosen as your advocate when you appeal against your sentence."

"What?" cried Ráby, in his excitement springing up, in spite of his weakness, from the couch. "You to be my defender! You who are already gravely impeached in the indictment I have formulated! Why such a false position is impossible; it is you who must stand at the bar. Do you mean to say you, who are my worst enemy, are entrusted with my defence?"

Petray smiled. He knew well enough he had a sick man to deal with, who was physically incapable of attacking him.

"Now you see how unjust it makes you, this misunderstanding. You shall know that the accused must have a counsel when he is confronted by the indictment. There are two of us, myself and the lieutenant, who have to take your case in hand; which do you prefer, him or me?"

"Neither," cried Ráby indignantly. "I am my own counsel, and I know how to defend myself, and do not need any of your help."

"My dear friend, be reasonable; see how unjust this is," said Petray in a wheedling voice. "You think I would defend you badly. But it is because I want to prevent you running your head against a wall that I am doing this. Listen, I'll read you the points of your defence."

And Petray proceeded to read the document in which he had set forth Ráby's case with such cunning adroitness, that black appeared white in his representations, and white wholly black. Such a web of sophistries, in fact, had he woven, that it had been difficult for a hearer to disentangle the truth. In it all the guilt was laid at the door of the dead "pope," and Ráby appeared as a too confiding victim of his wiles and misrepresentations. It was a tissue of false statements, yet Ráby listened to the end.

Then he said indignantly: "So you really believe I need all that for my justification, do you, that the guiltless are to be blamed and the criminal cleared, in order that the truth be made manifest; that I withdraw the impeachment already made against you, that I allow peaceable and harmless peasants to be attainted as rebels; that I disavow the responsibility of redressing their grievances, and that for this, a dead yet innocent man be blamed, and his memory be defamed. No such defence for me, thank you!"

Petray laughed patronisingly.

"My good friend, you are an idealist and always will be. What does the 'pope's' reputation matter to you, since he is dead? Do you suppose he troubles as to what men say of him now? And as for the peasants, we can make short work of them by putting them in irons. The defence is perfectly in order; you only have to sign that you accept it."

"Let my hand wither in its chains first," cried the prisoner, "ere I subscribe to such infamy!" and he stretched his wasted hand to heaven.

"Think twice, Ráby, before you decide thus," said his tormentor. "If you refuse, you may no longer rely on my help, and then you will just go back to the place you came from."

"Take me there," cried his victim, "but torture me no further, rather kill me outright. But as long as my soul is master of my body, no pains or persecutions shall cause me to forswear my honour and give the lie to truth!"

His anger lent the prisoner an unwonted energy, and Petray fairly quailed as Ráby dashed up to him and attempted to tear the document from his hand; between them it was torn in two, but the leaves were stained with blood!

Petray was beside himself with rage; he hastily called for the gaoler and the heydukes, who shortly entered, followed by Laskóy.

"He is an abandoned wretch, a traitor, a madman," cried Petray. "He has flown at me, and tried to murder me. Put him in irons again directly!"

"Out with the fetters," cried Laskóy. "Where are the heaviest ones?"

And they tore off the bandages from Ráby's wounded limbs, and called the locksmith to rivet them afresh.

But that functionary revolted at this fresh act of cruelty against a helpless invalid. "I won't do it," he said defiantly. "From this hour I serve the authorities no longer; I will have no part in such cruel injustice!" And so saying he left them, never to appear again.

At last, after searching Pesth in vain, they found a locksmith in Pilis to do the work.

But when they thrust Ráby back again into his icy dungeon, he cried, as the door closed upon his tormentors, "I am not dead yet."

CHAPTER XLV.

"But I'll take care that you soon will be," muttered the gaoler, as he fettered the prisoner afresh to the wall, "and I've orders to visit you twice every day, so that you may not carry on any of your accursed necromancy in the cell."

The next time his rations were brought him, it occurred to Ráby that the bread was strewn with a white powder. He had often complained of it not being salted, but this did not look like salt, and as he was not hungry, he did not attempt to eat it.

That evening when it was dark, he heard the well-remembered voice again from the floor above.

"Poor Ráby," it whispered, "are you there?"

And on his ready answer, came the caution: "Do not eat of the bread they have brought you, it is poisoned."

The prisoner had suspected as much, but what was he to do? There was nothing for it but to die of hunger, it seemed.

"Examine the cane I am pushing down" came the voice again, and a minute or two later, appeared the cane whose hollow had already brought him so much. This time it was filled with chocolate, and there was enough to last him till the morning. But what was he to drink?

"Pour the water out of the pitcher, and through the cane I will fill it with fresh," suggested the voice, and he hastened to obey.

The next morning the gaoler saw with dismay that his prisoner was still alive, and apparently uninjured by his supper, yet it would have killed most men. However, he had not eaten much of it to be sure, judging by the little that had disappeared.

And when his back was turned, once more came the voice calling to Ráby, and this time it brought bad news indeed.

"The Emperor has gone," it said, "he sought for you, but could find no trace of you. They told him you had been released, so he left in that belief."

"Only give me writing materials," pleaded Ráby earnestly.

"I cannot, as soon as you are convicted of having them in the cell, you are to be beheaded immediately. Besides, no one knows where the Emperor is; they say he is in Turkey."

The threat was for Ráby but one more spur to action, and he was defiant, and pleaded no longer with his protectress. He had hidden a morsel of paper in his wretched bed, and on this he wrote with a straw for pen, with a drop of his own blood for ink, for he had no other. When it was dry, he rolled it up and concealed it in a straw-stalk.

Then he waited till the next time his cell was being swept out by a heyduke, who was the one who had formerly brought him the pitcher with the false bottom. Ráby gave his missive to him, and whispered, "This is worth a hundred ducats." The man understood, and took the straw.

That was Mathias Ráby's last attempt at freedom.

From that day forward, all sorts of threats were used to make him sign Petray's paper, and sometimes they kept him so long under examination in the court, that he fainted from sheer exhaustion.

One night the door opened, and Janosics appeared with three men, one of whom bore a brazier of burning coals, another a pair of pincers, and in the third he recognised the public executioner of Pesth.

"I'll soon make the stubborn fellow yield," cried the castellan brutally; "let's see if this won't bend him! Now, gentlemen, do your duty; strip him, and torture him till he confesses his crimes."

Ráby was dumb with horror. They tore his clothes from him, but the sight of the prisoner's haggard face and emaciated figure smote the heart even of the executioner with a sudden pity.

"My good Janosics," he said, "I won't torment the poor wretch, not if you give me the whole Assembly House for doing such work."

And with that, he put on his coat, seized the water-pitcher which stood by Ráby's bed, and extinguished the coals, so that the cell was plunged in sudden darkness. Then the whole crew withdrew quarrelling among themselves.

When Ráby brought the occurrence to the notice of the court the following day, they only laughed, and said he had been dreaming!

CHAPTER XLVI.

One of the thoughts that tortured Ráby most was the anxiety as to what he should do for food, if his benefactress' daily supply of chocolate should fail him. He saved up a little store of it hidden in his black bread, and for water, he could trust to the ice which still, through the severity of the season, constantly formed in his dungeon.

And one day, what he had so long dreaded, happened, and the voice was heard no longer, and he had to take refuge in his hardly saved store of nourishment. Nor was there any sign of his protectress on the following day. But that night in the room above he could hear men's footsteps and the sound of a woman groaning, as if with pain, all the night long. A fearful suspicion crossed his mind that he dared not face, even to himself.

It was obvious that overhead someone was dying, and that someone a woman. He would not let his mind dwell on the presentiment that suddenly arose; it could not be, it must be a nightmare conjured up by his own fevered imagination.

The next morning the groans had ceased, but he could not hear what was being said by those talking. By the afternoon, his fears were changed into certainty, and he knew it was no dream.

Then he heard the sound of singing, the melancholy droning that the Calvinists use over the corpse, so charged with dreary forebodings, the horrible gloom of which is in such contrast to the touching Catholic ritual for the dead, where all tends to prayerful hope for the departed and to consolation for the survivors.

And then followed a series of dull thuds, as if they were nailing down a coffin-lid, and Ráby shuddered, but not this time with the cold.

Towards evening his gaoler came to visit his cell, and Ráby mastered his feelings sufficiently as far as to ask who it was they were burying.

The castellan read the real question in the prisoner's face as in an open book. It betrayed his one vulnerable point, and his tormentor was not slow to take advantage of his discovery.

So he wiped his eye hypocritically, and murmured in a sorrowful tone, "Alas, it is our beloved Fräulein Mariska, the head notary's daughter, that they are carrying to the grave. Heaven rest her soul!"

The prisoner uttered a sharp cry as if he had received his death-blow; then he burst into tears. Truly the dart had gone home this time, and nothing could ward it off. The gaoler laughed behind the prisoner's back; he had done better than the executioner for once!

But Ráby bowed his head on his knees, and clasped his fettered hands in prayer for the soul that had so lately taken flight from this valley of tears. But had he known it, Ráby was praying, not for the soul of Mariska, but for that of his wretched wife, for it was she whom they were bearing to the grave.

Fruzsinka had been, all unknown to him, a prisoner like himself, and this was the end. How she had come there we shall learn later, for meantime there are other factors in this strange history to be reckoned with, and Ráby is still languishing in his dungeon.

CHAPTER XLVII.

Ráby no longer dreaded the poisoned food that he expected his gaoler to bring him, but next morning, strange to say, Janosics appeared with empty hands and a malicious leer on his ill-favoured features.

"Do I have no food to-day?" asked the prisoner.

"Yes, indeed, my dear friend, from to-day you live like a prince. No more bread and water for you, but just a jolly good dinner of the best, and as much red wine as you like. And your fetters are to come off, and you are to be moved into better quarters. You know, I daresay, as well as I can tell you, what all this means."

Ráby shrugged his shoulders.

"Well, it means that to-day your death-sentence is to be formally approved in court, and that the scaffold is your destination. Till then, you are to be kept in the condemned cell, and have everything you like as befits a criminal under sentence of death, and enjoy yourself while you may."

It was too true, and no jest. The locksmith came and filed off the prisoner's fetters once more, and then the barber shaved him, but the closeness with which his hair was cut, signified only too clearly it was the "toilet of the condemned."

They did not stand on ceremony, but just carried Ráby into the court (for he could not walk), to hear that the capital sentence against which he had previously appealed was now confirmed by the higher court, and that he must prepare to die forthwith.

He heard the decision with strange indifference, but all now he longed for, was that they should get it over as quickly as possible.

He was taken, not into his former cell, but into a small cheerful, well-warmed room, where a table stood spread with all the delicacies imaginable.

This was the "condemned cell," and to it many a kind-hearted housewife in those days was accustomed to send the pick of her larder, to provide a good dinner for those whose earthly meals were numbered—a form of charity at that time very much practised by the housekeepers of Pesth.

"Now, Ráby, you can eat and drink to your heart's content," cried Janosics. "But it's no good trying to take any away with you, remember." And the gaoler pushed the table to the couch, so as to be within the reach of the prisoner.

But Ráby had no appetite, and had other preoccupations than those of the table, to fill his mind just then.

Meanwhile, Ráby's message had not been forgotten by the heyduke to whom he had entrusted it. Old Abraham had taken it to the Emperor who, he heard, was laid up sick in the capital, and it had been promptly read and acted upon. Three days later, Colonel Lievenkopp, just appointed the commandant at Pesth, sought out the governor, and demanded immediate audience on urgent matters of state.

He had, in fact, a message from the Emperor. "Thanks, Colonel, leave it there; I'll read it later on; there's no hurry," said his Excellency, airily, on receiving the imperial missive.

"Unfortunately, there is hurry, your Excellency! I have orders to have the mandate read in my presence."

The words staggered the governor. He, the virtual, if not the nominal ruler of Hungary, to be spoken to like this, and to have the law laid down in this fashion to him!

"Hoity-toity! I have other things to do! Suppose, too, I am not inclined to read it?"

"Then your Excellency will permit me to observe that I am empowered to proceed to extreme measures. In the event of your Excellency not reading that letter at once, I am commissioned to call in half a dozen officers of public health who are waiting outside, with a regimental surgeon, for the purpose of placing your Excellency in a strait-waistcoat, and escorting you to Vienna under surveillance—you will guess whither?"

The governor's face became crimson with rage.

"What do you say—For me, a strait-waistcoat? Me, the representative of the crown? Do you mean to say the Emperor said that, that he has written it? Impossible, man, impossible!"

And he tore the letter out of the envelope, and read its contents.

They were short, and his eyes became suddenly blood-shot as he read as follows:

"From to-day you are relieved of your office: make over your keys to the district commissioner at once.

"JOSEPH."

"And I have Mathias Ráby to thank for this," groaned his Excellency.

"Possibly," said Lievenkopp drily, "for his Majesty has entrusted me with a patent for the Pesth magistracy, whereby he demands the instant release of Mr. Mathias Ráby; in the case of non-obedience, by ten o'clock to-morrow, I am ordered to enforce its execution by a battery and a corresponding number of soldiers, and if the prisoner is not brought out, to storm the Assembly House forthwith, and release Mr. Ráby from captivity."

"Storm the Assembly House?" stammered the magnate, dazed with the suggestion. "Stir up civil war just for the sake of one miserable culprit. Oh, that fellow will be the death of me!"

And the wretched man staggered as with a sudden blow, and blindly clung to a chair for support to prevent him from falling. He was blue in the face, his clenched hand still grasping the letter; it was the beginning of an apoplectic fit.

Lievenkopp hastened to send one of the secretaries for a doctor, but it was already too late; when the surgeon arrived to bleed him, the governor was beyond such help. Thus passed one more actor in this memorable tragedy of Rab Ráby.

CHAPTER XLVIII.

It is time to return to Frau Fruzsinka, and to explain how she had come to be a prisoner under the same roof as her husband.

When Fruzsinka found that Ráby was, in spite of the efforts she had made to save him, a prisoner in Pesth, her rage and disgust knew no bounds. The abandoned woman still carried on her miserable masquerade in man's attire, and as a pretended highwayman, continued to strike terror into the hearts of the countryside.

One night, however, she was taken with what seemed a sudden faintness, and seeking shelter in a peasant's hut, was betrayed by the owner to the heydukes, and carried off by her captors to the prison in Pesth. By the time she arrived there, she was evidently seriously ill, and appeared to be in a high fever, although it never occurred to the prison authorities that her malady might be infectious.

Janosics, who had hailed her arrival with ill-concealed delight, perceiving his prisoner wore a richly embroidered kerchief round her neck, proceeded to annex it, and bind it round his own. But this rough undressing, to which she was subjected as a culprit, was too much for Fruzsinka, and she soon betrayed her sex by her tears at the rough treatment Janosics meted out to her.

As might be expected, the news soon spread that this was no highwayman, but a woman, and she too of noble family.

Tárhalmy recognised her at once, and he tingled with shame at the thought of Mathias Ráby's wife being treated as a common felon. And the case of a woman of Fruzsinka's position being sent there was so rare that there was literally no provision for such prisoners in the building, and so it came to pass that the disused "archive-room," as it was called, the room where Mariska had been able to communicate with Ráby, was that now appointed for Fruzsinka.

"You will be rewarded for this," gasped the wretched woman. "I shall not trouble you long, for I shall not live over to-morrow."

And when Tárhalmy, having found a maid to wait on her, was leaving the room, she called him back to whisper:

"I know you have a daughter you love dearly. Send her away immediately from this house, so she escape the contagion I have brought with me."

Tárhalmy hastened to warn Mariska that she might go to the house of her aunt at Buda, and told her who the prisoner really was.

But the girl was terrified at the thought of leaving Ráby, perhaps to starve, nor did she shrink at the idea of nursing Fruzsinka, but begged her father to let her remain at home, and tend the sick woman.

But Tárhalmy would not let her carry her self-abnegation so far.

Meantime, the doctor came, and deceived by the patient's symptoms, which seemed to him those of an ordinary fever, made a false diagnosis of Fruzsinka's case, and failed to recognise her malady for what it really was—the oriental plague, which was then raging in the near East.

But the plague-stricken woman would not allow a soul to come near her, and refused all attempt at help or consolation, for she, being a Calvinist, would not even see the kindly Capuchin friar who came to offer his services.

And Mariska was allowed to remain till the news of Lievenkopp's threatening mission determined her father to send her away.

As for that officer's demand, it was, deemed Tárhalmy, a question to be settled by the Pesth tribunal, and the still closed door of the prisoner's dungeon would be the answer to the Emperor's mandate, whilst the prisoner himself, when it came to the execution of justice, should know who was master in Pesth!

Surely Tárhalmy had good reasons for sending his daughter away.

Thus was Ráby bereft of his guardian-angel, and so it came to pass that his evil genius, his wretched wife, lay dying in the room over his dungeon.

But Fruzsinka's prophecy came true; she died the next day, and was promptly buried. No one mourned the dead woman, as no one had excused her.

CHAPTER XLIX.

The fateful day broke at last and found the Pesth authorities still in council; their vigil had lasted throughout the night. It was no light question to be decided: nothing less than the authority of the Hungarian constitution, and whether or not it should resist the armed force which menaced it.

Many among them pitied the prisoner and deemed him guiltless in their own hearts, but the law had to be justified—at whatever cost—and Ráby's acquittal would have embodied the breach of that law. Thus it was that no voice was raised on his behalf, and his condemnation was a foregone conclusion.

It was with difficulty the prisoner could stand, so exhausted was he; and when he looked in the faces of his judges, he found there no mercy.

Tárhalmy had hidden his face in his hands, as, at the stroke of ten from the great Franciscan church clock, the vice-notary (they spared Tárhalmy the office) began to read the sentence of the court on Ráby.

He read out the absurd charges which had been got up against the culprit, the résumé of the former trials, the judge's verdict, the prisoner's incitements to the peasants to revolt, his association with brigands, and resort to diabolical arts in order to escape from prison, all of which had rendered him amenable to death by the axe. But this sentence, said the speaker, could not be carried out, since the Emperor had abolished capital punishment, and so it had been commuted by the court into the galleys for life. Mathias Ráby was therefore adjudged to be chained that very day to the oar, to work out his just sentence.

"Chained to the oar!"

For that broken emaciated form what a mockery the sentence seemed! And Mariska, what had she said to it, had she heard it?

Ráby had to be supported by two heydukes, as he was compelled to listen standing to the sentence, but his face was deathly pale as he heard it.

All at once the blare of trumpets and beating of drums was heard without, and out of the neighbouring barracks came squadrons of infantry and cavalry. The heavy roll of the cannon and the rattling of the gun-carriages were distinctly audible as the latter rumbled along the cobbles. And high above it, Lievenkopp's command to load was clearly heard, and the rattle of the muskets as the soldiers obeyed.

The pale face of the prisoner suddenly glowed with hope, and an electric thrill of triumph convulsed his relaxed limbs, as he listened. Rescue was at hand then!

Now it is the turn of his judges to blench, for his persecutors to tremble. The sword is suspended over the judge's head, not over the culprit's. Who will first avert it?

"Now, gentlemen," cried the vice-notary, "the sentence, you know, must be read from the open window of the Assembly House, so all may hear it!"

The speaker (he was quite a young man) suddenly paled with terror as he took up the document, and hastily begged for a glass of water. Laskóy was too terror-stricken to take upon him the task before which his junior quailed.

Tárhalmy stepped forward and seized the paper. "I will read it," he said calmly.

And turning to the castellan, he cried, "Close the doors, and tell the heydukes to load their muskets at once."

As Ráby heard that command he shuddered. The first shot fired, the door of the Assembly House once shattered, would be the signal for the whole country to be aflame with revolt. Such a course would hurl the nation and the dynasty to the verge of ruin. And for what? For the sake of ensuring freedom to one miserable man. Was it worth it?

The prisoner suddenly broke away from his guards, and intercepting Tárhalmy as he reached the window, he threw himself at his feet.

"Your worship," he cried, "I recognise the justice of the sentence, I no longer defy you, I am utterly broken; let me die, but do not let me be further tortured or insulted. But do not on my account stir up bloodshed and strife in this land; trample me, kill me if you will, but do not let the innocent suffer. You shall never hear a word of complaint from me again!"

Tárhalmy tore his coat lappet from Ráby's trembling grasp, and strode firmly but proudly to the window. Below in the street, came the word of command from the officer in charge: "Load your muskets!"

Standing at the open window, Tárhalmy read aloud, in a clear unwavering voice, the judgment on Ráby from beginning to end. The prisoner had fainted. The cannon were in readiness, the muskets loaded; they only awaited the order to fire. All at once, an imperial courier, galloping at full tilt through the crowd, dashed through the trumpeters, rode up to the commandant, and handed him a sealed missive, crying "In the King's name!"

Lievenkopp hastily broke the seal of the letter, read it, and stuck it into his breast-pocket, then he shouted, "Shoulder your arms!"

The trumpeters sounded a retreat; the cumbrous cannon were wheeled back again, and the threatening convoy took their way back to the barracks, from whence they had so lately come.

But the red-coated courier stood beating on the door of the Assembly House with the knob of his riding-whip, and calling, "Open, in the King's name!"

CHAPTER L.

At the sound of those few words, "In the King's name," the door of the Assembly House was immediately opened; the formula acted like magic.

There are two words which are often written down together, "Emperor" and "King," wherein the outer world sees little difference, but for Hungarians there is all the difference in the world. For the Magyar, the first means only the foreign yoke, and all that it stands for; but the second represents that rightful regal authority which in Hungary never fails to win the loyalty and love of those to whom it appeals. And it is a distinction which the world outside Hungary is sometimes slow to recognise.

And so it was that when the red-coated courier appeared before the Pesth tribunal he was received with the utmost respect. It was the office of the head notary to open and read the missive, which he did first to himself. When he had finished, tears stood in the strong man's eyes. And as he began to read it aloud, his voice trembled audibly, and he was visibly moved.

"WORSHIPFUL CITIZENS!

"His Majesty the King herewith, by this present royal rescript, withdraws all vexatious edicts hitherto issued, with the exception of his edict of tolerance and that for the freeing of the serfs. He revokes the compulsory order for the use of a foreign language, and rehabilitates your council and restores your constitution. He concludes a war carried on against the will of the nation by an honourable peace. He asks you, the members of the Pesth magistracy, to call a general council and promulgate the constitution in Pesth, and further orders that the holy crown of Hungary be brought from Vienna to Buda, after which he will summon Parliament and will be crowned there."

The last words were drowned by loud cries of "Long live the King!" while the council members sprang up from their places huzzaing and cheering. They seemed like changed beings. Even Tárhalmy, the grave phlegmatic man, generally as cold as ice and a slave to duty, was transformed, and his set, serious face flamed with a sudden enthusiasm.

"Now, gentlemen," he cried, "comes the new order, now we shall have justice done. And before God and men can I now say, 'Woe to those who have done this foul wrong to Mathias Ráby.' I will justify him at the bar of our country, and none who helped to persecute this brave man shall escape unpunished. The nation shall judge him."

"Hear, hear!" shouted many voices, and the loudest of all was Petray's.

"Justice for Ráby," exclaimed that worthy, "yes, it is right he should have it. I have always told the lieutenant here what a sin and a shame it was thus to compass his ruin."

"What?" cried Laskóy, "I, compassing Ráby's ruin? What do you mean? Who but you managed the whole business, I should like to know!"

"That's a lie!" retorted his antagonist, and the strife promised to be endless, for the others now joined in lustily, and swords were all but drawn.

Tárhalmy took his documents under his arm. "I am going," he said, "I prefer to choose my own company."

Meantime, the news of the royal proclamation had spread like wild-fire, and nothing else was talked of. Nagy (otherwise "Kurovics") hastened to Janosics to impart to him the news that the members of the council were quarrelling as to which one was guilty of Ráby's condemnation, and that it would be as well at any rate, it should not be laid at the door of the prison officials.

So the two made for the condemned cell, where Ráby had been dragged all but unconscious.

The prisoner imagined they had come to lead him to the galleys.

"No, my friend, thank your stars you are not going there," shouted Janosics, "you are reprieved! You are free!"

And a sudden thrill of joy born of his regained liberty, shot through the exhausted frame of the prisoner, remembering he was not to be scourged at the oar. But then his unbending spirit reasserted itself, and he exclaimed proudly, "I need no man's grace, and I accept none of your favours, I would rather die here!"

"You won't then do anything of the kind," retorted the gaoler, "but you will just march! Here, thrust him out, you fellows," and he called up a couple of warders who roughly seized the prisoner between them, and carried him in spite of his struggles into the courtyard below. There was a small iron door which led into a side thoroughfare, and this Janosics opened and pushed Ráby through it, out into the street the other side.

There they left him on the cobbles, in a dead faint from the efforts he had made, and there he lay like a lifeless log. The prison authorities did not care on whom the blame for detaining Ráby fell, but they were determined it should not lay with them.

Janosics returned whistling into his room. But suddenly he ceased to whistle; something seemed to be throttling him. His limbs too were convulsed by a sudden tremor, and horrible spasms of pain shot through his whole body. When he tried to cry out, he failed to utter a sound, and only blood came from his mouth. And still that awful sensation of strangulation oppressed him, so that he tugged at the kerchief about his throat to get it off; it was the one Fruzsinka had worn. And the words of the dead woman, her warning that none should come near her, came back to him.

The doctor he sent for, directly he saw his patient, exclaimed in horror, "This is the oriental plague," for he recognised the symptoms of the fell malady.

And that word at once drove every living soul away from the unhappy man, and he was left writhing in his agony behind the door till he was still, for that meant he was dead. Then they sent two condemned felons to wrap up the corpse in a horse-rug and carry it out into the cemetery there to be buried like a dog. The only thing they troubled after was as to whether enough quicklime had been thrown into the grave.

But Ráby lay half-dead on the cobble-stones. There were no other houses in the alley, save the monster barracks, the university hospital, and the great stone rampart of the hinder part of the Assembly House.

As a rule, only one person went up that alley every day, and that was an old Jew named Abraham. He was no longer bound by law to wear the red mantle, and could go about in his black gown and kaftan. With him was a red-haired boy, his youngest son, an intelligent lad who had excellent legs and could run with the best.

But Abraham left him at the corner of the alley and went alone to the little iron door.

There he was accustomed to wait each morning till a heyduke appeared. Then he would push a paper containing a piece of gold under the door, and receive in exchange another morsel of paper. This contained the latest news of Rab Ráby, and Abraham promptly gave it to the youngster waiting at the corner, who forthwith would run with it to Buda, where Mariska was waiting for it.

But on this particular morning, the Jew found no news of Ráby, but instead, the prisoner himself, lying on the stones, as one dead.

The old man raised no alarm, nor did he utter a word, but bending over the prostrate man, laid his hand on Ráby's heart to see if it yet beat.

When he had satisfied himself that Ráby was still alive, Abraham wrapped him up in his warm fur-lined mantle, took him in his arms, and carried him to the corner of the alley, where he and his son between them dragged him into a sedan-chair, and bore him off—whither no one knew!

A voice like the voice of the angels themselves (so it seemed to the half-conscious man who heard it) sweet as the song of the spheres and thrilling with some unwonted harmony which did not seem of this earth, recalled the stricken soul of Mathias Ráby back from the shadows of death where it yet lingered.

"May heaven preserve you to us, poor Ráby," whispered the voice.

The ex-prisoner awoke from his swoon to find himself in a warm room, whose atmosphere was redolent with some refreshing fragrance, pillowed on soft cushions, while above him were bending two blue eyes that seemed as if they carried in their inmost depths, something of the light of paradise itself. Such eyes, and who could forget them, once having seen them?

But to this day the treasure-chest of Szent-Endre has never been found, so effectually was it hidden from all men.

THE END.

Milton Keynes UK
Ingram Content Group UK Ltd.
UKHW030905151124
451262UK00006B/1001